FRAMING THE RAPE VICTIM

FRAMING THE RAPE VICTIM

Gender and Agency Reconsidered

CARINE M. MARDOROSSIAN

RUTGERS UNIVERSITY PRESS
New Brunswick, New Jersey, and London

Library of Congress Cataloging-in-Publication Data
Mardorossian, Carine M., 1966–
    Framing the rape victim : gender and agency reconsidered / Carine M. Mardorossian.
       pages cm
    Includes bibliographical references and index.
      ISBN 978–0–8135–6603–0 (hardcover : alk. paper) — ISBN 978–0–8135–6602–3 (pbk. : alk. paper) — ISBN 978–0–8135–6604–7 (e-book)
    1. Rape victims—United States. 2. Rape—United States. 3. Women—Violence against—United States. 4. Rape in motion pictures. I. Title.

HV6561.M367 2014
362.8830973—dc23   2013029876

A British Cataloging-in-Publication record for this book is available from the British Library.

Copyright © 2014 by Carine M. Mardorossian
All rights reserved

No part of this book may be reproduced or utilized in any form or by any means, electronic or mechanical, or by any information storage and retrieval system, without written permission from the publisher. Please contact Rutgers University Press, 106 Somerset Street, New Brunswick, NJ 08901. The only exception to this prohibition is "fair use" as defined by U.S. copyright law.

Visit our website: http://rutgerspress.rutgers.edu

Manufactured in the United States of America

For Kathleen Lerusse

CONTENTS

	Acknowledgments	ix
	Introduction	1
1	Framing the Victim	24
2	Rape and Victimology in Feminist Theory	41
3	"Birth Rape": Laboring Women, Coaching Men, and Natural Childbirth in the Hospital Setting	68
4	Prison Rape, Masculinity, and the Missed Alliances of Hollywood Cinema	90
5	Rape by Proxy in Contemporary Diasporic Women's Fiction	112
	Conclusion	129
	Notes	137
	Works Cited	147
	Index	161

ACKNOWLEDGMENTS

I want to thank the activists and survivors, colleagues, and friends I met during my years as an anti-rape activist. These years overlapped with and extended into intense thinking and discussion surrounding feminist theory. To all those who were part of this journey in one way or another, I send my deeply felt gratitude: Amanda Anderson, Yves Clemmen, Sagari Dhairyam, Pascale Drianne, Anna Marie Gire, Kay Holley, A. J. Herzog, Stephanie Foote, Christine Levecq, Janet Lyon, Cris Mayo, and Faustina Robinson. Others have more recently been instrumental in helping me finish this project: Diane Christian, Robert Daly, Masani Alexis Deveaux, Bruce Jackson, Arabella Lyon, Carla Mazzio, Cristanne Miller, Gwynn Thomas, and Joseph Valente; my wonderful writing partner and friend Margarita Vargas; and my amazing graduate students. I thank the Humanities Institute at the University at Buffalo for a Research Fellowship that gave me time to write. I am also grateful to the many readers and critics of my work, especially the anonymous reviewers at the press, my amazing editor Katie Keeran, and my meticulous copy editor Kate Babbitt. It has been a genuine privilege to work with the staff at the press. Last but not least, I have to thank my family for their unwavering understanding and love. I am particularly grateful to Lonny Morse for his uncompromisingly scientific mind and his inexplicable humility. My children, Cédric and Delphine, fill my days with delightful, unimaginable moments, messes, and fresh perspectives that routinely help me think outside the box. In Dr. Seuss's memorable words, "If you can see things out of whack, then you can see how things can be in whack." My kids teach me this and more every day.

An early version of chapter 2 was published as "Toward a New Feminist Theory of Rape," *Signs* 27.3 (2002): 743–77; copyright 2002 Mary Hawkesworth; reprinted with permission from the University of Chicago Press. Portions of chapter 5 appeared as "Rape by Proxy in Contemporary Caribbean Women's Fiction," *Feminism, Literature, and Rape Narratives: Violence and Violation*, ed. Sorcha Gunne and Zoë Brigley Thompson (London and New York: Routledge, hb 2010; pb 2011), 23–38; reprinted with permission from Taylor & Francis Group, LLC. A portion of chapter 3 was previously published as "Laboring Women, Coaching Men: Masculinity and Childbirth Education in the Contemporary United States," *Hypatia* 18.3 (2003): 113–134; reprinted courtesy of Indiana University Press. Parts of chapter 4 and chapter 1 appeared in "Victimhood in the Carceral Culture of Women's Prisons," *International Review of Victimology* 19.1 (January 2013): 69–83; reprinted courtesy of Sage Publications, first published on June 4, 2012 doi: 10.1177/0269758012447214.

FRAMING THE RAPE VICTIM

INTRODUCTION

According to FBI statistics, the incidence of rape often increases at times when the incidence of other crimes is on the decline. For instance, the FBI's Uniform Crime Report of 19 September 2011 announced that "while [DC] saw a moderate reduction in 2010 violent crime levels, reports of forcible rape jumped 25 percent" (Skomba and Chen 2001). Similarly, in spring 2011, the New York Police Department reported "a significantly lower homicide rate and a decrease in the overall crime rate" for 2011 but a dramatic 24 percent jump in rape complaints from the year before (see Huffington Post 2011; Johnston 2011). These statistics show two things: first, that rape remains a significant social issue, and second, that it is often singled out as a special kind of crime that may even be conceived as distinct from other forms of violence such as homicide or mugging. The statistics pertaining to violence in society thus sometimes remain unaffected by the high incidence of rape, which is treated differently for ideological reasons. Although it would be inconceivable to offer "overall crime rates" that did not include murder or gang violence (which mostly affects men), it is conceivable to cite "overall crime rates" that exclude rape. In other words, when statistics reflecting the rate of violent crimes that include rape are not offered alongside those that single out rape, we know the crime of rape is not weighted similarly to other crimes.[1]

Rape may be a ubiquitous phenomenon, but because it mostly affects women, it is not seen as a crime that concerns the social body as a whole (unlike violent crimes that predominantly victimize men). It is the event women have to fear, experience, avoid, and deter and whose pervasiveness, feminists argue, has shaped women's bodily comportment whether they are conscious of it or not (Bartky 1988; Cahill 2001; Young 2011). Victims often blame themselves when they are raped, and they are routinely blamed when it occurs. Bestsellers published by conservative commentators such as Katie Roiphe and Christina Hoff Sommers outline the myriad ways that women and their misconceptions should be held responsible for the high incidence of rape, which, these authors argue, has itself been inflated by years of feminist brainwashing. Women are now repeatedly accused of triggering if not of causing rape through their misguided behavior (drinking, partying), their indoctrination (by a feminism whose representation of women as victims is blamed for producing their victimization), or their own lack of will (which allegedly leads to a complicit passivity). As one of the slogans of the SlutWalk movement puts it, "Society teaches us 'don't get raped' rather than 'don't rape.'"

Such configurations of rape have furthered ghettoized sexual violence along gendered lines. Since its emergence on the public agenda in the 1970s, rape has been perceived as a crime that is perpetrated by men and that affects women. In fact, it has been "naturalized" as the social crisis that concerns women (in both senses of the term: it is about women, and they are always concerned by it). While it is true that the statistical reality of rape as a crime marks it as a gendered crime (and 98 percent of its victims are indeed women), I believe that we have let these statistics limit our response to the problem and essentialize rape as a woman's issue.

The goal of this book is to contest the notion that rape is a woman's problem. Rape, I argue, is not a woman's issue. Neither is it a man's issue, as is sometimes maintained by anti-rape activists who point to the fact that the statistical

FIGURE 1. Chicago SlutWalk, 4 June 2011. Photo by Michael Courier.

majority of perpetrators are male. Rather, it is an issue pertaining to masculinity, an ideological construct that cannot and should not be reduced to biological sexual difference and whose authority in culture derives from its structural and relational positioning vis-à-vis femininity. *Framing the Rape Victim* therefore restores masculinity to gender in response to the dominant culture's reductive and debilitating approach to gender as primarily of and about women. It recasts rape as primarily a problem of and with hegemonic masculinity and only secondarily (to the extent that femininity is structurally related to masculinity) as a woman's problem. I start with the premise that masculinity and femininity are structural positions rather than biologically derived ones. The position of dominant masculinity can be occupied by either men or women, while structural femininity is a position that may define and subordinate men, minorities, and other marginalized groups just as effectively as it does the category women. Furthermore, I argue that the current form that gendering rape has taken obscures rape's defining role in our culture of violence, including by well-meaning (sometimes feminist) voices that claim to have its victims' best interests at heart.

In other words, analyzing victimization through the lens of a reframed masculinity means bringing rape to public attention not as "a woman's issue" but as an issue that saturates culture and defines structural masculinity's relation to femininity and not women's relation to men. This reframing is important at a time when the FBI—no doubt in response to the Penn State sex scandal—finally expanded its long-standing definition of rape to include sexual assaults on males. In November 2011, former Pennsylvania State University football assistant coach Jerry Sandusky was indicted for forty counts of sex crimes against young boys, and important officials such as Penn State athletic director Tim Curley and senior vice president for finance and business Gary Schultz (who oversaw the Penn State police department) were charged with perjury and failure to report suspected child abuse. In July 2012, when the Louis Freeh Report was finally released, it revealed that the most powerful men at Penn State, including Vice President Gary Schultz, Athletic Director Tim Curley, former president Graham Spanier, and the late Joe Paterno, had failed to take steps to protect the children for fourteen years (Freeh Sporkin and Sullivan, LLP 2012). They had even gone so far as to repeatedly conceal critical facts relating to Sandusky's child abuse from the authorities in order to avoid bad publicity. When the news of the scandal broke, the media was at a loss for what words to use to describe the crimes under investigation: child molestation, child abuse scandal, involuntary deviate sexual intercourse, indecent assault, unlawful contact with minor, corruption of minors, child sexual abuse, sex scandal, sexual misconduct, and child sex-abuse scandal were all phrases that circulated in a media that was reluctant or unwilling to call rape rape.

To the extent that the incidents were seen as legitimate instances of violence (because they were directed at children) but not of rape, they expose the culture's difficulty with reconciling sex and violence. Similarly, the much-mediatized cases of bullying in the media over the last few years show that in cases concerning adolescents, the violence involved was not adequately addressed as a legitimate form of violence since so many bullying incidents led to suicides. Sexual elements in cases of violence seem to muddy the ability of people to recognize violence as violence, because sex and violence are still seen as antithetical to one another.

It is a function of the ghettoization of rape in culture that Sandusky's assaults were not discussed as instances of rape but as crimes that stood apart from their feminized counterpart. And it is this book's goal to rectify such a compartmentalized approach to sexual violence. Not only is the Sandusky sex scandal an instance of rape (which the FBI's new definition of sexual assault finally acknowledges), but it also reveals the extent to which the function of rape as *the* visibly gendered and sexualized crime in our social imaginary has become to conceal the inherently sexualized nature of all violence in culture. The proliferating and conflicting formulations surrounding various instances of rape in culture reveal that it is structural femininity, not the female subject, that is rape's victim. They also show that rape's social function today is to naturalize violence as an unmarked social relation: because rape is compartmentalized and marginalized as *the* visibly sexualized crime, the profoundly sexualized nature of violence is rendered invisible.[2] Recognizing the sexualized dimension of all violence will help remove this stigmatization.

Framing the Rape Victim is thus predicated on the idea that sexual violence is not separate but integral to our understanding of violence in the contemporary United States, that all violence is, in fact, sexual(ized) violence. As Teresa De Lauretis put it, "The representation of violence is inseparable from the notion of gender.... Violence is engendered in representation" (1985, 33). And this gendering is inseparable from the dominant generalization that "becoming gendered" leads to the heterosexuality of people gendered as men and women. Heteronormativity is therefore built into the cultural understanding of sexualized violence and is mediated by gendered expectations at every level (including, paradoxically, in cases of same-sex violence).[3] By contrast, *Framing the Rape Victim* shows how gender is always already constructed through multiple relations of class, race, and context that mediate the experiences, representations, meanings, and possibilities of what constitutes "the sexual" and sexual violence in culture.

This book thus proposes an intersectional approach to gender and sexualized violence that involves all the experiences and meanings that flow from racialization, culture, class, and sexuality. Social realities are embedded in multiple levels of complexity, and the recognition of their interweaving needs to replace any one-dimensional approach to "becoming gendered." This entails not only the understanding of questions of culture, class, race, nationality, and sexuality as interwoven forces but also the refusal to prioritize one social force (race, class, gender) over another in its imbrication with sexualized violence. For instance, the way one becomes "a man" or "a woman" interacts differently with "becoming racialized" according to context and history. Throughout *Framing the Rape Victim*, I will highlight the changing social forces that interact most forcefully with sexualized violence and the processes of gendering, racialization, and class on which it is based.

But what does it mean to argue that all violence is, in fact, sexualized violence? I am certainly not suggesting that all violence is a form of rape. Rather, I argue that irrespective of the gender of those involved in a violent interaction, the violation itself entails the mobilization of a relational and structural paradigm of masculinity/femininity that is not only operative in rape per se but of which one particular form *is* rape as we know it. In other words, even in cases of gang violence, which typically involve men, a structural relation between masculinity and femininity defines the relationship of the antagonists. The 2009 death of Salum Kombo, the eighteen-year-old who was stabbed to death in Bow, East London, after he called his friend a "pussy" on Facebook, is a case in point. Nurul Ullah, a youth worker who served as a mediator between local youths at the time, had to intervene to stop a gang war from erupting after the tragic event (see Hamill 2012; Pidd 2010). Even in a situation that stages a face-off between two men, the structural paradigm of masculinity and femininity is at work, since each of the two actors is striving to occupy the dominant masculine position while casting the other in the subordinate feminine one (first through insult, then through stabbing).

Similarly, in his research on gang violence in the United States, Lewis Yablonsky has uncovered the ways in which the "macho-syndrome," an extreme form of "tough-guy behavior," is explicitly present in much of the violence committed by gang members. The gangster's insecurity about his masculinity results in a verbal or physical "machismolike superman" posturing (Yablonsky 1988, 18) that leads to violence when the gangster feels disrespected: "Any comment of disrespect to a gangster that implies femininity, like, 'You're a pussy' or 'You're a faggot' will quickly produce a violent response" (ibid., 19). In a later work, Yablonsky notes that "implying that a gangster has feminine characteristics is sufficient grounds in a gang culture for a violent—even homicidal retaliation" (Yablonsky 2008, 124). Violence does not have to be of an explicitly sexual nature or even entail verbalized gendered invectives to implicate a subject who seeks to occupy the dominant masculine position through the subordination of another (who is in the feminine position). The consistent devaluing of terms associated with the feminine in Western culture ("you are such a girl," "sissy," "whore," etc.) testifies to the prevalence of this paradigm, which also operates when the slurs are of a racial nature.

Framing the Rape Victim goes further, however, than identify rape as the extreme form of a sexualized violence that defines all violent social relations in the twenty-first century. It also demonstrates that rape is the paradigmatic form of a defining violation that constitutes normative subjectivity at its core. The book is premised on the idea that our sense of the self as a fully actualized, autonomous, and embodied subject (derived from the Enlightenment) is tied to a normative form of masculinity that ultimately grounds sexualized forms of violence. Indeed, in a culture where the abled and whole body is considered the norm, the violated, disabled, and victimized body inevitably becomes the term against which the normative body constitutes itself. The forms of selfhood considered normal in Western culture thus depend on gendered polarities that rationalize sexual violence by promoting a form of hegemonic masculinity that alternative subject positions are subordinated to. This defining violation is always sexualized because the dominant masculine position is produced and consolidated through the social, historical, and discursive exclusion of structurally—as opposed to biologically—feminine subjectivities implied in the category of victim (Kramer 2000; Žižek 1994).[4] As cultural critic Lawrence Kramer puts it, the threat of violence is built into the "very structure of identity" (2000, 8) in an indelible way, all the more so since the subject position of absolute masculinity is a fictitious notion of embodied autonomy and absolute self-possession that no one—not even men—can hold but that is nonetheless presumed and performed endlessly. Rape is a phenomenon that is therefore fundamental to Western culture and that defines "the very core of ordinary subjectivity like a bone in the throat" (ibid., 2). It is also a phenomenon in which the unequal relation between the "man" and the "woman" refers not to a biological distinction or gender roles but rather to the symbolic dimension of language in which elements (signifiers) have no essentializing existence. That is, they are constituted through their mutual differences. In the critical assessment of rape, viewing masculinity and femininity as structural positions rather than as biological designations is crucial if we want to dislodge rape from its essentializing and compartmentalized association with women and women's bodies. We need to challenge the saturation of the feminine with the sexual and thereby decouple women from an implicitly and inherently victimized position.

By highlighting the sexualized dimension of all violence on the one hand and the paradigmatic role sexualized violence plays in the constitution of the normative self on the other, *Framing the Rape Victim* thus revisits Michel Foucault's controversial call for the decriminalization of rape as defined as a sexual crime. In 1977, the French theorist claimed that

> when one punishes rape one should be punishing physical violence and nothing but that. And to say that it is nothing more than an act of aggression: that

there is no difference, in principle, between sticking one's fist into someone's face or one's penis into their sex . . . there are problems, because what we're saying amounts to this: sexuality as such, in the body, has a preponderant place, the sexual organ isn't like a hand, hair, or a nose. It therefore has to be protected, surrounded, invested in any case with legislation that isn't that pertaining to the rest of the body. . . . It isn't a matter of sexuality, it's the physical violence that would be punished, without bringing in the fact that sexuality was involved. (1988, 200–202)

Foucault was concerned that defining rape as a sexual crime would compound the saturation of the social with the sexual. This stance was in keeping with his investment in exposing and undermining the construction of sexuality as a core feature of people's identities. According to Foucault, since the nineteenth century, the proliferation of discourses (medical, legal, psychoanalytic, educational) concerning sexuality has worked predominantly as a means of disciplining social and political power: people have been so preoccupied with checking, controlling, confessing, and managing sex and sexuality that all kinds of inequities go unaddressed as a result of this obsession with what has been discursively but effectively manufactured as their "core identity." Thus, he saw the singling out of rape as a sexual crime as another symptom of this "ruse of power."

Like Foucault, I believe that treating rape as exceptional because explicitly sexualized ultimately plays in the hands of power. In fact, it hides how saturated with the sexual all forms of violence truly are. I argue that rape should therefore be put on a continuum that recognizes the central role gender and sexuality play in the structuring of all social power relations. The cultural recognition that the sexualized nature of all violence is, like Edgar Allan Poe's purloined letter, hidden in plain sight will, I believe, remove rape from the marginalized status to which it has been relegated in the contemporary United States. It will then be prosecuted not because of its exceptional singularity but because of its representativeness as an extreme form of the always already sexualized violent relations that saturate and define the social body. By this, I do not intend to dilute the significance of rape or take women out of an equation that predominantly affects them but rather to reveal the representativeness and centrality of both rape and women in a culture where violence is always sexualized.

Unlike Foucault, who was calling for a reform of the penal code, however, I believe that this intervention needs to occur at the cultural rather than the legal level. The reason why legal redress in rape cases has been ineffective is, I believe, because the cultural understanding of rape misrepresents it as a special-interest issue rather than as the tip of an iceberg that saturates all social and power relations. Indeed, according to the Rape, Abuse, and Incest National Network, 54 percent of all sexual assaults continue to go unreported to the police, while

97 percent of all rapists will never spend a day in jail (Rape, Abuse & Incest National Network, n.d.).

My call for the recognition of the sexualized nature of forms of violence that are viewed as nonsexual is thus a cultural intervention that will remove rape from the special-interest niche it has been occupying "at home." We need to put rape on a continuum that recognizes the central role of sexuality and gender in the "making of culture" in the United States (to borrow from Lawrence Kramer's title). If we live in a "rape culture," it is not because U.S. culture is inherently in the business of normalizing sexual violence against women but because violence is an inherently sexualized phenomenon of which rape is the extreme form. Rape is an issue that primarily affects women not because they are women but because they often—although not necessarily—occupy the position of the structurally subordinate in relations of domination. Men, children, other categorical minorities, and senior citizens can and do also occupy this "feminine" position.[5] As Monique Plaza puts it, "If men rape women, it is precisely because they are women in a social sense; and when a male is raped, he too is raped 'as a woman'" (1980, 31). Similarly, child rape, which has been so prominently in the news at the beginning of the twenty-first century, provides the perfect example of the extent to which the position of being dominated is conducive to this phenomenon.

The abuse of Iraqi prisoners by members of the U.S. military at Abu Ghraib is another salient example of the workings of such sexualized violence and of the obscuring of its racialized and sexualized dimensions. In response to the abuse, rape, sodomy, and homicide of prisoners in the Baghdad correctional facility, the decision of the U.S. Department of Defense to remove seventeen soldiers and officers from duty and charge eleven soldiers with dereliction of duty, maltreatment, aggravated, assault and battery worked to obscure the profoundly sexualized nature of the violence committed.

Ironically, the Department of Defense's ruling in this case is aligned with Foucault's controversial move to define rape as an act of violence rather than one of sexuality and hence as an act that is indistinct from other types of assaults. It also surprisingly echoes second-wave feminist Susan Brownmiller's similar call, in 1975, to purge rape of its sexual content (Cahill 2001, 144). However, as Cahill explains, while Foucault's statement is about striking a blow to the workings of power, Brownmiller's position emerges from her concern that emphasizing the sexual elements of rape may invite assumptions about the culpability of feminine sexuality (since femininity is equated with passivity). Unlike these two thinkers, who each stressed the desexualization of rape for different reasons, I propose to highlight the larger economy of a socially constructed sexualized hierarchy of which rape is one instance, albeit a paradigmatic one. To expose this economy, we need to trace its workings not by singling out rape in isolation but by placing it on the continuum of a sexualized violence that it brings to light, signifies, and epitomizes, both as a trope and lived experience. If we recognize that there is, as psychoanalysis shows, no escaping the sexualized (see Žižek 1994), that the very making of the self in Western culture is founded on a paradigm of sexual violence whereby the structurally masculine overpowers and defines itself against the structurally feminine, then rape and the threat of rape stop functioning as ghettoized practices that concern only "victims" (and, increasingly, certain types of allegedly "passive" and "weak" women) and become instead paradigmatic phenomena of modernity to which society as a whole should attend.

MASCULINITY REDEFINED

Masculinity in this reframed dimension is no longer a set of gendered characteristics that define mostly men but a structural position that seeks to dominate by subordinating the feminized (feminine) position through sexual, class-based, and/or racialized practices of othering. The subordinate position, in other words, may be occupied by black men (chapter 4) as well as white and nonwhite women (chapter 5), or, for that matter, by white men. The dominant position of masculinity is also one that both men and women may actively seek but whose absolute instantiation no one, not even the most domineering human being, can ever wholly embody. The "machismolike superman" posturing of gangsters in gang culture is one gang members constantly need to reaffirm and perform in their attempts to compensate for the alienation they feel in the social body (Yablonsky 2008, 124). Their posturing is constantly under threat and has to be enacted and reenacted. Gangsters fall back on violence as a means of realizing their superiority precisely because the absolute masculine position is never attainable. It is a position that they always struggle to ascertain and can never unambiguously occupy because it is relational and requires a process of sexual and racial othering in order to exist. I argue that we need to widen the wedge between masculinity and maleness that these dynamics help expose lest we remain mired in an economy that legitimizes sexualized violence (and by extension rape) by essentializing the yoking of maleness with violence and femaleness with victimization.

According to Todd Reeser, masculinity is a diffuse and complex a phenomenon whose meanings vary according to the historical, cultural, and theoretical contexts in which it operates (2010, 3). The structural dimension that *Framing the Rape Victim* aims to identify as the core element of masculinity has indeed been expressed in multiple and changing ways historically. During the European Renaissance, for instance, expressions of male-male intimacy were the purview of the masculine rather than of the effeminate or homosexual man with whom they later came to be associated (2). Feelings of superiority and vulnerability can both constitute expressions of structural masculinity. Also telling in this respect is the contrast between the treatment of gang rapes in the United States and in

India, where gang rapes have also been occurring with alarming regularity over the last few years. In his article "The Crisis of Indian Masculinity" (2012), law professor Ratna Kapur highlights the 2003 gang rape of a seventeen-year-old Delhi University student in Buddha Jayanti Park, the 2005 Dhaula Kuan gang rape of a student from Mizoram in a moving car, the 2010 gang rape of a young BPO employee from the northeast, and the 2012 gang rape of a 23-year-old physiotherapy student on a Delhi bus, among others, as the cultural expression of a generation of young men who cannot adjust to having to compete with women in the workplace. As is illustrated by the wave of protests that have shaken the country since the 2012 rape and murder of medical student Jyoti Singh Pandey, the country as a whole has been able to recognize rape as a social issue that saturates relations of class and gender. According to Kapur,

> Over the past several decades, women's rights have proliferated and they are claiming their subjectivity, asserting their identity as women as opposed to being someone's wife, daughter, or sister. And with the opening up of the market, women are more visible in the workplace. That they are entering male bastions of power has challenged the sense of superiority and entitlement of the traditional Indian male. This idea of a woman as a fully formed human subject remains a difficult concept to embrace. The grooming of young men to have a feeling of entitlement by Indian parents breeds a sense of masculinity and male privilege. . . . When women do not cower or display their vulnerability—thereby inviting the protection of the virile Indian male—what follows is a sense of emasculation and aggrievement on the part of these men. . . . We need to think about how we can handle women's equality in ways that are not perceived as threatening. That demands greater responsibility on the part of parents as well as society not to raise sons in a way in which they are indoctrinated with a sense of superiority and privilege. (Kapur 2012)

Kapur's bold linking of the "sense of superiority and privilege" that constitutes one expression of normative masculinity with the normalization of sexual violence in culture is similar to the connection *Framing the Rape Victim* is establishing between normative forms of subjectivity that increasingly define themselves against the victim and the feminine on the one hand and the prevalence of rape as a social problem on the other. Society breeds sexualized violence when it promotes normative rather than deviant forms of identity. This is what distinguishes my intervention from equally compelling ones that condemn "toxic masculinity" in culture. According to Jaclyn Friedman, for instance, rape is "enabled by a deeply entrenched, toxic masculinity. It's a masculinity that defines itself not only in opposition to femaleness, but as inherently superior, drawing its strength from dominance over women's 'weakness.' . . . Or, as former NFL quarterback and newly-minted feminist Don McPherson recently put it, 'We don't raise boys to be men. We raise them not to be women, or gay men'" (Friedman 2013). While this feminist critique recognizes the relational aspect of structural masculinity, its use of the qualifier "toxic" risks obscuring the fact that rape is an extension of normative (able-bodied, heroic), not deviant, masculinity. The problem is the toxicity of normative masculinity rather than a particular form of "toxic masculinity."[6] In strong contrast to India's response to gang rape as an expression of culture, the United States has been increasingly focusing on rape as an issue of criminal deviance, as an exceptional occurrence rather than as a pattern of violence. The contrast could not be wider between the nationwide outrage and anti-rape rallies that shook India in the wake of the 2012 Delhi gang rape and the quietism that characterizes the U.S. response to rape.

This is deeply ironic since rape is no less unusual in the U.S. context as it is in the Indian one. Think of the twenty men who were sentenced in November 2012 for the gang rape of an eleven-year-old in Cleveland, Texas, in December 2011; of the instigator of the gang rape of a sixteen-year-old in Richmond, California, who was sentenced in October 2012; of the four men who were sentenced in April 2012 for the gang rape of a fifteen-year-old near New Orleans; of the six men who are still at large after raping a fourteen-year-old in 2012 in Chicago; of the rape of a developmentally disabled woman on a Los Angeles bus in November 2012; of the kidnapping of an autistic sixteen-year-old on the regional transit train system in Oakland, California, also in November 2012; and last but not least, of the much publicized sexual assault of an inebriated sixteen-year-old girl by two high school football stars in Steubenville, Ohio, during a night of partying on 11 August 2012. As Rebecca Solnit argues, "We have far more than 87,000 rapes in this country every year, but each of them is invariably portrayed as an isolated incident. We have dots so close they're splatters melting into a stain, but hardly anyone connects them, or names that stain. In India they did. They said that this is a civil rights issue, it's a human rights issue, it's everyone's problem, it's not isolated, and it's never going to be acceptable again. It has to change" (Solnit 2013).

Kapur goes further to stress the problems associated with the effort to address what is a fundamental cultural issue through mere legal reform: "Indians need to understand that gang rape is not just an aberration committed by inhuman men. We need to address how we as a society are implicated in producing such appalling levels of violence against women, which is increasingly being tolerated and even normalized.... [And because this is] a deeply ingrained societal problem... more law will only serve to give a sense of something being done, when in fact very little is being done. Law reforms in the area of rape have been taking place over three decades but they do not appear to have arrested the appalling levels of violence to which Indian women are subjected" (Kapur 2012). I agree that the reframing of rape as inherent to the "making of culture" and its underlying crisis of masculinity cannot be addressed through legal reform if such reforms do not derive from a radical cultural reframing of rape. In fact, they may actually contribute to the quietism that defines the response to rape in the United States, since they create the illusion of safety and change by generating the idea of the state as a neutral arbiter between two parties—the perpetrator and the victim. As Rose Corrigan (2013) argues, the history of rape law reform actually reveals that the bureaucratic intransigence and standard operating procedures of gendered state institutions have undermined the central claims of anti-rape and feminist advocates since the second wave of the women's movement. Rape is an issue of culture that cannot be reduced to the individualizing rhetoric adopted in law reform.

The meanings and associations surrounding particular expressions of structural masculinity are shifting and context specific but, as the example of gang rape reveals, the core element of structural masculinity continues to operate regardless of its varied expressions or the sex of the subject. To echo Reeser, even "the most basic assumption about masculinity . . . , namely, that it belongs to men," is far from a given (2010, 2). The very phrase "men and masculinities," which is so commonly used in titles of journals and anthologies in the field of masculinity studies, points to the automatic yoking of the two concepts of "man" and "masculinity" in culture and, simultaneously, to the denaturalization of this association in scholarship. Indeed, if their yoking is not tacit and has to be reiterated through the repeated juxtaposition of the two words, then the very staging of the combination undermines its naturalization.[7] Men and masculinity do not go hand in hand anymore, all the more so since "although men may have more to gain from masculinity than other groups, the cause or the origin of masculinity cannot be directly linked to the male body in any simple or stable way" (17–18). In fact, women may have as much if not more of a vested interest in defending or occupying a hegemonic masculine position as men do (17).[8] By similarly capitalizing on the distinction between maleness and masculinity, sexed body and ideology, *Framing the Rape Victim* seeks to challenge the age-old associations and oppositions that have mobilized if not paralyzed the field of anti-rape activism and theory. As Joseph Valente (2011) explains through his provocative distinctions between maleness, manliness, and masculinity, while these concepts are not disjunctive, they are also neither coterminous nor coextensive, to the extent that the ideological formation of dominant masculinity that was historically designed to contribute to male power has become increasingly structural and less personal. Although women today still disproportionately bear the burden of sustaining the fiction of gender polarity, they too can and increasingly do support and promote the unambiguous subject position of masculinity that grounds normative subjectivity. *Framing the Rape Victim* intervenes in this widening space between sexed body and ideology to remove rape from its problematic and limiting yoking to the vicissitudes of the female psyche.

In stark contrast to the recent focus of anti-rape discourse on destabilizing the constructs that have defined femininity (passivity, victimization), I propose that we challenge the meanings that have historically buttressed hegemonic masculinity and its association with agency. Indeed, in asking women to change their relationship to codes of femininity as a way of deterring rape, anti-rape scholars and critics have inadvertently contributed to anchoring masculinity's hold on an unambiguous form of agency. I am calling for a paradigm shift that will redress the victim-blaming repercussions of this approach by breaking masculinity's violent hold on culture as a site of desire and agency. We need to remember that domination and agency are not the same thing and that one can dominate without exercising agency and vice versa.

Feminist historians have long exposed the ways the grand narratives of history traditionally represent men as the mover and shakers of nations, the sources of life-transforming, history-making, and heroic activities, while women are relegated to the role of more or less passive cultural transmitters. As McClintock points out, most nationalist discourses equate women with an "atavistic and authentic body of national tradition (inert, backward-looking, and natural), embodying nationalism's conservative principle of continuity," while they identify men as "the progressive agent[s] of national modernity (forward-thrusting, potent, and historic)" (1997, 92). According to this narrative, women are repositories of men's stories and deeds and as such function as available surfaces upon which the relations that constitute our culture of violence get scripted both physically and metaphorically.

Feminism has responded to this set of associations either by (re)claiming the same sense of agency for women (women as historical agents) or by revising the definition of agency as it pertains to women (resistance or passivity as agency). While *Framing the Rape Victim* partakes of the second approach to the extent that it too challenges and dismantles the way the passivity/agency dyad has been used to define femininity, it also takes issue with the ways that both responses (reclaiming or revising agency) remain focused on femininity's relation to the concept, thereby naturalizing the association of masculinity with an unambiguous form of domination that is then conflated with agency. In relation to sexual violence specifically, feminists either urge women to deploy the kind of self-determining and mountain-moving agency that has historically been associated with the masculine (so as to deter rape), or they call for the recognition of a different form of women's agency to alter our response to rape. For instance, they may ask women to stop rapes by refusing to enact the "script" of the passive female victim (Marcus 1992), either by fighting back against their assailant (through a masculine form of agency) or by using verbal strategies that may distract and dissuade (a more feminine form of agency). While these two approaches are no doubt well meaning, they risk inadvertently essentializing the cultural association of femaleness with the subordinate position of victimization because the constant enactment of subversion reinforces and reproduces the ubiquity of masculine power. They also put the burden of overhauling normative masculinity's investment in sexualized violence squarely on women's shoulders, because—one can only surmise—masculinity's yoking to agency is fixed and uncontested.

By contrast, I propose that we challenge the often-unquestioned historical association of masculinity with an ennobled or vilified form of self-reliant and categorical agency and rethink the implied conflation of domination and agency this formulation perpetuates. We should highlight the ways that hegemonic masculinity's repeated performance of supremacy through sexualized forms of violence are not an enactment of agency but the result of a passive if not "terrorized" acquiescence to scripts of power and domination that are uncritically sustained and embodied by its "masculine" subjects. We need to understand that the will to dominate is not an expression of free will or of a subject exercising agency so much as it is the expression of a subject bound to gendered expectations that have turned the will to dominate into identity itself. Indeed, the failure to dominate produces a "terror machine" because it threatens the subject with complete annihilation: once one subscribes to the tenets of this identity-making machine, one is nothing if one does not dominate.[9]

To the extent that the heroic masculinity of post 9/11 nationalism, which continues to be summoned after every mass shooting that shakes this country (Columbine, Aurora, Newtown), is defined through its relational and structural distinction from a subordinate feminine/victimized position, it too is part of a culture that legitimizes sexualized forms of domination and ultimately violence. Because normative forms of masculinity are defined by categorical notions of wholeness, self-possession, fully embodied and abled autonomy, they cannot ever be attained or sustained by any member of the social body and thus lead to sites of crisis and violence that will be directed against the vulnerable through the masculine's foundational structural relation to the feminine. This is a matter of ideology, not personality. It is no surprise, then, that the very political party that has been most vocal about the need to remasculinize the country since 9/11 is also the one whose members made the most aberrant and abhorrent victim-blaming statements about rape in the context of the 2012 presidential election (see chapter 1 for a discussion of rape and politics).

The hegemonic form of masculinity that ultimately grounds sexualized violence needs to be reframed and understood as what it is, namely a form of passive if not terrorized reenactment of a script that grounds and justifies social domination. The fact that the coupling of terror and passivity I am suggesting feels oxymoronic in relation to masculinity but the association of fear and passivity in relation to femininity is now almost completely normalized in critical responses to rape is a function of the disjunctive modes in which masculinity and femininity operate. I argue that far from functioning as an instantiation of unambiguous agency, hegemonic masculinity is therefore the symptom of an uncritical reproduction of an unreachable and unsustainable "norm." The association of the "absolute" masculine with domination and power should thus be ruptured not by advocating that we replace a destructive form of masculinist agency with an ennobled one but by exposing the arbitrary conflation of embodied agency with domination. *Framing the Rape Victim* calls for a reframing of both passivity and agency as a means of challenging the sexualized dimensions that ground violence today.

The outcome of such a shift in perspective is similar to the reframing of "vulnerability" Judith Butler offers in her post-9/11 work. In *Precarious Life: The Power of Mourning and Violence* (2004a), for instance, Butler discusses the ways vulnerability (to others) should be viewed as the prototypical human condition. In other words, rather than being viewed as a state of being that characterizes only certain people due to character or circumstance, vulnerability would be seen as a function of human beings' permeability to others. It is no longer, then, to be seen as the purview of the weak but as a function of our humanity and a condition that none of us can ever fully control and that we share with nonhuman life. This understanding of "vulnerability" is significant because it not only helps us reframe our understanding of agency as something that can no longer be conflated with individual will and subjectivity, it also helps us reconceptualize the notion of victimization itself. If we begin to see victimization as an extreme form of the vulnerability to others that we all share, we would have to address it in ways other than through the anti-victimist stance that has recently dominated discussions of social relations in U.S. culture. Victims are people whose vulnerability to others has been abused rather than people who, as they are now increasingly defined, let themselves fall prey to a condition (vulnerability) to which the rest of us are supposedly impermeable. For instance, news sources often depict the rape and murder of young women using the passive voice "in a way that almost makes it sound as if women were just out there playing the rape-victim role" (Pullum 2012). If we came to terms with the fact that we are all, by definition, characterized by vulnerability, then it becomes more difficult (if not impossible) to hold it against people that they are vulnerable.

Rethinking vulnerability as something we all share necessarily renders moot the question of whether a particular victim's vulnerability was warranted or not. Similarly, if we view rape as an extension of a violence that is always sexualized rather than as the only form of violence that is sexualized, we would stop seeing it as a condition that only affects the (defective) few and we would begin to respond to it as the extreme form of a pervasive condition to which we are all vulnerable in one form or another. As a result, the shaming and guilt-tripping that has in recent decades accompanied anti-victimist discussions of rape would also be redressed.

RAPE (IN) CULTURE

The representation and understanding of rape in U.S. culture today is inflected by a series of polarized perspectives: rape is either sensationalized as an extraordinary occurrence or naturalized as part of our culture (through the coining of the term "rape culture," for instance). The public is either outraged by its existence or desensitized to it. People can be deeply sympathetic to its victims or they are automatically suspicious of claims of sexual victimization. Rape is seen as a human rights violation and a politicized issue in contexts such as wartorn Third World countries, whereas at home it is viewed as an individualized and interpersonal problem. In fact, it may be that rape as a *social* issue has been eclipsed domestically precisely because of the increasing media attention to rape as a "weapon of war" in Third World countries. This militarization of rape as a barbaric act perpetuated in war-torn foreign settings works to ensure that rape in the national setting, where it is not used as a weapon of war, loses legitimacy as an issue that requires a social rather than an individualized response. It also reinforces constructions of war-torn countries as backward, barbaric, and inferior and consolidates the imperialist image of the United States as a beacon of equality and democracy. As a result, sexual victimization that results from non-militarized aggression becomes delegitimized as the purview of the few; that is, the weak and/or the manipulative.

What is more, the tropes of rape in culture are also divided into metaphorical or literal representations. As a metaphor, rape can signify either violent historical encounters such as colonialism (the "rape of the land") or benign cases of political discord. Conservative commentators such as Rush Limbaugh, Glenn Beck, and Michael Savage have no qualms about using rape as a metaphor when discussing progressives or progressive policies. For example, Beck said that New Yorkers are "being raped by [their] government," while Limbaugh, during a discussion of health care, told his listeners: "Get ready to get gang-raped again" (Frederick 2009).[10] Last but not least, when studies turn their attention to same-sex sexual violence or male victims of rape, a new division emerges in our approach to rape since that discussion often takes place separately from the case of women victims, even warranting distinct works of scholarship altogether.[11]

Because of our academic and disciplinary affiliations, scholarly studies of rape often cannot help but reinforce the mainstream's polarized understanding of the issue. Some studies focus on the representation of rape in film (Heller-Nicholas

2011; Horeck 2004; Projansky 2001; Russell 2010) or literature (Doyle 2007; Graham 2012; Gunne and Thompson 2011; Sielke 2002; Stockton 2006), and highlight it as a representation or metaphor we analyze to expose particular ideologies that affect our response to rape. Other studies approach rape as a sociological or psychological reality, a traumatic event that affects real women and demands interventions of one kind or another in their lives (Gavey 2005; P. Y. Martin 2005). The authors themselves bridge these two angles of approach through their interdisciplinary interventions: scholars focusing on the representation of rape reveal how it necessarily affects the societal response to actual victims, while the concern of sociological feminist scholars for "real" victims always accounts for the ways cultural representations of rape affect them. However, insofar as these studies approach rape from two seemingly opposed perspectives, they compound the dominant assumption that the representation of rape is separable from its reality (notwithstanding the fact that the studies themselves challenge this separation).

It is this book's contention that the compartmentalization of rape into metaphorical or referential phenomenon, representation or reality, exceptional or ordinary occurrence, women's or men's issues is what enables and reflects the social, gendered, and racial inequities of power that ground Western notions of selfhood. To expose this process, *Framing the Rape Victim* examines both how rape and victimization are culturally conceptualized today (in feminist theory, cinema, or fiction) and how these representations impact victims of violence and social responses to the crime. The book thus aligns analyses of literal sexual victimization (as pertaining to rape victims in chapter 1 and 2) with discussions of more metaphorical meanings of rape (the rape of the nation in chapter 1 and "birth rape" in chapter 3); of cinematic with journalistic representations of prison rape (chapter 4); of feminist activist and theoretical responses to rape (chapter 2); and of men-on-women rape (chapter 2) with representations of female-on-female rape in recent immigrant novels (chapter 5).

These juxtapositions are not meant to imply that every instance of violation in culture is a form of what we have heretofore been thinking of as rape (in what would amount to a "rape culture"). Rather, I seek to identify the continuum of "sexualized" violence that defines *all* forms of violations and violence in culture, the extreme form of which is rape as we know it. It is not, then, the case that every form of violence is rape but that rape is the paradigmatic form all violations (including "birth rape") take in a culture where all violence is sexualized (whether in its metaphorical or literal instantiation) and where normative subjectivity itself is produced through a reliance on an economy of dominance and violation. Specifically, I bring into relief the collusion of contemporary narratives of sexual victimization with the discourses of masculinity and whiteness that buttress exclusionary forms of U.S. nationalism. Thus, I show how sexual violence is not incidental but integral to the ways we make sense of ourselves in the contemporary United States.

Despite the saturation of Western culture with this economy of sexual violation, I have argued that rape and victimization have paradoxically been increasingly ghettoized as a social reality. *Framing the Rape Victim* examines how this marginalization occurred in part through the homogenizing and enduring effects of the encoding strategies that the politically correct debates of the 1990s brought to victimization. Special attention is paid to the position of victimhood in U.S. culture following the terrorist attacks of the World Trade Center on September 11, 2001. I show that the sociocultural shift toward neoconservatism initiated in the 1980s has reinforced the view that the United States was "violated" and emasculated and that its sovereignty has been rendered vulnerable to attack. The trope of sexual violence, which has been mobilized for over a decade by media representations of this national tragedy, is now increasingly mediated by neoconservative configurations of victimization that have molded U.S. culture's response to sexual violence. In this discursive space, the culture's views of victimization are increasingly aligned with a binary conceptualization of passive (and feminized) victimhood on the one hand and of resistant agency (masculine self-sufficiency that is allergic to vulnerability) on the other. The sociopolitical space of neoconservatism has pilloried claims to victimization as signs of moral weakness, individualized failures, and lifestyle issues (D'Souza 1992; Paglia 1990; Roiphe 1993; Sommers 1994). As a result, victimhood is no longer a political category aimed at the mobilization of policy and law reforms such as the Violence Against Women Act (1994) and the Battered Immigrant Women's Protection Act (2000). Not surprisingly, in 2012 and 2013, the first attempt was made to undo many of the protections enshrined in the Violence Against Women Act (VAWA), which had been reauthorized with bipartisan support and very little controversy for close to two decades (Selverston 2012).

I argue that this 1990s reframing of the term "victim" as an unwanted symptom of moral failing to be devalued has played a fundamental role in constructing notions of agency that support exclusionary models of (especially masculine) American selfhood. To elucidate fully the ramifications of this dominant and regulating discourse of sexualized victimhood, *Framing the Rape Victim* relies on an analysis of "victim" as a dynamic and rhetorical term that produces meaning rather than containing it in a uniform, stable, and referential manner. Both a critical analysis and a call to action, the book offers a more capacious notion of agency that promotes engagement with rape as a social issue that pertains to violence in the culture as a whole rather than just to women. I argue that rape is not—as it is now often portrayed in both popular and academic circles—about feminine weakness, passivity, or comportment but about normative identity in a culture where agency and autonomy are valorized as the purview of a hegemonic form of masculinity. It is only when we see rape as a problem that results from normative rather than deviant identities that its deterrence will stop being marginalized as a special-interest issue.

CHAPTER BREAKDOWN

In line with the idea that sexual(ized) violence is key to the ways we make sense of ourselves in the West, *Framing the Rape Victim* examines the appropriation of the trope of sexual violence in contexts as divergent as Hollywood cinema, the maternity care industry, diasporic women's fiction, and feminist theory. I analyze unorthodox and hence controversial representations of rape in twentieth- and twenty-first century U.S. culture instead of the typical images of female victimization rape evokes in order to tease out the ideological implications of such portrayals of victimization for our understanding of agency in the contemporary United States. The proliferating and conflicting formulations of rape in culture reveal, I argue, that the masculinity/femininity dyad does not stop operating when the agents behind the deed become interchangeable.

Chapter 1 offers a theoretical overview of the term victim and highlights the ways the concept has evolved. Whereas victim and its concomitant oppression were once terms around which feminists rallied to protest patriarchal domination, it is now a condition that is blamed for reinforcing if not producing the structures of power that were once identified as its source. The genealogy of the term victim offered in the first chapter reveals, however, that the hermeneutics of suspicion that defines contemporary academic and mainstream responses to victimization is no less vulnerable to ideological appropriation and manipulation than previous allegedly unreflexive deployments of the term. Indeed, to claim that representing people as victims has the power to or the effect of masking their agency assumes that victimization as it is conceptualized precludes agency and vice versa. Conversely, to believe that representing subjects as agents will work to prevent their victimization merely reproduces the assumption that victims are not agents and vice versa. Indeed, if the point of portraying people as agents is for them not to become victims (which it is in current mainstream and academic interventions), then it stands to reason that this new injunction in no way challenges the conceptualization of agency and victimization as opposites.

The next two chapters expose the pitfalls of the two models of agency—liberal individualist and postmodern—through which rape and victimization have been consistently analyzed and that have dominated both academic and public discourses since the 1990s. The liberal model in its most extreme form sees the subject as an unencumbered agent of change, capable of acting independently and making choices in the world. In contrast, the postmodern approach tends to highlight the social structures that shape, constitute, and often hinder the free expression of the subject's will and decision-making power. The two chapters reveal the pitfalls of each approach and pave the way for the alternative model of agency this book promotes, one it has gleaned from the unorthodox representations of sexual violence in recent diasporic novels by Caribbean women writers.

In chapter 2, "Rape and Victimology in Feminist Theory," I discuss the paradoxically widespread negative coding of victimhood within U.S. feminism. In keeping with mainstream culture's rampant aversion for the term "victim," postmodern feminist theorists in particular have emphasized the ways that women's agency is negatively affected by representations of women as victims. Their model of agency focuses on the structures (such as language) that limit the opportunities subjects have and their capacity to make choices. I argue that postmodern feminists (Brown 1995; Gavey 1999; Rentschler 2011) mistakenly assume that their critical perspective on victimization is somehow exempt from co-optation by what Foucault identified as "the ruse of power." Specifically, I argue that influential analyses of rape by Brown (1995), Cahill (2001), Heberle (1996), and Marcus (1992) collude with conservative victim-blaming discourses by inappropriately subjecting feminist political strategies to psychoanalytical or psychological assessments. By viewing rape as a socially scripted but interpersonal interaction, these feminists emphasize victim psychology and agency as a deterrent to rape, but their approach reinscribes the agency/victim binary they are claiming to undo. This has led to postmodern feminism's unavowed and uncritical valorization of agency at the expense of victim subjectivities. I call instead for a retheorization of the shifting meanings of categories such as "victim" and "experience" that would not measure success solely with reference to the fully actualized, unalienated Enlightenment subject.

Chapter 3, "'Birth Rape': Laboring Women, Coaching Men, and Natural Childbirth in the Hospital Setting," deliberately suspends the natural impulse to want to deliberate about whether rape is a legitimate or outrageous metaphor for hospital childbirth. Instead of deciding whether the name fits the crime, I propose that we first examine the ways that women's experience of hospital delivery may illuminate the conundrum surrounding agency in discussions of rape. Answering the questions the hospitalized birth experience raises surrounding women's agency is a prerequisite, I argue, before we can truly determine the legitimacy (or lack thereof) of the use of the rape metaphor in relation to hospital birth. We should pursue this line of inquiry if only because the question of whether "birth rape" is not simply a natural birth gone awry ("bad birth") strongly echoes discussions by conservative pundits of rape as "bad sex." Specifically, this chapter takes to task the health care industry's appropriation of family-centered maternity care rhetoric and the plethora of choices it offers expectant parents in the hospital setting (natural childbirth, epidural, narcotics, personal birth plan, etc.). I argue that this liberal rhetoric of choice and agency only serves to compound and obscure women's disempowered status in relation to the birth experience via the staging of a normative form of masculinity in the delivery room: the husband as "coach." Indeed, this individualist and interpersonal model fails to account for the ways actors can be thoroughly constituted by their social context *while* acting as agents. This chapter exposes how the gendered power dynamics that underlie the practices of hospital delivery reinforce a form of victimization that is all the more pernicious for being veiled by a rhetoric of choice.

The next two chapters show how alternative representations of rape and agency in culture can either reinscribe dominant forms of hegemonic masculinity (chapter 4) or contest them (chapter 5). Chapter 4, "Prison Rape, Masculinity, and the Missed Alliances of Hollywood Cinema," focuses on prison rape to show how Hollywood cinema's representation of male rape gives way not to a feminist alliance with subordinated forms of femininity but to a reification of a damaged yet heroic masculinity that defines itself against a feminist ethos through an appropriation of racial dynamics. The construction of a masculinist nationalist identity is again and again made possible through the social and historical exclusion of structurally feminine and minoritarian subjectivities that are implied in the very category of victim. Even the "softened" masculinity of 1990s Hollywood cinema does not forgo this structural relation since it resorts to processes of racial othering when the apparent dismantling of gendered polarities threatens its dominance. These representations further testify to the fact that victimhood is no longer a viable political or progressive category in the twenty-first century. Rather, victimhood provides the context through which the recent public outcry surrounding male prison rape has led to the reinscription of a heteronormative understanding of sexual violence, in part because men are seen as "undeserving" victims of "homosexual" rape. This response contributes to the overshadowing of sexual violence against incarcerated women. Indeed, despite national efforts to address the prevalence of (male) prisoner rape, the reality of sexual violence against women in prison remains obscured.

Chapter 5, "Rape by Proxy in Contemporary Diasporic Women's Fiction," examines the unorthodox representation of female-on-female rape in the latest wave of immigrant fiction by African diasporic women writers. While such controversial representations fly in the face of the statistical predominance of male-on-female sexual violence, I argue that they work not as contestations but as extensions of the heteronormativizing violence rape epitomizes. The brutal rape of women by women depicted in this fiction functions as what I call a form of "rape by proxy" that ironically succeeds in exposing the very paradigm of hegemonic masculinity and subordinate femininity it seems to undo. It also offers a more capacious notion of agency than the Western notions of embodied autonomous subjectivity that are derived from Enlightenment thinking. In so doing, these novels show us a way out of the agent/victim binary that has dominated discussions of sexual violence and trauma in the popular and academic scenes. Through a focus on "doubling" and double consciousness, they expose the Western logic whereby the recognition of agency has come to depend on the outcome and deterrence of violence. Instead, they create a hybrid form of subjection and subjectification, of coping and healing that does not reinscribe trauma through representation but rather transforms it. Instead of being conceived as feminine passivity, which, in the Western imaginary, is cast as a form of giving up or, worse, implied consent ("not quite rape" [Coetzee 1999, 25]), doubling is represented as a form of *cultural* survival and strategizing (conscious or unconscious) that derives from cultural resistance (vodou) rather than individualized resignation. This reframing of what the West would call pathologized passivity as culturally derived resistance legitimizes victim subjectivity as a more complex state than the normalized contemporary devaluations of victimhood as a morally reduced, fixed, monolithic, and self-inflicted state. It is this book's contention that if the culture could recognize in vulnerability and victimization (rather than in self-aggrandizing agency) forms of empathetic affiliation and community, the victim-blaming rhetoric that dominates our understanding of cultural and national cohesiveness would be remedied in important ways.

Framing the Rape Victim examines how contemporary narratives of victimization are fundamental to the discourses of dominant masculinity that define U.S. nationalism. Specifically, through the analysis of representations of rape as both lived experience and metaphor in various sites of U.S. culture, I examine the rhetorical appropriations and misappropriations of the trope of sexual violence in the construction, consolidation, and contestation of normative national, racial, or gendered identities in the post-9/11 United States. I use the trope of rape as a lens through which to study contemporary U.S. culture. I also single out sites of culture and cultural anxiety to crystallize how rape and victimization are conceptualized today as "deviant" rather than as the necessary outcomes of a normative economy of meaning. This two-pronged approach brings into relief the processes of "framing" (to use Lakoff's term) to which the term victim has consistently been subjected over the last two decades. It also reveals the fundamental role this process has played in the construction of a notion of agency that supports exclusionary notions of American selfhood. I conclude by arguing for a more expansive notion of agency than the ones that dominate popular and academic, conservative and liberal representations of sexualized power relations in the contemporary United States.

In her survey of feminist criticism in the October 2006 issue of the *Publications of the Modern Language Association* (*PMLA*), the influential critic Toril Moi bemoans feminist theory's current domination by poststructuralist theory, "a theoretical doxa that no longer has anything new to say" (2006, 1735) and cites instead Simone de Beauvoir's *The Second Sex* as "a magnificent example of what feminist theory can be at its best" because it "analyzed the world she lived in" (1739). Moi's exhortation that we need to analyze the world we live in resonates with *Framing the Rape Victim*'s assessment of the impasse reached by current conceptualizations of agency and oppression in the United States. The book paves the way for a new approach to issues of victimization, and because it uses the everyday as the springboard for its scholarly and political intervention, it not only offers a new way of thinking about rape and discourse but also models uses of particular kinds of evidence for creating new paradigms for cultural analysis.

1 · FRAMING THE VICTIM

> Frames are mental structures that shape the way we see the world. As a result, they shape the goals we seek, the plans we make, the way we act, and what counts as a good or bad outcome of our actions. In politics, our frames shape our social policies and the institutions we form to carry out policies. To change our frames is to change all of this. Reframing is social change.... Reframing is changing the way the public sees the world. It is changing what counts as commonsense. Because language activates frames, new language is required for new frames. Thinking differently requires speaking differently.
> —George Lakoff, *Don't Think of an Elephant!*

This chapter uses two examples to illustrate how the concept of "victim" in U.S. culture has been framed in discussions that either directly or indirectly pertain to rape. Both events took place in 2004. The first, a particular response to the tragic events of 9/11, is metaphorically linked to sexual violence. The second, the Kobe Bryant rape case, focuses on the legal developments that surrounded a literal case of alleged sexual violence. Both "current events" reveal the hermeneutics of suspicion through which the term "victim" has been framed over the last two decades and the reactionary consequences of this discursive development. They highlight how the critical devaluing of the term "victim" today is represented as a salutary response to previously unreflexive yet ideologically loaded endorsements of the concept. Whereas the underlying assumption in both cases is that the critical assessment of the term "victim" that currently prevails in both the academy and the media corrects the ideological bias that previously defined appropriations of the term, I show how the negative devaluing of the term is itself part of an ideological agenda whose parameters can be traced back to the 1990s political correctness debates. The current distancing trend in discussions of victimization and sexualized violence is no less saturated with a strategic and reappropriative ideology because it is critical. Rather, I argue that far from representing a freeing from ideology, it is actually a reflection of the backlash against the substantial gains made by minority groups over the last few decades.

At the end of March 2004, Karen P. Hughes, one of George W. Bush's longest-serving and closest advisers, began a sixteen-city tour promoting her book *Ten Minutes from Normal*, an account of her life as the president's most trusted employee. Hughes, who had retired from service in 2002, was such a key member of President Bush's team that in 2005 she was asked to return to office as undersecretary of state for public diplomacy and public affairs, a position created in an attempt to change foreigners' negative perceptions of the United States. During her 2004 tour, she appeared on numerous TV and radio shows, where her hosts seemed invariably keen on having her discuss the same passage from her memoir, namely the one describing her reaction to 9/11. As she explains in the book, when the time came for the president to give his first speech to the nation after the tragedy, Hughes insisted that he not describe the event in the terms that had been originally planned. To quote Hughes, "When [Ari Fleishman] read it, the first line made me apoplectic: 'America today was the victim of. . . .' 'We are not victims,' I interrupted, 'we may have been attacked but we are *not* victims.' Ari agreed, and put [White House communications director] Dan [Bartlett] on the phone" (2004, 238). The sentence was subsequently altered to "America today was under attack," a change that elicited the approval of every radio host and—we can only surmise—listener during Hughes's interviews.

This example powerfully illustrates the problematic status "victim" has come to occupy in the United States since the 1990s, a status that has everything to do with how the term operates as a representation. In rejecting the term "victim," Hughes is not suggesting that the United States was not actually the victim of a terrorist attack or that there were no casualties as a result of it. What is at stake in her visceral reaction is how the language might represent the United States as a shamed victim. She is concerned not with the event itself but with the framing of the event in relation to a crisis that was very much perceived and repeatedly cast as a metaphorical form of sexual violence. In light of the fact that 9/11 was a tragedy for which, significantly, the crime of rape served as the "central paradigm for framing events" (Cole 2008, 118; Hawkesworth 2005, 132), it is not surprising that for Hughes, the negative connotations and stigma attached to the concept of victim would similarly taint the target of violence (the United States) rather than its source (the terrorists) in relation to the national tragedy. In other words, Hughes is echoing an understanding of the term "victim" that the political correctness debates of the 1990s turned into common usage and that the response to rape further popularized, namely as the "perception of one who is weak and was overcome or manipulated by an external source possibly due to his/her own negligence or helplessness" (Andrews quoted in Underwood and Edmunds 2002, 5–6). These negative connotations are compounded in cases that are metaphorically or literally associated with sexual violence, a crime for which victim-blaming attitudes are the norm. By insisting that "we [Americans] are *not* victims," Hughes thus challenges what was once a tautology, namely that any innocent bystander who is killed in the course of an attack is indeed a legitimate victim, and instead adopts an understanding of the term "victim" as a sign of "individual powerlessness over internal resources and a dependence on others to rectify the situation" (ibid.). She thus embraces a view that reveals the incompatibility of the concept with the U.S. nation and U.S. nationalism. Victims are what the United States and its inhabitants cannot be. That is, victimhood is a condition in opposition to which American identity is defined. Americans help victims, they do not become victims. They may identify *with* but not *as* victims.

George Lakoff describes the process that defines what counts as "commonsense" as "framing." The listeners' and radio hosts' tacit approval of Karen Hughes's rejection of the term "victim" illustrates the kind of "commonsensical" framing of the term Lakoff evokes. Not once was Hughes asked to explain why saying that the United States was "the victim of a terrorist attack" was such an outrageous statement. Not once did the callers ask why people who are killed by a terrorist act are not actually victims. The unavowed logic behind Hughes's reaction works at the level of her listeners' collective "cognitive unconscious," that is, at the level of the "structures in our brains that we cannot consciously access, but know by their consequences: the way we reason and what counts as commonsense" (Lakoff 2004, xv). To Hughes and her listeners, the use of the word automatically suggests an acceptance of defeat and an internalization of failure that are highly gendered and are taken for granted when the term "victim" is used. These associations have now become "simply" incompatible with the myth and "imaginary community" of the nation.

The release of Hughes's book in 2004 coincided with another current event that showcased a similar rhetorical debate surrounding the concept of victimization. This time, the debate took place in the country's courts, and it was about a literal rather than metaphorical case of sexualized violence. During the 2004 legal proceedings of the rape trial against the NBA superstar Kobe Bryant, "victim" was the "identity" that, ironically, both the defendant and the accuser were claiming best defined their status in court. In an effort to shift the blame from the basketball star to his accuser, defense attorney Hal Haddon argued that referring to the female plaintiff as a victim would impair jurors' ability to consider evidence impartially. He insisted that its use would necessarily inculpate their client as the agent behind the deed while denying the accuser's own sexual agency: "Until Mr. Bryant is acquitted, he is a victim, or at least, arguably is." Judge W. Terry Ruckriegle granted the defense's request and ruled that Bryant's alleged victim could no longer be called "victim." She had to be referred to by name in the courtroom and as a "person" in jury instructions. Bryant's team of attorneys also asked the judge to prohibit use of the term "defendant" in reference to the Lakers' guard, but Ruckriegle rejected that request, because, he thought, the term "defendant" was "an accurate reflection of his legal status" (Cypher 2004).

As Cynthia Stone, a spokeswoman for the Colorado Coalition Against Sexual Assault, noted at the time, this was the first time that what the judge had termed "this semantic debate" had ever become an issue in the courtroom, since until this case, the term victim had been routinely used in the criminal justice system "where legalistic definitions of victim and offender are an important aspect of the system's functions" (Underwood and Edmunds 2002, 6). However, according to Larry Pozner, former president of the National Association of Criminal Defense Lawyers, this terminology fight was a major issue that went beyond semantics: "In a courtroom, only a jury can decide whether she's a victim and to call her a victim is to prejudice the jury," he said. "Only when a jury decides guilt or innocence will her status be decided" (quoted in Cypher 2004). Whether one thinks this semantic dispute is well grounded or not, it shows the discursive power the term "victim" has accrued in the eyes of most Americans today, so much so that routine court proceedings have been altered in reaction to it. In other words, a word that was consistently and inconspicuously used in court is now ascribed an ideological power it never previously had. In what seems like a symptom of what Joan Didion means by magical thinking in her book *The Year of Magical Thinking*, it is as if the mere use of the term has the power to influence decision making and make things happen.[1] Or, to borrow De Lauretis's terms, it is as if the court suddenly and selectively became aware that the rhetoric of violence may entail the violence of rhetoric, that violence is "engendered in representation" (De Lauretis 1985, 33). Most importantly, however, Bryant's defense lawyers rejected its use because in questioning the woman's status as a victim, they corroborated her representation as a sexual agent; that is, a consenting adult whose promiscuity they sought to emphasize through repeated references to her past and subsequent sexual relationships.

Whether we believe, as Bryant's attorney intimated during the trial, that the white nineteen-year-old's accusation stemmed from a history of "black men hav[ing] long been falsely accused of rape by white women" (Associated Press 2004) or rather, that Bryant did occupy the position of dominant "white" masculinity in relation to a girl whose class, age, and gender subordinated her to him,[2] the mobilization of the agent/victim opposition as a way of undermining rape allegations by the prosecution reveals the contextualized ways that the term "victim" gains visibility as an ideologically loaded word in the twenty-first century. It also echoes Hughes's visceral and categorical refusal to refer to the U.S. nation as "victim of" a terrorist attack. Hughes's reaction stemmed from her unwillingness to conceive the United States as both agent and victim. Victimization was incompatible with her view of the United States as a superpower.

It is no coincidence that both of these incidents took place in 2004, the year of the first presidential campaign after 9/11. Presidential races are transitional times when nationalist narratives become magnified, rhetorical strategies surrounding national identity gain visibility, and discursive patterns and structures of feeling are elaborated, refined, repeated, crystallized, and revised for the voting public's benefit. During the 2012 presidential campaign, for instance, rape was again brought to the forefront of political discussions and became a primary way Republicans and Democrats distinguished their political agendas from one another. When Congressman Todd Akin (Missouri's 2nd District) claimed that rapes that were "legitimate" would not lead to pregnancy because the woman's body has a way of "shut[ing] down the whole thing" through a stress response, or when Indiana's senatorial candidate Robert Mourdock claimed that a pregnancy after rape was "something that God intended to happen," these comments soon stopped being "a few errant remarks from insensitive politicians" (Filipovic 2012) and became part of a political platform that repeatedly reinforced the view of women as passive vessels of God's will or man's sperm.[3] Other comments included Wisconsin state representative Roger Rivard's assertion that "some girls rape easy"; Tennessee state senator Douglas Henry's comment that "rape, ladies and gentlemen, is not today what rape was. Rape, when I was learning these things, was the violation of a chaste woman, against her will, by some party not her spouse"; Republican activist Phyllis Schlafly's declaration that marital rape doesn't exist; and South Dakota Republican Bill Napoli's contention that "[a] real-life description to me would be a rape victim, brutally raped, savaged. The girl was a virgin. She was religious. She planned on saving her virginity until she was married" (quoted in Filipovic 2012). On 23 January 2013, the Republican lawmaker and state representative in New Mexico, Cathrynn Brown, introduced House bill 206, which would have legally required victims of rape to carry their pregnancies to term in order to use the fetus as evidence for a sexual assault trial. This bill would have charged a rape victim who ended her pregnancy with a third-degree felony for "tampering with evidence" (Bassett 2013). Last but not least, on 1 March 2013, Celeste Greig, the president of the conservative California Republican Assembly, the state's oldest and largest GOP volunteer organization, and the person Ronald Reagan once called it "the conscience of the Republican Party," told the *San Jose Mercury News* that pregnancies by rape are rare "because it's an act of violence, because the body is traumatized" (quoted in Harmon 2013).[4] These examples powerfully show how central rape has become to this country's cultural narratives about agency and identity.

The narratives of gender identity and social meaning that are constructed around sexual victimization "speak" to voters from all walks of life and are, during election time, routinely appropriated by both the left and the right. During the 2004 presidential campaign, both Republicans and Democrats deployed a strikingly similar narrative in their attempts to convince voters that their party was the most adept at protecting America in the War on Terror. Ironically, at a time when the United States had actually become the victim of a terrorist attack, politicians and presidential candidates from both parties became most keen to distance the country and its citizens from the concept of victimization. Drawing on the anti-victimist discourses that had been popularized during the previous decade, both Republicans and Democrats sought to portray themselves as masculine heroes rather than feminized victims. Bush was represented as the "cowboy" president Ronald Reagan had made popular in the 1980s, while Democrats worked hard to convince Americans that their candidate was the real man "reporting for duty" (Cole 2008, 123). In the context of the War on Terror, the concept of victim came to be mobilized as the condition and representation to mistrust, vilify, abhor, and reject. It is no surprise, then, that one of the legacies of such a rhetorical development is that in the 2012 campaign, politicians no longer had any qualms about publicly and repeatedly making demeaning remarks about rape victims or trying to withdraw heretofore unquestioned bipartisan legal protections reserved for victims of violence. The Violence Against Women Act (VAWA), which was enacted in 1994 to provide greater legal protections and other services to survivors of domestic violence and their families, had passed the House of Representatives uncontested for nearly twenty years, but in January 2013 it expired due to bipartisan gridlock. One could argue that in the aftermath of the War on Terror, the word "victim" simply became pure rhetoric with no content.

The trope of sexual(ized) violence in the United States is now mediated by neoconservative configurations of victimization that work to obscure the gendered and correlatively racialized dimensions of forms of violence. The meaning of the term "victim" over the last few decades has undergone significant rhetorical and ideological developments that have affected victims along deeply gendered and racialized lines. Specifically, since the terrorist attacks on the World Trade Center on 9/11, a renewed sociocultural shift toward a neoconservatism that was initiated in the 1980s has consolidated the view that the United States has been emasculated and its sovereignty rendered vulnerable to attack. In this discursive space, victimhood no longer functions as a political category that can be successfully deployed to support the adoption of policy and law reforms but rather as one that the neoconservative media has successfully reframed as a sign of moral weakness and self-generated failure.

The discursive and ideological processes involved in demarcating "good" and "bad" victims in U.S. culture work, I argue, to reinforce hierarchical relations based on raced, gendered, and classed power. To expose these processes and bridge the divide between representation and reality in representations of sexualized violence requires a contextualization and historical analysis of the anti-victimist stance that has defined discussions of rape. The Hughes and Bryant examples, which mobilize rape as a metaphor on the one hand and as a crime on the other, are cases in point. Significantly, both instances mobilize a particular devaluation of victimhood that has entered the realm of "commonsense" in the U.S. national consciousness.

THE DEVALUING OF VICTIMHOOD

To fully understand the negative connotations associated with the concept of victim in the United States today, we need to look back at the "political correctness" debates of the 1990s from which they derive. The last decade of the twentieth century witnessed the emergence of a virulent anti-victimist discourse, notably with the publication of Richard Bernstein's essay "Ideas and Trends: The Rising Hegemony of the Politically Correct" in an October 1990 issue of the *New York Times*. The article marked the emergence of the term of "political correctness" in public discourse and the beginning of a rampant devaluation and degendering of victimhood and minority claims in the mainstream. Dinesh D'Souza's attack on the "victim revolution" (1992) on university campuses was probably one of the most popularized versions of this discourse, and both higher education and radical feminism soon became the prime target of such conservative criticisms. In *Tenured Radicals* (1990), for instance, Roger Kimball (1990) singled out radical feminism for promoting special interests that were antithetical to the acquisition of the kind of core and universal knowledge needed to shape the future citizens of a modern democracy. Similarly, for Ellen Klein (1998), academic feminism constituted a threat to rigorous scholarship, while Carolyn Mooney (1988) echoed a large number of conservative commentators when she accused feminists of having abandoned rational thought in favor of their own political agenda. As Alyson Convery notes, "Feminist ideas were positioned at the very foundations of the edifice labeled 'political correctness.' What has to be stressed here is that these critics created the very entity that they attributed to feminist and other politically progressive theorists. The 'political correctness' code emerged as a mechanism for undermining minority challenges to the status quo, firstly by discursively collapsing all claims of disadvantage as being about victimhood and victimization (whether or not such claims were couched in precisely these terms), and then by devaluing victimhood as a morally, and not just a practically, reduced state" (2011, 6).

Convery's analysis highlights the enduring and homogenizing effect of the encoding strategies of politically correct discourses over the last two decades. Not only is invoking the term "victim" enough to trigger negative and devaluing connotations about a person, but all self-proclaimed victims are now subjected to disapproval (at best) or distrust and condemnation (at worst). The "innocent" victim of the past can now only ever be the victim who rejects that status. Drawing attention to or identifying victimization as a platform for solidarity and social change is immediately recast as a ruse of power rather than as a legitimate critique of it. Convery's detailed survey of eight influential Anglo-American feminist journals between 1987 and 2007 reveals that the denigrated term "victim" has become so paradigmatic today that, ironically, even feminist theorists participate in its devaluing. While most feminists see their sustained critique of the concept of victim as a form of theoretical and interventionist contestation, Convery's research shows instead that the delegitimization of the concept is not only shared across national and cultural boundaries of the Anglo-American academy (Australia, Britain, and the United States) but also bridges the gap between conservative critics and a large number of academic feminists. Interestingly, one of the best-selling books in France in 2006, Elizabeth Badinter's *Dead End Feminism*, echoed the Anglo-American suspicion that women's victimization was a symptom of the "cult of victimhood" to which feminism has fallen victim and that depicts women as defenseless and oppressed. This cult, Badinter argues, conflates real and fake victims and is the reason why contemporary feminism has lost all credibility. Badinter also situates the emergence of this new sensibility in the 1990s after women had made some real advances in social and political life. What these transatlantic examples repeatedly show is that the undermining of the category of victim goes hand in hand with an uncritical ennobling of agency and resistance as markers of the kind of self-reliance, sense of responsibility, and complexity that victims purportedly lack.[5]

Whereas victimization once referred to something tragic or criminal (outside the self) that affected one's life experience, it is now increasingly used to denote a problem that is intrinsic to the self and that makes one partly if not wholly responsible for the regrettable experience to which one was subjected. I mentioned earlier that the term now evokes resignation, passivity, subordination, weakness, powerlessness, and dependence. Victims of sexual violence, for instance, now balk at being "victims" and want to be called survivors instead.[6] Self-help gurus repeatedly warn their listeners not to indulge in a victim mentality. Perhaps, as suggested earlier, it is the grueling tragedy of the terrorist attacks of September 11, 2001, that triggered an even more virulent anti-victimist discourse. As Cole explains, "We might assume that the tragedy of 9/11, which brought forth in the U.S. new groups of victims . . . would curb anti-victimism. On the contrary, efforts to embrace and commemorate those who perished during the attacks, to assess national and individual responsibility, and to validate warmongering abroad, all relied on anti-victim discourse" (2008, 118).

What is more, the combination of anti-victimist and anti-feminist backlash has led to the entrenchment of victimization as a feminized concept. Victimhood is irretrievably coded as feminine, no doubt because of its reframing as a sign of weakness and passivity, traits that have traditionally been ascribed to femininity in Western culture. The prototypical victim "has become a woman," to evoke an epigrammatic phrase used in the 2004 movie *In My Country* (based on Antjie Krog's 1998 novel *Country of My Skull*), a film about the Truth and Reconciliation Commission Hearings in South Africa.[7] Today, the concept of "victim" automatically summons the image of a downtrodden, helpless, and usually female individual in need of assistance or counseling, all the more so since feminists themselves have acquiesced to the reframing of victimization as a characterological or psychological trait rather than the result of experience. In the United States, this development has been further reinforced because the tradition of connecting women to the discourses of the psyche is, as Dana Becker (2000) states, 200 years old and has historically been key to the disempowerment of women.[8] This explains why even such an incontestable victimization as the World Trade Center bombing paradoxically led to endlessly recycled anti-victimist statements by both Republican and Democratic administrations. According to conservative pundits such as William Bennett, the terrorist attacks were the price we paid for the feminization of the United States in the hands of "victimology mongers" who left the country vulnerable and weak. The only hope out of this quagmire, they claimed, was the remasculinization of the country and the restoration of patriarchal power (see Cole 2008, 119).

Considering the prevalence of anti-feminist conservative ideology in U.S. culture, it is not surprising that gendered views of victimization that align with a binary conceptualization of passive (and feminized) victimhood and resistant agency (masculine self-sufficiency) should define the response to sexual violence. To fully understand the ramifications of the dominant and regulating discourses of victimhood in relation to rape, it is important to move to an analysis of "victim" as a dynamic and rhetorical term that produces rather than contains meaning. We can thus be attentive to the contingent ways that preconceived notions about who is or is not a "victim" reinscribe normative power relations based on race, gender, and class. Such a cultural analysis allows for a more complex and nuanced understanding of the gendered and racial dimensions of victim subjectivities in representations of sexualized violence.

ENNOBLING AGENCY

Whether rape is represented as metaphor or reality, its analysis typically centers on the question of the agency of the victim. Agency and victimization are conceptualized in opposition to one another, and the presence of one automatically implies the absence of the other. Agency is valorized as a mark of self-reliance, resistance, and moral worth, a valorization that is increasingly enabled today through the devaluation of victimhood's association with passivity. This opposition is present, for instance, in the international best-selling mystery trilogy—*The Girl with the Dragon Tattoo, The Girl Who Played with Fire,* and *The Girl Who Kicked the Hornet's Nest.* In 2010, all of these titles were in the top ten highest-selling e-books of all time. Stieg Larsson's protagonist Lisbeth Salandar is tellingly subjected to a gruesome rape when she is identified as a victim in the text and as an avenging feminist heroine when she disavows the term. Her sadistic guardian and rapist, the narrator tells us, picked her because she *was* a victim ("The sadist specialised in people who were in a position of dependence. Advokat Bjurman had chosen her as a victim" [Larsson 2008, 253]). Later, however, we are urged to admire Salandar for her refusal to remain the victim her perpetrator identified her as, a diminished state that is symbolized through an association with women's centers: "Even though she was well aware of what a women's crisis centre was for, it never occurred to her to turn to one herself. Crisis centres existed, in her eyes, for *victims*, and she had never regarded herself as a victim. Consequently, her only remaining option was to do what she had always done and take matters in her own hands and solve her problems on her own. That was definitely an option. And it did not bode well for Herr Advokat Nils Bjurman" (ibid., 237). The emphasis on Lisbeth Salandar's subjectivity in the text makes the enactment of rape dependent on her inner strength and character or the lack thereof.

The frequent use of the term "survivor" instead of "victim" in U.S. culture also testifies to people's inability to see victims as capable of agency. When I was completing my 40-hour training as a rape crisis volunteer in the mid-1990s, I attended a panel that included four women who were to tell us about their experiences as victims of sexual assault. As could be expected, the organizer introduced them all as "survivors." One of the panelists, however, immediately spoke up to object to the term on the grounds that she did not feel like a survivor *yet*. What was striking about that moment was that in reclaiming a word that had been forsaken in the name of her agency, she was not only contesting the fixed, monolithic meanings ascribed to "victim" ("yet") but ironically reclaiming her agency through the reappropriation of the very word that was supposed to deny it.

By contrast, Karen Hughes's visceral reaction to the representation of the United States as "victim" was very much grounded in the "Cult of True Victimhood" that defines most anti-victimist discourses (for the "cult of true victimhood," see Cole 2007). The underlying message of Hughes's rejection of the term "victim" was that true victims will always deny being victims. Similarly, the Cult of Victimhood was operative in the Kobe Bryant rape case since the defense attorney was arguing for the removal of the term from the proceedings even as he was explicitly claiming the status of "real" victim for his client. Anti-victimism occurs in the name of the pure, innocent victim who denies being one.

The Cult of True Victimhood is incompatible with the image of the United States as a superpower and agent in world affairs. The opposition of (a masculinized) agency and (feminized) victimization that grounds this conceptualization is the process through which the nation generates "other" (abject) bodies and posits itself as their opposite, namely as an inviolable, unimpeachable, and homogenous entity.[9] The trope of the "victim," which is increasingly framed as a repository of passivity and weakness, cannot be reconciled with the American nation's foundational identification with heroism; that is, "the brave" and (un)sung heroes the national anthem celebrates. As a cartoon by Daryl Cagle, "How We Remember September 11th," puts it, the "Heroes" of 9/11 were firemen, while the "Victims" were young girls in pigtails, weeping. The nation and its iconic representatives make it their business to rescue victims, but they cannot themselves be victims even if they actually were victims of the terrorist attack. This explains why some commentators began referring to the dead as heroes rather than victims even when no heroic act was involved. This may also explain why the very firefighters and 9/11 first responders who have been celebrated as the nation's heroes were all but abandoned when they needed help to pay for the long-term and sometimes deadly physical afflictions (heart disease, respiratory disease, cancer) that resulted from the time they spent in the foul air of Ground Zero.

Heroes-turned-victims are not an identity the nation's representatives could respond to or support. In December 2010, Republicans in the Senate staged a successful filibuster to keep the James Zadroga 9/11 Health and Compensation Act of 2010, which sought to provide $7 billion in benefits to workers who responded to the 9/11 terrorist attacks, from coming up for a vote. If it had not been for Jon Stewart's excoriation of that betrayal on his final *Daily Show* of the year, with a panel of four first responders, each of whom had a potentially deadly condition (one of them had stage 4 throat cancer), that legislation would not have passed. It was after Stewart's show that Fox News came out for the legislation and Rudolf Giuliani began endorsing it. Republicans then joined Democrats in a unanimous vote to fund the legislation for the heroes-become-victims.

The dualism of victim/agent that grounds these reactions to national crises defines the Kobe Bryant case as well: the defense's argument that the use of the term "victim" would unjustly inculpate their client and deny the accuser's sexual agency similarly assumes that victim and agent are mutually exclusive states. This argument is an all-too-familiar one for feminists who have historically worked to expose the ways this opposition perpetuates gender inequality. The two diametrically opposed options women are traditionally offered with regard to sexual subjectivity are "innocent" victim or "guilty" sexual agent. This is the same norm that continues to make it difficult to prosecute cases of sexual assault against prostitutes and erotic dancers.

In Buffalo, New York, in 2007, the arrest of the Bike Path Rapist, a man linked to eleven cases of rape and three murders over twenty-six years, confirmed the persistence of this binary in the popular imaginary. In September 2006, the discovery of the body of a white middle-class suburban mother twelve years after the Bike Path Rapist's previous attacks led the authorities and the press to puzzle over the uncharacteristic gap that separated his latest crime from his previous ones. Speculations were made all over the news about the reasons for this hiatus. Only one source (to my knowledge) dared suggest that the Bike Path Rapist's decade of silence coincided with a series of murdered prostitutes in the Niagara Falls, Ontario, area. In other words, while it was conceivable to all that the Bike Path Rapist might have attacked many more women, it took years and an incidental hit based on DNA by the local lab before the possibility that the same man might also be responsible for attacks on prostitutes was considered. No doubt such a possibility was all the more difficult to envisage because it would create a connection between women who are "innocent" and those who are "guilty" and associate a crime against normative femininity with the rape of a prostitute, which is seen by the dominant discourse as a contradiction in terms (see Becker and Beebe 2009).

This kind of binary framing has made it difficult for people to recognize that one may have sexual agency, even be extremely "promiscuous," and still be the victim of rape or that a person does not have to be or act "innocent" to be a victim, that completely immoral individuals can be victimized too. Drawing attention to the victim's "innocence" or lack thereof shifts the focus away from the circumstances that subordinate the subject to her inability or supposed "unwillingness" to prevent them, her unexpressed agency. It creates the faulty assumption that a person's general moral fiber has a bearing on their status as the victim of a crime. The most unethical or criminal person can clearly be the victim of a crime no less than the most ethical one. The conditions surrounding the subject are what matters and needs to be changed, not the subject's propensities.

The conundrum evoked by the status of victim today can be partly explained by the tension between the two models of agency that have dominated both social theory and public life for the last few decades. Agency within social constraints is defined in diametrically opposed ways, depending on the degree to which individuals are perceived as able to free themselves from the hold of social conventions and expectations. As Convery notes, it is part of the ennobling of agency and the attendant denigration of victimhood that agency is the term that is always theoretically analyzed and complicated while victimhood is typically posited as a fixed, unsophisticated, and one-dimensional term:

> The elaboration believed capable of achieving the required analytical complexity is to the notion of agency—the brief is to develop a concept of agency that

can coherently accommodate an awareness both of structural impediments to action, and of possibilities of action. There is no such call to similarly complicate the notion of victimhood, so that it might be considered as multi-layered, as marked by inaction at some points but propelling to action at others, or as being applicable in some respects to women who occupy simultaneous oppressed/oppressor roles depending on their positioning within intersecting axes of power—in other words, one that could also coherently incorporate elements of agency. (2011, 187)

On the one hand, liberal individualism in its strongest form sees individuals as preceding the forms of social discipline to which they are subjected and hence as capable of "robust agency" (Carle 2005, 307). The liberal individual is perceived as capable of making choices, bringing about change, and achieving his or her life goals. On the other hand, postmodern approaches tend to emphasize the socially constructed nature of human aspirations, values, and decision-making processes, so much so that they come close to denying the possibility of agency altogether. In *Thinking Fragments: Psychoanalysis, Feminism, and Postmodernism in the Contemporary West*, Jane Flax sums up the postmodern position in the following oft-quoted sentence: "Man is forever caught in the web of fictive meaning, in chains of signification, *in which the subject is merely another position in language*" (1990, 32; Flax's italics).

The tension between the liberal and postmodern accounts has haunted feminism in particular since the 1990s, all the more so since the strongest version of the postmodern "death of the subject" has been deemed incompatible with feminism's project of female emancipation (Benhabib 1995, 20).[10] If the subject is the product of the language of which it is supposed to be the source, how can it have the distance necessary to alter its symbolic structures and narratives? As Seyla Benhabib has compellingly pointed out, this position dissolves concepts of intentionality, self-reflexivity, accountability, and autonomy (Benhabib 1995).

Framing the Rape Victim joins the ranks of scholars and feminists who have worked to mediate between these two models of agency. For instance, in her influential work about the social construction of gender identity, Judith Butler maintains the importance and possibility of a space for individual and collective agency. Similarly, in "Theorizing Agency," Susan Carle finds in classical pragmatism's theory of the self a useful paradigm to acknowledge both the socially constructed nature of the self and the possibility of agency: "To the classical pragmatists, selves in interaction with each other constantly reconstruct the social environment, just as this social environment, itself composed of selves in interaction, constantly constructs, or gives social identity to, these selves" (2005, 307). In so doing, these scholars offer a critique of both the liberal version's implausible notion that subjects "choose" their identities or fates and of postmodern feminism's unacknowledged and unresolved contradictions when it comes to theorizing agency in relation to sexual violence.

By questioning the sustained challenge the term "victim" has been incurring over the last few decades, I do not mean to imply, however, that we should not interrogate the ways the term, like any other concept (including democracy), gets deployed and (mis)appropriated in cultural life. It is, for instance, crucial to question the premises of the victims' rights movement in the United States. The history of the emergence of this movement betrays its reactionary ethos; the victims' rights campaign entered the world of politics under right-wing patronage, never to leave it. In 1982, President Reagan and Attorney General Edwin Meese created the President's Task Force on Victims of Crime, which issued a report that proposed that a victims' rights provision be added to the Sixth Amendment. This emotional report, which did not include documentation of its claims, included the story of the rape of a 50-year-old woman. The report convinced Congress to start an Office for Victims of Crime in the Justice Department and secure funding for various services for victims (President's Task Force on Victims of Crime 1982). Since then, the victims' rights campaign has increasingly worked under the aegis of right-wing funders and politicians who push for increased executions and longer prison sentences and whose vengeance-rights agenda isolates crime from broader social and economic issues (see Shapiro 1997; Rapping 2003).[11] In such contexts, the concept of victim and the implications of its use must be challenged because they create the illusion that the state functions as a neutral arbiter between individuals. Similarly, the link that was historically established between white victimization and black aggression requires the same kind of radical debunking, all the more so since its roots lie in the fraudulent rape charges that were routinely invoked as grounds for the lynching of black men at the turn of the last century. According to Bevacqua (2000), the racism through which rape was brought to the public's attention in the nineteenth century also characterized the arrival of rape on the public agenda in the 1970s, since the rape policies that were adopted then were meant to protect the nation's (white) women against black criminality.

The critical scrutiny that challenges the ideological deployment of victimization in these contexts is both crucial and emancipatory. While I am in no way advocating a return to unexamined uses of the term "victim" (or of any term, for that matter), I am suggesting that the relentless and abstracted rejection of the word "victim" in contemporary cultural and academic life today has become part of the problem rather than the solution. Far from functioning ad infinitum as evidence of deep theoretical acumen or social consciousness, it has now become appropriated by the same rhetorical and ideological apparatus that the original critics of victimization sought to debunk. This reappropriation reminds us how common anti-victimist conceptions of oppression have become since the 1990s.

It also reminds us that, as Stuart Hall (1980b) argues, cultural texts and representations, no matter what their provenance, produce meanings in society that are necessarily circumscribed by their conditions of production. Cultural meanings surrounding victimization today ironically work at the intersection of the popular and academic scenes to transmit ideologies of race, gender, and class that normalize sexual violence and hierarchies of power.

It is remarkable that the metaphorical, rhetorical, and ideological appropriations of victimization should not have received more attention from cultural studies scholars. While commentators of widely divergent persuasions agree that calling someone a victim is problematic, few have paused to examine how the terms of this remarkably uniform critical consensus fail to account for the different contexts in which the victim/agent dichotomy is naturalized, implicitly assumed, or contested. It could be that because everyone knows that women and nonwhite populations are disproportionately the most disenfranchised sections of the world population, the language and associations used to discuss their victimization are not examined (after all, they are victims, aren't they?). As a result, the production of a form of naturalized referentiality in relation to victimization and its imbrication with race and gender fails to be scrutinized. By contrast, I want to highlight the rhetorical ways victimization has in fact implicitly and inherently become a woman's or minority issue (or "problem") in the national imaginary. This is not to intimate that women and minorities in general do not experience injustice on a larger scale; rather, I suggest that the ways that victimization invokes gender and race (and vice versa) today is often detrimental to the very people suffering from it. In other words, we should not merely assume that it is because women and nonwhite populations in general are the most disenfranchised both within and across national boundaries that the notion of victimization is gendered and racialized. Neither a correspondence between representation and the reality behind it nor the absence thereof should absolve us of the responsibility of investigating the terms of the production of a particular representational politics. For instance, despite the "fact" that U.S. women are four to six times more likely to die of heart disease than of breast cancer and are less likely to survive an attack than men, heart attacks are still largely represented or perceived as the result of a "male" disease. Women account for nearly half of all heart attack deaths (heart attacks are the number one killer of both women and men nationwide), and more women over sixty-five die of a heart attack than from all forms of cancers combined. Similarly, the gendering and racialization of the term "victim" is not just a reflection of actual experiences of poverty and oppression but functions as a contributor to them. Associating the status of victim with certain segments of the population ensures that oppression becomes an issue of identity rather than one of structure, an issue of ethnics rather than ethics, and one of individualized behavior rather than governance.

Similarly, when so-called postmodern feminists strive to have women change an allegedly internalized script of rape or a so-called feminine comportment as a deterrent to rape, they cannot help but reinscribe the victim-blaming effects of neoliberal conceptualizations of oppression. Making the prevention of rape about women's psychological or physiological inclinations still relies, albeit cryptically, on an ontology whereby subjects precede their relations. In so doing, it also obscures the structural difference that defines the masculinity/femininity paradigm in representations and experiences of sexual violence by replacing it with a psychological one.

The pitfalls of the liberal and postmodern models of agency discussed in chapters 2 and 3 illustrate the importance of expanding our understanding of agency in representations of sexualized violence. Chapters 4 and 5 work in tandem to show how alternative representations of rape can work to either reinscribe the dominant regime of hegemonic agential masculinity (chapter 4) or to contest it (chapter 5). All four chapters point to the importance of challenging the conflation in both feminist theory and the public sphere of victimhood with passivity and of subjectivity with agency. I argue that the erasure of victimhood as a viable subject position in feminist theory has failed to advance the cause of women's empowerment. It has merely created an updated version of the agent/victim binary whereby the once-positive valences attached to victim subjectivities have been replaced by negative ones, while what was once criticized as a masculinist version of agency (self-defense, for instance) is now advocated as a deterrent to rape. Feminist theory has ironically aligned itself with neoconservative narratives about rape that locate the source of the problem in psychology or in the wrong choices (female) victims make in their interactions with men. To evoke Lauren Berlant's important work (2008), victim subjectivity has thus become yet another way the dominant culture both creates and confronts the female complaint; that is, when women's public voice is allowed to enter the public sphere, it does so only in an extremely reduced form.

By analyzing the languages and rhetorical justifications surrounding victimization in U.S. culture, *Framing the Rape Victim* seeks to expose the iconography of legitimation and delegitimation through which forms of sexual(ized) violence are framed, reframed, and contained along gendered and racial lines. We live in a historical moment when power is consolidated through received language and structures of rhetoric whose operations are particularly evident in the contradictory yet "commonsensical" uses of the term "victim" over the last few decades. These rhetorical structures have affected everything from individual consciousness to identity-forming institutions such as health care, Hollywood cinema, academic discourse, and popular culture. Through an analysis of pertinent popular, literary, political, and academic arenas such as hospital birth, Hollywood melodrama, "feminist" bestsellers, and contemporary immigrant novels, this book thus brings into relief how the rhetorical strategies surrounding victimization have worked to regulate national anxieties about the shifting boundaries of nationality, gender, and race in the contemporary United States.

2 · RAPE AND VICTIMOLOGY IN FEMINIST THEORY

In the late sixties and seventies, the second wave of the women's movement became the site of emergence of a pro-victim approach to rape in public policy.[1] Specifically, the second wavers worked to undermine the dualistic representations of victimization and agency that informed discourses of rape and challenged the diametrically opposed options of "innocent" sexual victim and rational (and hence "guilty") sexual agent that were traditionally offered women with regard to sexual subjectivity. The second wavers were instrumental in exposing this configuration as an extension of what they called "rape culture." In the same way that queer politics worked to turn "normal" into just one among many other forms of "performing queerness," they reclaimed victimization and oppression as terms that should be yoked to activism and self-empowerment rather than to pity and passivity. In fact, second-wave feminists proclaimed women's status as victims of patriarchal oppression *in order to* bring about social change.

Today, in stark contrast to this appropriation of "oppression" and its concomitant "victimization" as instruments of social transformation, the very act of identifying people as "victims" is ironically perceived as part of their problem. It is seen as a speech act with negative discursive and material ramifications that keeps its referents in suspended helplessness while freezing unwanted social relations in time. Calling people "victims" is often seen as a willful misrecognition of people's power of self-determination, as an ideological instrument of subordination that encourages them to remain stuck and conceals their ability to change the unfortunate circumstances of their lives. Phrases such as "anti-victim" feminism, also known as "neo," "post," "dissident," or "post-ideological" feminism, permeate the airwaves, contending that women need to stop focusing on oppression and start enacting their own power. In an effort to debunk what is now labeled "victim feminism," the phrase "power feminism" which Naomi Wolf originally coined in Fire with Fire, has gained credence among academic and nonacademic feminists alike. Yet this current obsession with the ideological repercussions of a term people would often no longer be caught dead using obscures the fact that this negativity is not inherent in the term itself. As I explained in chapter 1, its critique, like its earlier allegedly "naïve" endorsement, is a rhetorical and discursive development that needs contextualization. This is all the more ironic, since for second-wave feminism, being a victim did not signify a lack of agency. Identifying and rallying *as* victims was all about reappropriating the concept for women's empowerment and about exposing the arbitrariness of the supposedly fundamental dichotomy between victimization and agency that defined approaches to sexual oppression.

In other words, the objection to the use of the term today overlooks the fact that its implications and ideological repercussions are context bound and fluctuate. In criticizing a previous generation of feminists for rallying around "women's oppression," we are assuming that they were operating in the context of the same meanings that were subsequently attached to the concept of victim. The development of "victim" into a sign of resignation and self-willed subordination turns feminism's subject of change into a "subject of feeling," thus neutralizing the emphasis of the late 1960s on transforming the subject of feeling into a subject of change.[2] This is all the more ironic since this postmodern intervention occurred in the name of the progressive ideals it has since failed to serve.

This chapter takes to task a particular subset of feminism, so-called postmodern feminism, for debunking the concepts of "victim" and "oppression" without accounting for its own complicity with the rhetorical strategies of the neoconservative political correctness movement of the 1990s. I use the term "postmodern" to refer to feminists whose work on sexual violence, beginning in the 1990s, began locating the source of women's sexual oppression in the representational and rhetorical codes of feminism rather than in societal norms. In stark contrast to the neoliberal model, the postmodern model of agency emphasizes the linguistic, representational, and cultural structures that constitute the subject. In relation to sexual violence specifically, it focuses on "rape scripts" that are supposedly and paradoxically generated and/or reproduced by feminism itself and that female victims supposedly follow and should instead work to subvert. I will show how this exhortation ironically resurrects through the back door the Enlightenment subject and along with it the liberal model of agency that postmodernist feminists had initially set out to challenge.

In the 1990s, postmodern feminist theory was instrumental in challenging existing paradigms about the category of (women's) "experience" that too often constituted the unproblematized basis of a positivist feminist politics. Following Foucault, feminist postmodernists argued that using women's experience as the source of explanation rather than as what requires analysis often reinforces the very categories (man/woman, sex/gender, etc.) whose origins and effects we should be questioning. As Joan Scott put it in her influential essay "Experience" (1992), "The project of making experience visible precludes critical examination of the workings of the ideological system itself, its categories of representation (homosexual/heterosexual, man/woman, black/white as fixed immutable identities), its premises about what these categories mean and how they operate, its notions of subjects, origin and cause" (25). In other words, instead of justifying our critical discourse through examining women's experience of rape, for instance, we should examine what the category encompasses in different spaces and times and investigate its relation to other areas of women's lives in the public sphere.

In light of postmodern feminism's germinal contribution to the theorization of "women's experience," it is surprising that it came to the theorization of sexual violence so reluctantly. In a 2002 essay published in *Signs*, I took feminist theorists to task for their lack of attention to an issue that constituted, after all, one of the most prevalent aspects of women's existence and of second-wave feminist scholarship. A survey of feminist articles published in the 1990s (the decade that saw the blossoming of feminist theorizing and self-critique) revealed a puzzling scholarly neglect of the topic in the pages of some of the most influential journals in the field.[3] Rape had become academia's most undertheorized issue: feminist theory tended to bypass the topic in favor of more ambivalent expressions of male domination such as pornography and sexual harassment. The kind of theoretical and genealogical scrutiny that other aspects of women's lives (such as the body, gender performativity, eating disorders, transgender politics, etc.) occasioned was remarkably absent from studies of sexual violence. The topic had been predominantly relegated to issue-oriented and experiential analyses such as introductory women's studies courses.

Today, my call for more theorizing of rape seems to have been heeded since there is no shortage of scholarly and theoretical engagements with the topic. If I have nonetheless decided to revisit and extend the arguments I made in 2002, it is because I believe that 1) the topic continues to be marginalized in new ways; and 2) the fundamental challenge I posed more than a decade ago about the need to reconceptualize agency as something other than the opposite of victimization has still to be worked out in the discipline.

Rape may no longer be the "taboo subject of feminist theory today" (Mardorossian 2002, 743), but as I explained in the introduction, the humanities/social sciences perspectives that "divide" studies of rape today seem fated to consolidate the mainstream's investment in keeping the ideology and the reality of rape separate. Scholars themselves may successfully reveal the link between victims' experiences and the representation of rape in various areas of cultural life, but the fact that our point of entry into the analysis of rape remains rape as either trope or crime further contributes to the problem. For instance, studies focusing on the ideological work performed by rape in film have revealed how the film industry reproduces the "ideology of rape" by depicting women as powerless and subordinated to the will of men. They reveal that when films stage rape or its retelling by a victim on screen, they often fall into the trap of representing the suffering (and usually beautiful) victim in terms of pathos and horror, thereby reinforcing feminine stereotypes that affect "real" victims.[4] But because these studies focus on "representations" while others function as self-help books for "real" victims, the perception that rape theory is separate from experiential women's studies approaches to the issue persists.

Here I am striving to challenge the facile and untenable opposition between representation and reality that defines current discussions of rape. At the same time, I am also cognizant of the fact that while it is true that relations of power and the political are always mediated by representative practices, we need remember Stuart Hall's warning that "there are ways of constituting power as an easy floating signifier which just leaves the crude exercise and connections of power and culture altogether emptied of any signification" (1992, 286). In this chapter, I draw conclusions about how the "crude exercise and connections of power" operate in relation to the dynamics of sexual violence and its processes of signification in feminist inquiry. If I tend to single out "postmodern" feminists among academics who analyze rape, it is because their appeals to the theorization of experience has helped make the problems with the negative valuing of victimization all the more visible. Specifically, I focus on theorists whose work has problematical implications for anti-rape politics whether they are directly (Cahill 2001; Heberle 1996; Marcus 1992) or indirectly (Brown 1995) tackling sexual violence. I argue that the incompatibility between feminist research and activism does not simply, as postmodernists claim, derive from activists' denial of the discursive nature of rape or their reluctance to problematize women's experience but also from the regressive implications of contemporary approaches to rape. When contemporary feminists do tackle rape and anti-rape politics, they seem unable to do so in any other way than in the psychologizing and victim-blaming terms that dominate hegemonic approaches to gendered violence in contemporary culture. As a result, there is paradoxically more continuity between contemporary postmodern feminists and the "backlash" than between postmodern and activist feminism. What is more, contemporary feminists who expose the ways women's representation as rape victims victimizes them further by denying their agency cannot help but themselves reinscribe the very agent/victim binary they claim to undo.

This critical focus on the conventions with which women and the issue of rape have been represented is undoubtedly an important contribution to feminist scholarship. However, this concentration has failed to render explicit and theorize the relationship between these signifying practices and anti-rape politics and activism in and outside of academia. Here I place this development in the context of the general (re)turn to interiority that animates cultural theory today. I investigate the problems associated with this renewed focus, which, I argue, too often reduces anti-rape politics to a psychic dimension. I conclude the chapter by calling for an alternative and more capacious model of agency that challenges the contemporary overemphasis on subjectivity and interiority without falling back on the unproblematized category of "experience." While the impasse academic feminism seems to have reached in its analysis of rape might point to the limit of postmodern theory, it does not invalidate theory per se.

Theory means speculation, and speculating about traumatic experiences has always been a contentious agenda. As Slavoj Žižek (2008) explains, "The overpowering horror of violent acts and empathy with the victims inexorably function as a lure which prevents us from thinking.... There is a sense in which a cold analysis of violence somehow reproduces and participates in its horror" (4). What should be questionable, however, is not theory itself but the assumption that offering anything but the same unequivocal explanation for an experience amounts to denying that experience's traumatic impact or even its "reality." We have now moved beyond thinking that subjecting the same experience—that is, the violation of a woman's body—to different explanations is a suspect gesture. An alternative analysis does not necessarily amount to denying the victim's suffering or their account of the incident, since victims' accounts cannot be so neatly separated from the signifying practices and discursive frameworks that culture makes available to them for making sense of their experience(s). It is clear that victims' account of their experiences does not exist in a vacuum of authenticity awaiting a feminist revolution to be able to safely express itself, since victims, like all of us, get their cues from the intersecting and conflicting discourses through which the world is understood and shaped. Victims of rape are not impervious, for example, to the victim-blaming rhetoric that underwrites, I argue, postmodern feminist responses to rape.

My call for more theorizing of sexual violence in 2002 aimed to challenge not only reductive issue-oriented approaches that had been dominating the field but also the politically reactionary implications that characterize postmodern academic treatments of victimization. We needed a new theory of rape that supplements feminist accounts of women's experience with a contextual analysis of the ways experience is given meaning at a particular time and space. But we also needed to reconceptualize the term "victim" so that the contemporary emphasis on the ennobling of victims' agency ceases to extenuate the threat of violence in women's lives.

⋯

As a result of the notable lack of theoretical engagement with sexual violence at the turn of this century, it is media-friendly conservative writers such as Katie Roiphe, Camille Paglia, and Christina Sommers who set the tone and the parameters for the analysis of rape in the public sphere, so much so that any discussion of the issue has since seemed inevitably locked in terms established by the backlash. These self-proclaimed feminist writers all have one thing in common besides the fact that their books have been bestsellers: they downplay the severity of the problem of rape by blaming the high incidence of rape in the United States on the warped and unnecessarily alarmist representations of "radical" feminism. They go to great lengths to debunk the rape statistics offered in feminist surveys and anti-rape literature and argue that the problem is really not as widespread as we are led to believe. Victims in fact owe their victimization not to the experience of rape but to a feminist propaganda that has brainwashed women into thinking of themselves as victims. For Camille Paglia, the main proponent of the gender-wars theory, the battle of the sexes is a natural phenomenon that is here to stay, so women might as well quit trying to bring about any systemic change to this incontrovertible aspect of men and women's relationships. They should instead stand up, learn the rules, and participate in this perennial war game they have been willy-nilly playing with the other sex. Rape is only one aspect of this game that has been misnamed as a crime and should be returned to its original and healthy natural definition. Similarly, Katie Roiphe, the author of the controversial and extremely popular *The Morning After* (1993), attacks feminists working against sexual violence and more specifically against date rape, for goading women to keep their panties up and their dress down. According to Roiphe, because feminists promote a "Victorian" version of female virtue, they deny female sexual agency and infantilize women. Thus, feminist propaganda is ultimately what brings women to rename a harmless, albeit confusing and unsatisfactory sexual experience (bad sex) as date rape.

It is certainly important to debunk such unresearched and polemical conservative attacks against radical feminism. For instance, representatives of the backlash relish questioning the validity of the alarming rape statistics offered by feminist organizations. In fact, they spend so much time debunking feminist data that, according to Roiphe, one can only conclude that "the rape epidemic on campus is more a way of seeing, of interpreting, than a physical phenomenon" (1993, 57). The results attained in the survey of thirty-two colleges by Mary Koss, Christine A. Gidycz, and Nadine Wisniewski (1987) is a favorite target of the acrimonious attacks of conservatives. According to this well-known survey, 1 in 4 women is victim of rape on campuses, while the FBI offers a 1 in 8 statistic; hence the accusations of distortions against feminists. What the backlash never considers, however, is how these statistics will inevitably change depending on the definition of rape that is adopted. Legal definitions of sexual assault vary from state to state: some only include vaginal penetration by a penis, others consider forced oral sex or penetration by objects or fingers as part of the definition, and on and on. The FBI statistics are also always based on reported rapes that are deemed legitimate by the police taking the report, while the *Ms.* survey also included experiences that the students themselves did not classify as rape but that fit the legal definition of rape. What is of course petrifying about the efforts of the backlash to deflate feminist statistics is the assumption that a statistic of 1 in 8 or 1 in 10 invalidates rape as an important social issue. What is more, Koss's findings have been replicated again and again by other researchers (see, for instance, Tjaden and Theonnes 1998).

Others have convincingly revealed the backlash's dubious distortion of statistical data, its blaming of the rape crisis on feminist "hysteria" or alternatively on the victims themselves, its dangerous conflation of bad sex and date rape, its use of undocumented and anecdotal sources as evidence, and its "paramnesiac" reduction of feminism's complex past to a homogenizing and essentializing narrative.[5] I am less interested here in exposing the rhetoric and arguments of "patriarchy's prodigal daughters" (to use Elizabeth Minnich's [1998] spirited term) than in trying to understand the popular acclaim this kind of polemical writing has received in the public sphere. How can we explain the immense popularity of these distorting bestsellers? I contend that what attracted such a large audience is not false consciousness so much as these writings' destabilizing and speculative effect on a field (rape theory) that was ignored for so long.

Insofar as these authors make us look at the dynamics of sexual assault from a different angle and hold feminists accountable for our own implication in the available discourses concerning rape, they were doing "theory" in the broadest conceivable sense. It was the worst kind of theory, unresearched, undocumented, and polemical, but it was theory nonetheless. And in a field that had not been theorized in the booming decade of theory, the 1990s, theorizing of any kind, even of the worst kind, was bound to attract and fascinate. The fact that victims of sexual assault are themselves sometimes drawn rather than repulsed by such conservative accounts of their own experience also reveals that feminism needs to reconsider some of its truisms about rape and rape victims.[6] This forces us to acknowledge that there is no homogeneous standpoint among rape victims that is available in an unmediated fashion. Their experiences themselves are steeped in historically and culturally contingent constructions and require that we attend to the signifying practices (including feminist ones) through which they are given meaning.

Let me clarify that I am in no way implying that we need to reread these texts more carefully in order to appreciate an argument whose theoretical complexity escaped us the first time around. These bestsellers are based on the petty and undocumented impressions of archconservative pundits, and no reading between the lines will throw a more favorable light on their methods and goals. Christina Hoff Sommers, for instance, was paid six figures by the right-wing John M. Olin and Harry Bradley Foundations to publish her antifeminist tract *Who Stole Feminism? How Women Have Betrayed Women*. Nonetheless, these conservative writers have succeeded in dislodging rape from the issue-oriented and experiential perspectives that circumscribed its examination. They ironically echo postmodern feminist critiques of "standpoint theory" insofar as they too challenge the assumption that the "authentic" truth about gender subordination lies in women's "voicing" of their own experiences. Like postmodern feminism, they offer instead a bold account of women's existence whose grounding is not in women's experience but in the discourses constructing it. The "dutiful daughters of patriarchy" inadvertently highlight the impossibility of separating the "reality" of rape from the feminist institutions and ideologies through which the experience is given meaning. They thus not only unsettle feminism's positivist explanations of women's lives, they also turn the spotlight from victims of rape to the operations of feminist epistemology. Their account is problematic, however, because while they hold feminists accountable, they ignore that feminism does not exist in a vacuum and cannot be studied independently of the cultural environment in which it operates. They also flatly deny the reality of the "rape crisis."

Theorizing rape is all the more important if we want to stop the writers of the backlash from setting the terms of the debate. The pervasiveness of the reductive opposition between power versus victim feminisms both outside and within academia is only one example of how the terms have been reconceptualized.[7] And unfortunately, the ways some feminist scholars have engaged the issue have only contributed to reinforcing such oppositions by making rape and its prevention about women's interiority and self-reflexivity.

In *Feminists Theorize the Political*, a collection of essays edited by Judith Butler and Joan Scott, Sharon Marcus provides one of the very few academic attempts to engage rape theoretically during the 1990s. Her influential essay "Fighting Bodies, Fighting Words: A Theory and Politics of Rape Prevention," which remains one of the most-quoted essays in anti-rape scholarship, is sophisticated and lucid, and her desire to offer a more efficacious theory of rape prevention is extremely laudable. Yet her reasoning and conclusions are also disturbingly reminiscent of popular antifeminist manifestos like Katie Roiphe's *The Morning After*. As I stated earlier, according to Roiphe, the "rape epidemic" on campuses is a linguistic phenomenon generated by feminist extremists who cry wolf when their female protégés encounter a wolf behind bars on a harmless tour of the local zoo. She claims that women are the naive dupes of a feminist propaganda that infantilizes them by representing them as virginal beings who could not have themselves initiated sexual pleasure. A guided tour at her local library would have disabused Roiphe of her preconceptions about radical feminism's relation to female sexuality and agency. Feminists have spent well-documented years fighting against the court's use of the victim's sexual daringness, visibility, and promiscuity as evidence of "consent." Until 1988, Illinois courts, for instance, allowed the prior sexual activity or the reputation of the victim to be used against her. This allowed the defendant to have community witnesses come into court to testify to the victim's "reputation." The assumption was that a woman could not be raped if she had had prior sexual activity. Until 1 January 1992, the victim's manner of dress could also be used as a sign of "consent." And to this day, I have yet to hear of a state's attorney agreeing to take the case of a raped (and living) prostitute to trial.

Sharon Marcus does not go so far as to accuse women of misnaming their experiences because of feminist prudishness. However, she too holds feminist discourses of rape partly responsible for the high incidence of sexual assault and abuse. Specifically, she takes issue with feminist anti-rape literature and activism for representing women as always already raped and rapeable. The "apocalyptic tone" adopted in feminist political action, she argues, reinforces the "rape script" that presupposes masculine power and feminine powerlessness and that society more or less successfully inscribes on men's and women's psyches. Rape victims are thus women whose minds are colonized by a sexual scenario they could instead learn to recognize and use to prevent the scripted experience: "To speak of a rape script implies a narrative of rape, a series of steps and signals whose typical initial moments we can learn to recognize and whose final outcome we can learn to stave off. . . . The narrative element of a script leaves room and makes time for revision" (Marcus 1992, 390–391).

According to Marcus, the rape script predates the act of violence and only "momentarily" creates the identities of rapist and victim when it is enacted. Rape is thus "a scripted interaction in which one person auditions for the role of rapist and strives to maneuver another person into the role of victim, . . . a process of gendering which we can attempt to disrupt" (391). In other words, it is up to the woman to recognize that her assailant does not simply have the power to rape but that his power is created by the extent to which she succumbs to the social script's efforts to secure her participation. Marcus sees each individual rape as comprised of various stages such as verbal threats and other forms of action and harassment and argues that the time and space between these threats and rape constitute "the gap in which women can try to intervene, overpower and deflect the threatened action" (389). Thus, she takes the very notion of continuum that feminists use to describe "rape culture" and applies it to individual rape and nothing else. Women need to identify the various parts of their interaction with the would-be rapist as stages on a continuum. They need to get their act together, be on the alert, and take their cue rather than conform to the "self-defeating rules which govern polite, empathetic feminine conversation" and that generate their "noncombative responses to rapists" (389).[8]

The assumption that rape occurs because of women's "noncombative response" to the social script of gender is dubious. It is extremely problematic to assume that victims share a similar psychological makeup or relation to the social script before the rape takes place, that all victims are "women." It is true that victims themselves often corroborate the assumption that they could have done more to prevent the rape in the gap between the threat and the act: they typically blame themselves for what happened and list all the ways they could have avoided the situation had they acted differently.[9] This retrospective response, however, is a coping mechanism in reaction to the rape and to social responses to sexual violence and not a testimony of the victim's participation in gender socialization before the assault. Self-blame occurs systematically, whether the victim fought back or not, whether the rape occurred or was thwarted, whether in fact s/he did try to subvert the sexual script or not. The assumption that rape is successful because of women's passive compliance with a sexual and linguistic script is problematic on two counts. First, it implies that women who get raped do not strategize prior to the rape and therefore that their rape necessarily signifies their enactment of the pregiven role of victim. Second, because it focuses on women's reaction or lack thereof during an attack, it necessarily takes the focus

FIGURE 2. New York City SlutWalk, Union Square, 1 October 2011. Photo by Peter C. Gravelle.

off the rapist and places it—along with the "responsibility" for the outcome of this scripted interaction—on the victim and the victim alone.[10]

This tendency is so ingrained that when political analyst Zerlina Maxwell appeared on the *Sean Hannity Show* on 5 March 2013, to argue that the best rape prevention is not about what women can do to protect themselves but about raising men who don't rape, what ensued was an onslaught of misogynist and racist attacks. Conservative viewers who interpreted Maxwell's remarks as a threat to gun rights proceeded to express their outrage on social media Web sites, with some even claiming that she deserved to be gang raped and murdered (Millhiser 2013). Maxwell insisted that Hannity's suggestion that women should carry guns to prevent themselves from being raped would easily devolve into a victim-blaming mentality. If we want to stop rape, she explained, it stands to reason that we should focus on the rapists rather than on the victims. And, she added, "If firearms were the answer, then the military would be the safest place for women, and it's not" (ibid.). Ironically, postmodern feminism's exhortation that women get in touch with their agency as a way to deter rape aligns them with the hateful viewers and host of the show. Most importantly, it would fail to accommodate Maxwell's courageous stance as a mark of agency.

In 2001, Ann Cahill's *Rethinking Rape*, a theoretical intervention that set out to challenge unproblematized histories of the body and subjectivity, seemed to be the answer to the absence of theorization of sexual violence that had plagued contemporary feminist theory in the 1990s. Like Marcus's theory of rape, however, Cahill's book resurrects through the back door a model of liberal agency that not only relies on the subject's consciousness (victim as analytical reader of scripts) but also presupposes a gendered arrangement that precedes the rape act rather than, as I suggest, one that is produced by it. For Marcus and Cahill, "women" have a preexisting gendered identity or propensity that makes them vulnerable to the rape act. By contrast, I argue that it is the rape act that produces the opposing positions of femininity and masculinity that people would otherwise move in and out of depending on the context in which they find themselves.

Cahill begins with an analysis of two major schools of feminist philosophy. The first one defines rape as "violence, not sex" and is characterized by the work of Susan Brownmiller, while the school associated with Catharine MacKinnon and Andrea Dworkin represents rape as an extension of compulsory heterosexuality. For Cahill, both schools wrongly establish an opposition between the violent and the sexual and perpetuate in doing so the nature/culture binary. Woman is seen as a slave to biology on the one hand and the dupe of patriarchal culture on the other. Neither theory adequately addresses the sexed body, which is what Cahill seeks to remedy in *Rethinking Rape*. She then gives an overview of recent feminist scholarship in the area of corporeality and embodiment, which, she argues, provides the foundation for her own theory of rape. She discusses the work of Rosi Braidotti, Elizabeth Grosz, Judith Butler, Moira Gatens, and Luce Irigaray before proceeding to analyze rape as a sexual act that affects the body, agency, and subjectivity of its female victim. Conspicuously, however, her overview of feminist theories focuses on embodiment in general without addressing the relevance of these theories to rape, while the elaboration of her own theory of rape as embodied experience hardly engages the theories she just reviewed. Cahill concludes by addressing the ethical ramifications of rape as well as the possibilities for resistance embodied in self-defense.

Cahill's historically minded theory of rape illustrates the need for further theorization of the issue. Like Marcus, she reproduces the now-axiomatic claim that rape is grounded in men's socialized aggression and women's socialized passivity. Male aggression and female passivity are treated as if they occurred in a neat binary that explains rape as a social problem. As a result, the transformation of women's comportment and psychic orientation becomes as crucial a response to rape as the curbing of male violence. This approach to rape and prevention is problematic, because while masculinist aggression is an invariable source of sexual assault, female passivity is neither a constant nor a cause of rape. Passivity is only sometimes a response to rape; it may or may not be an (un)successful deterrent. It never is, however, the cause of an aggression that can only be uprooted by addressing the problem itself rather than its symptoms. Infelicitous phrases such as that used in Maria Bevacqua's description of a political system that excused "the most brutal of rapists and blamed the most innocent of victims" (2000, 102) reflect the dynamic I am talking about; that is, one that shifts the responsibility for the crime and for its eradication to the victim. The juxtaposition of the degree of aggression of the rapist with the level of innocence of the victim necessarily obscures the fact that a victim cannot be more or less innocent of a crime she did not commit.

Similarly, despite her exhortation that agency and passivity should not be dichotomously defined (2001, 134), Cahill cannot help but reproduce conventional binary thinking about gender when she urges women to cultivate the instinct of self-defense that is encouraged in men. She argues that this "recodification of the female body would involve not an emulation of the male body, but rather the development of particularly feminine kinds of strength and power.... Women would be able to stand ... free from their dependence on men" (207). As with Marcus, I fail to see how living one's life in perpetual preparation for the worst is a liberating proposition. According to Cahill, whether we are aware of it or not, the pervasiveness of rape in our culture has already deeply affected feminine bodily comportment. What is unclear is why we would further entrench this influence by promoting self-defense, which is yet another way the threat of rape and violence shapes and limits our bodies (albeit as bodies with a "particularly feminine" kind of power). Self-defense posits an attack one tries to resist, and as such, preserves the centrality of rape in women's lives. Making the threat of rape the basis for reshaping one's body and mind is no less problematic than the way it marks and constrains one's body in the first place. Cahill's insistence that we move beyond the discursive configurations that keep us locked within the existing social order cannot be reconciled with a model of resistance that maintains the centrality of rape in women's existence. Women's adoption of a ready-for-battle mode buttresses more than it challenges the dichotomous thinking of the sex wars.

As with most feminist scholarship on rape, Cahill and Marcus focus on the variable that is female passivity as the site for change. Such well-meaning feminist politics ultimately advance the causes of a culture that is too eager to locate the source of the problem and its solution in women's putative inability to take action. In representing female passivity and male aggression as two sides of the same coin (the sum of which is rape), we further limit the horizon of women's choices and fail to problematize agency and passivity as dichotomously defined. As long as feminist analyses focus on overcoming female passivity as if it were the mirror image of male aggression, we will contribute to a climate that turns victims into the source of their own problems. For instance, what about victims whose passivity was a result of inebriation (Riley 2012b)? In July 2012, seventeen-year-old Savannah Dietrich, a Louisville, Kentucky, teen, faced contempt charges, up to 180 days in jail, and a $500 fine for tweeting the names of the two minor teenagers who sexually assaulted her. The teenage boys had pleaded guilty to first-degree sexual abuse and misdemeanor voyeurism for sexually assaulting Dietrich while she was inebriated and for subsequently distributing photos of their exploit on the Internet. Dietrich tweeted the boys' names because she was outraged by the plea bargain and light sentence they were offered. Dietrich's violation of the confidentiality of the juvenile hearing is a sign of this young woman's indomitable agency following her alcohol-induced "passivity" (Riley 2012c). On 11 August 2012, the same scenario played out in the Steubenville case, where pictures of the inebriated sixteen-year-old girl's violated nude body were circulated on social media after her sexual assault, and in two other cases of similar cyberbullying that resulted in the tragic suicides of fifteen-year-old Audrie Pott (S. E. Smith 2013) and seventeen-year-old Rehtaeh Parsons (Molland 2013). Cases such as these should make us rethink any attempt to make victims responsible for preventing their own rape in the name of an ennobled agency they supposedly lack. In light of the global attention the Dietrich case received, the defense attorneys withdrew their motion that the victim be held in contempt. The Steubenville case, however, led to disturbing media reports, one of which emphasized the victim's inability to recall the rape as if that jeopardized rather than reinforced the prosecution's case, while the other focused on how the guilty verdict "ruined the promising lives of the Steubenville rapists."[11]

Why isn't the culture promoting and locating the "possibilities for resistance" in self- or rape-awareness courses for men rather than self-defense training for women? At least then the blame for not having the time, money, or desire to take such courses would be directed against the group that most disproportionately generates perpetrators. What if women's decision not to take self-defense courses is deliberate rather than symptomatic of a passive adherence to gender roles? What about victims whose passivity constitutes a strategic choice?

Cahill assumes that "the woman who is able and willing to defend herself" would be far less likely to blame herself (2001, 205). What this statement overlooks, however, is the degree to which self-blaming is not a function of the victim's actions or beliefs but of societal attitudes that locate the source of rape in women's passivity. To claim otherwise would be to argue that women's actions are the ultimate determinant of how they make sense of particular events independently of their surrounding social structures. This assumption is all the more ironic in light of Cahill's own emphasis on intersubjectivity in her theory of rape. It is simply not the case that the trauma experienced by survivors is proportional to the degree or success of resistance they offer. Neither is self-blame: rape survivors who successfully resist an attack sometimes blame themselves more than the "passive" victims feminism is so anxious to whip back into shape. When feminists advocate self-defense as a solution to rape, they cannot help but provide more fodder to a culture that is already too eager to promote change one woman at a time rather than to root out sexual violence. Placing the responsibility for deterring rape on women without a guarantee of success individualizes the problem; it also merely shifts the ground on which victims blame themselves and get blamed.

For the last four decades, representations and discussions of rape and domestic violence have almost exclusively concentrated on the suffering of victims and have all but ignored the few studies of the behavioral and psychological traits of perpetrators. This lopsided focus originated out of concern for the welfare of victims and as a means of alerting the public to the destructive effects of sexual violence. Yet this focus cannot be dissociated from the reversal of cause and effect that characterizes responses to rape in our culture. Responsibility is still laid on the victim. Years of educating the public about these issues seem to have only resulted in the expectation that women should now know better than let themselves get raped. Popular discourse is more than ever invested in transforming this social problem into a personal transaction, while psychologists, psychiatrists and sociologists continue to study the issue of sexual violence . . . by studying women. Experts examine women's physical and mental health, attitudes to gender ideology, personalities, religious beliefs, interpersonal skills, previous experiences with violence, and, last but not least, "low self-esteem." They explain the issue of male violence by invoking the victim's psyche and create new categories such as "self-defeating personality disorder" to explain the rape (away).

This is taken to an extreme in one of the most recent psychological studies of rape that advocates holding perpetrators accountable for their actions so that "victims can then take a realistic look at themselves, and we can feel free to acknowledge some of the assertion, free will, *and yes, blame,* that also belong to victims" (Lamb 1996, 8, my emphasis). Ironically, Sharon Lamb supports her point by turning feminist standpoint theory on its head. She makes the familiar claim that we should "honor their [the victims'] perspective," but what she means is that since victims blame themselves, "by informing them that they are sadly mistaken in their perception of choice and free will we do them an injustice" (ibid., 22). Thus, out of respect for their point of view, we too should blame victims. Far from challenging the stereotype of victims as "passive, incapacitated shells," this standpoint model would be hard pressed to provide any other reason for not challenging the victim's perception than consideration for her because of her status as a victim. It thus not only entrenches the status of victim as an identity but also wrongly assumes that the victim's perspective does not change over time.[12]

At the risk of raising some eyebrows by appealing to my "experience," five years of volunteering as a hospital and hotline advocate for a local rape crisis services convinced me of the futility of looking for common characteristics among women who are victims of a sexual assault. I met and talked to women whose demeanor or religious beliefs made them the most likely candidates for reproducing the social script that underlies rape but who resisted their assailant in a way others who were more self-conscious about gender roles did not. I sat with a ten-year-old who could make no sense of the strange requests made by the man who appeared in her room in the middle of the night. Yet despite her confusion, the words "you did nothing to justify his actions" jolted an emotional reaction when she had shown none. I accompanied a war veteran who had been raped by another homeless man. He would certainly not have found his way to the hospital had it not been for the police who picked him up half-naked on the railway tracks and brought him there. Mentally imbalanced, homeless, and clearly haunted by visions of the war, the rape was the least of his concerns. After the rape kit was administered and a pair of pants was provided, he went on his way, hollering at his internal demons rather than at the crime he thought nothing of. I met women who fought or talked their way out of a rape and felt their victimization more keenly than women who had been raped and badly injured. I saw women who were bruised and beaten for having resisted; prostitutes raped by a pseudo-client whose violence both they and the hospital staff considered a side effect of that line of work; teenagers who had been raped after passing out at a party and blamed themselves for drinking; other victims who, while undergoing the evidence collection kit and various bureaucratic procedures in the hospital emergency unit, were shocked by the magnitude of the institutionalized response to an experience they had only thought of in interpersonal terms; and still others who were cracking jokes and holding conversations about errands they had to run even as they were being administered the morning-after pill and treated for the venereal disease they had contracted during the rape.

While I am all for disrupting processes of sexist gendering, advocating that victims do so during the process of getting raped not only has limited political efficacy, but it would also ultimately entrench existing social relations and gender inequalities. It assumes a category of women unified by a common psychic orientation to social gendering where there simply isn't one. Some victims stop fighting back because they are afraid they might get killed; others fight back for the same reason. Some get frozen. Others weigh their options and decide not to resist. Arguing that the dynamics of sexual violence can simply be reversed through a more self-reflexive attitude assumes that women have a linear and simplified relationship to the social codes that constitute them. A model like Marcus's therefore downplays the "materiality of gender" and ignores that social inscriptions—that is, our physical situatedness in time and space, history and culture—do not simply evaporate because we are made aware of them. Susan Bordo's pointed critique is also true of Marcus's approach to rape: "Many postmodern readings of the body become lost in the fascinating, ingenious (and often, prematurely celebratory) routes that imagination, intellect, and political fervor can take when looking at bodily 'texts' without attention to the concrete contexts—social, political, cultural, and practical—in which they are embedded. And so they need to be reminded of the materiality of the body" (1997, 185).[13]

As Bordo points out, cultural discourses "impinge on us as fleshly bodies, often in ways that cannot be determined from a study of representations alone" (1997, 183). The cultural, institutional, bodily and practical realities of our culture are not "transcended or 'transgressed' just because we can 'destabilize' them in theory" (185). We need to consider the effects of our preventive politics in the discursive context of contemporary configurations of power. Making women's behavior and identity the site of rape prevention only mirrors the dominant culture's proclivity to see rape as women's problem, both in the sense of a problem women should solve and one that they caused. Any discourse on rape needs to take into account the reversal of cause and effect that rape is constantly subjected to and that retrospectively constitutes effects as origins and causes. While enlisting the help of potential victims in preventing a variety of crimes is common practice, only gendered crimes generate the kind of victim-blaming responses rape and domestic violence produce. Whereas forgetting to set the burglar alarm or getting robbed despite the "neighborhood watch" does not exculpate the thieves, getting raped always elicits an investigation into how a victim might ultimately have been responsible for what happened. Bad judgment becomes cause, and victimization becomes manipulative or concealed agency. The responsibility of the rapist is seen as inherently linked to the victim's behavior and as a result often is erased. Somehow rape always comes to be grounded in the victim's behavioral or emotional dynamics rather than in the perpetrator's actions.

Ironically, the Foucauldian paradigm that postmodernists often evoke to buttress their claims helps make visible why making women's psyche the site of the analysis of rape or of rape prevention is a depoliticizing gesture for feminist politics. As Foucault's work has shown, the history of the modern subject has been one of depoliticization carried out mostly through the construction of a psychologized and ahistorical subject. In the nineteenth century, medical, legal, religious, and social discourses came together to construct the now-naturalized idea of sex as the secret of the individual's being, thus concealing the "power/knowledge" involved in creating the notion of sex as essence. Turning the "minor chronicle of sex" and "inconsequential bucolic pleasures" (Foucault 1978) into the pre-discursive core of the individual was a successful "ruse" of power that would keep the subject focused on changing the inner self rather than on addressing power relations. A whole system of institutional, cultural, and economic practices and social inequities was obscured when inner transformation was established as the only genuine means of achieving social change. The psychological and inner realm—that is, the individual's "center"—overrode material considerations. Similarly, Nancy Armstrong's (1987) Foucauldian reading of the history of the novel reveals the domestic novel to have been instrumental in producing the ideal of the modern individual as psychological reality. Written representations of the self replaced the aristocratic ideal of family name with moral value and of attractive and opulent surface with psychological and emotional depth. Armstrong explains that with its presumptions of naturalness, this new female ideal (which would become the prototype of the modern individual) removed subjectivity and sexuality from the realm of the political. In emphasizing inner life as the source of being and happiness, the middle class could justify social hierarchies in moral rather than economic terms.

It is ironic that when postmodern analyses locate rape prevention inside women's psyches, they replicate modern techniques of power even as they seek to challenge them. Nineteenth-century hegemonic culture has left an indelible mark on our own times. Although postmodern feminism problematizes the last century's assumptions by replacing naturalizing with social constructionist premises, it too runs the risk of displacing the subject's locatedness in history and culture when it advocates an inner revolution as the more efficient site, for instance, of rape prevention. As Wendy Brown points out in her critique of identity politics, "The question here is not *whether* denaturalizing political strategies subvert the subjugating force of naturalized identity formation, but *what kind* of politicization, produced out of and inserted into *what kind* of political context, might perform such subversion" (1995, 55). In the current political context, locating rape prevention in women's self-reflexivity vis-à-vis their imbrication in wider cultural dynamics runs the risk of becoming a new form of panopticism, an interiorized and individualized system of surveillance by which every woman becomes her own overseer. It is as if, having noted the failure of the panopticon project to individually reform criminals, we now applied it to their victims by gradually asking women to police their own behavioral and mental maps. Rather than question the principle of self-surveillance itself, we thus merely change its object.

The focus on power over one's social and discursive conditioning vacates the conflict between power relations and the autonomy of the self. It makes victims' lack of reflexive examination the new grounds for explaining masculinist domination and for holding them responsible for their subordination. The "technologies of the self" (to use Foucault's later terminology) thus overcome the materiality of the body because they locate the source of sexual violence in the feminine subject's failure to reinvent the self.[14] This individualistic mode conflates social contestation and self-constitution and undermines the social and political solidarity necessary to combat relations of domination such as rape. Representing victims as the peacekeepers of rape culture will result only in making them responsible for the war they could not prevent. Although it highlights the constructedness of identity, this process of self-scrutiny is no more liberating than the Christian tradition of inwardness.

Grounding rape prevention in the reinvention of the female self implies that the fight against sexual violence depends on and has to be preceded by the individualized questioning of normalized female subjectivity. Such a critical hermeneutics of the self will not only fail to diffuse male violence, it will also only corroborate the cultural narrative of victims as the source of their own problems. Hegemonic culture typically represents women as dominated by inner and complicated compulsions that require personalized self-help rather than political transformation. Advocating the microlevel cultivation of feminine self-knowledge and inwardness as a deterrent to rape is bound to compound this slide into therapeutic discourse. Feminists need to stop casting their anti-rape politics in terms of women's inner and psychological change. This further compartmentalizes rape as women's problem and marginalizes male victims as anomalies. As the backlashers have shown, victim-blaming assumptions based on women's internal proclivities flourish whether the subject's interiority is seen as derived from nature or from a social (or feminist) script. The question is no longer whether women's identity is immutable or constructed or whether they need to discover or continually produce their inner self but whether an emphasis on interiority and self-reflexivity is not itself a technology of domination that pathologizes the victim and displaces masculinist agency.

This emphasis on the "psychology of power" in academic treatments of rape is so pervasive that it sometimes extends from the characterization of "victims" to that of feminist politics. In *States of Injury*, Wendy Brown uses a psychologizing framework to critique the feminist reliance on identity politics as the means of recognition by the state. Like Foucault, she takes issue with legislative proposals (like MacKinnon's) to construe sexual subordination through pornography, harassment, or rape as a violation of women's civil rights.[15] Writing sexual subordination into the law, she argues, ultimately creates an identity politics that reinscribes "femaleness as sexual violability" and "injury as identity" and keeps us locked in a logic of recrimination and *ressentiment*: "Foucault (along with certain strains of psychoanalytic thought) reminds us that the law produces the subjects it claims to protect or emancipate. How, then, might a formulation of women's civil rights as violated by pornography or sexual harassment produce precisely the figure MacKinnon complains we have been reduced to by sexism, a figure of woman wholly defined by sexual violation, wholly identified with sexual victimization?" (1989, 131).

Besides fixing women's identity as "wounded," the effort to seek legal redress for injuries also "legitimizes law and the state as appropriate protectors against injury" while obscuring the masculinist state's own power to injure. Injury "is thereby rendered intentional and individual, politics is reduced to punishment" (Brown 1995, 27). This critique highlights how the best-intentioned projects, including feminist ones, can betray their emancipatory goals by creating "dependent subjects" and by reproducing the depoliticizing and regulating social norms of neoliberalism. Brown's argument is important and persuasive. Her work reinforces the scholarship produced over the last few decades on the critique of the "subject" and "identity politics." It also helps expose once again what is wrong with the victim's rights movement and its efforts, for instance, to enact a victims' rights amendment to state constitutions and to the U.S. Constitution. This type of lobbying has already been quite successful in twenty-nine states whose constitutions have been amended to legislate the rights of victims. Yet the guarantees included in such amendments, such as the right of victims to be present at all public proceedings, to register objection to negotiated pleas and releases, or to receive financial restitution from the offender, ultimately reinforce victim status. They personalize and hence preserve the relationship between victim and assailant. They turn crime victims into a vengeance-rights squad and the state into a neutral arbitrator ready to intervene when, for instance, constitutionalized restitution does not occur (and it often does not). The state then responds by increasing the offender's prison sentence. I agree with Brown that feminists should be critical of such rights-based agendas, all the more so since the history of the emergence of the victims' rights movement in the United States betrays its reactionary ethos.

What I take issue with is thus not Brown's acute and cautionary account of feminist entanglements with the state but the Nietzschean framework in which she casts it. Brown argues that the politicized identity of feminist struggle is structured by a Nietzschean logic of *ressentiment*; that is, it is "an effect of domination that reiterates impotence, a substitute for action, for power, for self-affirmation that reinscribes incapacity, powerlessness, rejection" (1995, 69). Feminist moral claims are a symptom of weakness, of their incapacity to action and thwarted "will to power" that leads to vengefulness and "toxic resentments." Thus, Brown sees feminist rights-based politics as turning powerlessness into "a dissimulated political discourse of recriminations and toxic resentments parading as radical critique" (xi). While her critique of rights discourse is well taken, her characterization of feminist scholarship and practice reproduces the tradition of inwardness through which women and feminists are typically discredited. Attributing feminist practice to a logic of resentment applies a trait Nietzsche uses to define individual character to a political movement and thus personalizes and psychologizes the latter. While I agree that the effects of politicized identity might lock us into a politics of recrimination, resorting to the Nietzschean notion sets up *ressentiment* as the driving paradigm in feminist thought. It is not a critique of the negative effect of a well-meaning but limited political strategy but a critique of the source of negativity from which feminist politics derive. From this one might conclude that feminism is endowed with a "slave morality" that makes it react to pain emotionally by inflicting suffering in return.

Brown's account of resentment as reaction to hurt or, in Nietzsche's words, "as a desire to deaden pain by means of affect" is a forceful description of the effects of capitalism and the bureaucratic state on the individuated and "impotent" late modern liberal subject (68–69). As a characterization of feminist reformist strategies, however, it succeeds only in pathologizing and individualizing an oppositional political movement that is made to sound like it is more in need of therapy than of a renewed emphasis on the political. *Ressentiment* in Nietzschean terminology is too closely associated with instinctual and affective conditions for it not to invoke an internalized and pathological interiority that takes a life of its own above and beyond the injury it seeks to address. As a result, feminist politics is seen not in terms of the potentially antidemocratic effects of its prescriptions but in terms of its underlying motivations. Nietzsche's account of the workings of *ressentiment* Brown cites in *States of Injury* highlights the psychologizing tendencies I am pointing out here: "For every sufferer instinctively seeks a cause for his suffering, more exactly, an agent; still more specifically, a guilty agent who is susceptible to suffering—in short, some living thing upon which he can, on some pretext or other, vent his affects, actually or in effigy. . . . This . . . constitutes the actual physiological cause of ressentiment, vengefulness, and the like: a desire to deaden pain by means of affects, ... to deaden, by means of a more violent emotion of any kind, a tormenting, secret pain that is becoming unendurable, and to drive it out of consciousness at least for the moment: for that one requires an affect, as savage an affect as possible, and, in order to excite that, any pretext at all" (Nietzsche quoted in Brown 1995, 68). It may be worth noting the selectiveness of Brown's quote here. Had she included the rest of the paragraph from Nietzsche's text, the seeming reasonableness of her argument about the workings of *ressentiment* in feminist politics would have been undermined. Nietzsche continues: "This kind of reasoning is common to all the sick, and is indeed held the more firmly the more the real the cause of their feeling ill, the physiological cause, remains hidden. (It may perhaps lie in some disease of the *nervus sympathicus*, or in an excessive secretion of bile, or in a deficiency of potassium sulphate and phosphate in the blood, or in an obstruction in the abdomen which impedes the blood circulation, or in degeneration of the ovaries, and the like)" (Nietzsche 1967, 127). The irony of a postmodern analysis that rests on such an essentializing and sexist account should not be lost.

Postmodern feminist discussions of the anti-rape movement seem more drawn to an examination of the "psychology of power" than to the discursive study of rape and victimization. They analyze rape victims and the anti-rape movement by looking at or implying hidden depths and inner meanings lodged in an individualized configuration. Ironically, this approach is also grounded in the very tradition of feminist scholarship and activism from which feminist postmodernism likes to distinguish itself, that of the second wave. According to Curthoys, the women's liberation movement of the 1960s and 1970s was primarily aiming, through the activity of consciousness-raising, at exposing the psychological effects of power. Its "liberation theory" provided "an account of the psychological workings of power, where power is seen straightforwardly as the ability of one person or group to determine the behaviour of another person or group.... The account is of the destructive psychological effects of power but it is also about how it can be confronted and undermined" (1997, 6). In trying to undo the distinction between psychic and social lives however, postmodern feminists today contribute to subordinating the effects of gender and social differences to the interiority of the self.

Not surprisingly, a similar displacement also characterizes their critiques of the practice of consciousness-raising. Postmodern feminists including Wendy Brown and Renee Heberle have singled out consciousness-raising and speak-outs as two sites where unproblematized experience takes on dangerous proportions as the basis of feminist epistemology. They invoke the women's liberation movement to critique the positivist assumptions of feminists whose main representative today seems to be Catherine MacKinnon.

Brown argues that most contemporary North Atlantic feminists "seek to preserve some variant of consciousness-raising as a mode of discerning and delivering the 'truth' about women" (1995, 41). She then singles out speak-outs against sexual violence as one such "forum for feminist truth-telling" (42), where the project of making experience visible consolidates categories of representation such as man/woman instead of denaturalizing them. Similarly, Renee Heberle warns us that feminism's "project of exposure" and its aim at piecing together "the ever-enlarged map of women's sexual suffering" reinscribes the gender norms that enable the victimization of women and "becomes, in effect, the social insignia of male power" (1996, 63). Like Wendy Brown, Heberle specifically takes issue with speak-outs against sexual violence as sites where, in telling their stories of sexual suffering, women reinscribe the tropes of masculinist dominance and feminine vulnerability feminism claims to seek to undo. In her discussion of the anti-rape movement, Heberle also echoes Sharon Marcus and Ann Cahill when she takes issue with feminism's focus on victimization. Just as Cahill advocates self-defense as a way of triggering a "recodification of the female body" (2001, 207) as a site of strength and power, Heberle calls for more stories of women who successfully practiced self-defense so that "society may take this as an opportunity to place greater onus on women to resist" (Heberle 1996, 72).

Brown (1995) goes on to draw an analogy between the "voicing of women's experience" staged in speak-outs and Foucault's genealogy of confession.[16] As mentioned earlier, for Foucault, sex was constructed as the secret of our being in the nineteenth century, by confessional, medical, psychiatric, legal, and other institutional forces that represented it as pre-discursive even as they were producing it through discourse. This was how, for instance, homosexuality was transformed from a sexual act into an identity: "There is no question that the appearance in nineteenth-century psychiatry, jurisprudence, and the literature of a whole series of discourses on the species and subspecies of homosexuality, inversion, pederasty, and 'psychic hermaphrodism' made possible a strong advance of social controls into this area of 'perversity'; but it also made possible the formation of a 'reverse' discourse: homosexuality began to speak on its own behalf, to demand that its legitimacy or 'naturality' be acknowledged, often in the same vocabulary, using the same categories by which it was medically disqualified" (1978, 101). Thus, the unearthing of the "hidden" histories of repression and silence in the world of homosexuality ultimately reinforces both the category itself and the transformation of "the homosexual" into a species. This is why, Foucault explains, sexual liberation is not a transgressive move, because it simply works within the terms set by power and reinforces the idea of sex as key to our identity.

Following the same logic, Wendy Brown argues that "truth-telling about our desires and experiences is construed as deliverance from the power that silences and represses them (rather than as itself a site and effect of regulatory power)" (1995, 42). Her critique of speak-outs and of their process of revealing the "hidden" histories of silence and repression also echoes Joan Scott's warning that "the project of making experience visible precludes critical examination of the workings of the ideological system itself, its categories of representation . . . its premises about what these categories mean and how they operate, its notions of subjects, origin, and cause" (1992, 25). It is true, for instance, that sexual violence as a violation of the self has a different valence in the West, where sex has come to be defined as key to one's identity, than it does in other parts of the world.[17] In other words, because the destructive psychological effects of rape are indissociable from the production of sex as our deepest identity, exposing rape as a violation reproduces the assumption that sex is the core of our identity. By contrast, in ultratraditionalist contexts where rape is marked as the defiling of the honor of the family and the village rather than of the victim's right to self-determination (which she does not have), marrying the victim to her rapist is perceived as an adequate redress, not for the harm done to the victim but for the debasement incurred by the clan. In some Muslim countries, when such a match fails to occur, shamed families have resorted to the "honor killing" of the rape victim. In his essay "Arab Honor's Price: A Woman's Blood," Douglas Jehl (1999) discusses the prevalence and acceptability of this practice in Muslim countries. (Self-)revelation as liberation in such a context is not only life-threatening but completely meaningless. We need to be wary, however, of conceptualizing the Arab world as the monolithic "other" of Western culture in relation to gendered violence. As Uma Narayan (1997) points out, the "cross-cultural connections" Western feminists make on issues of violence against women tend to foreground fatalities in Eastern contexts as examples of "death by culture," whereas similar forms of violence in the West are not related to culture or religion. In fact, domestic violence murders in the Western context are often not even given the kind of prominence that characterizes discussions of sexual violence in the "Third World."

I am very sympathetic to postmodern appeals to rigorous historical and critical examination of the workings of ideological systems and their categories of representation. The point that we need be attentive to how our own assumptions might reproduce the very terms we should be questioning is well taken. Nevertheless, I fail to see the "homology" Brown identifies between confession and speak-outs against sexual violence. Surely the experience of confessing a sexual act or "sin" one commits that involves the "truth" of one's own identity is a far cry from speaking out against a transgression committed by an agent exterior to oneself. This would simply amount to confessing someone else's "sin." Such conflation is all the more unfortunate because it reproduces reactionary beliefs that rape is a reflection of the victim's identity. It yet again collapses differences such as rape and sex by establishing an equivalence between the process of telling about one or the other. An alienating and violating experience such as sexual assault is not the equivalent of sex, the modern producer of identity. In "The Politics of Responsibility," Kathleen Jones (1997) deconstructs these false dichotomies and their victim-blaming consequences and illustrates the conflation of experience and identity in the description of her reaction to the murder of a feminist activist student trained in self-defense: "From the moment I received the first phone call . . . I have been in the middle of a tale unfolding in more than one direction at once. Here was Andrea the activist, and there was Andrea the victim. . . . Here was Andrea the self-defense instructor, and there was Andrea the 'battered woman.' What had any of us seen or known of Andrea after all?" (15). This is a typical cultural response that sets up victimization and agency (activism/self-defense) as mutually exclusive terms at the same time that it presents them as on a par with each other and in so doing turns victimization into an aspect of the victim's identity.

Unlike confession in the Christian tradition that Foucault had in mind, the speak-out is a site of collective enunciation. In this context, "truth-telling" is no longer a confession about the self, nor are the debated "truths" perceived as "the secrets to our soul" (Brown 1995, 42). Instead, what is made visible is precisely how "linguistically contained, socially constructed, and discursively mediated women's experiences are and how they are never just individually 'had.'" Through consciousness-raising and speak-outs, women come to understand that an experience they might previously have perceived as interpersonal in nature is in fact rooted in historical and social relations. The forum does not preclude so much as foster the analysis of the processes of subject construction. As a site of collective enunciation, it politicizes rape even as it allows victims and survivors to examine the very terms they use to describe their experience. Some reject the very term "victim" and its attendant connotations, others raise similar concerns about the word "survivor." They discuss how societal responses to rape shape their own, and so forth. Making the experience of rape visible at speak-outs or in other feminist forums does not, as Brown contends, obscure the workings of the ideological system or preclude their analysis. In fact, it often entails precisely the kind of denaturalizing postmodernists advocate, namely that of the equivalence of sex and identity or correlatively of sexual violence and self-loss.

The sense of empowerment women derive from speak-outs or consciousness-raising does not presuppose a unified and pre-discursive sense of self whose recovery is staged by these events. While the consensus about speak-outs remains that they are empowering to the participants, I would like to suggest that this is the case not because they provide access to an inner space and foundational "self" that is being unearthed and validated. Most rape victims' narratives of their experience vary over time, ranging from self-blame to anger directed at the assailant, relatives, and others. Their feelings are far from continuous or consistent, and no scenario of rape, no matter how saturated with evidence of the crime, guarantees victims' definitive adherence to one script over another. Nonetheless, speak-outs remain sites where victims feel empowered by their vocalization of a narrative they know to be fluctuating and confusing. What is at issue is not, as Brown claims, the recovery of a "foundational center," a "hidden truth" through the "confessional" discourse of the speak-out so much as voicing of the experience, the act of narrativizing itself.

What ultimately empowers survivors of sexual assault at speak-outs is not the process of reclaiming a unified self so much as the production of narrative itself. In her analysis of the incest survivor movement, Jan Haaken makes a similar claim about the controversial issue of recovered memory. She argues that instead of emphasizing the literal truth of the memories of childhood sexual abuse, feminists should acknowledge the transformative process such recollections necessarily entail: "We must recognize how feminist memorial projects mobilize a wide range of psychological and social meanings, some of which are woven unconsciously into the fabric of memory. We need not be embarrassed to acknowledge this deeply social aspect of remembering or the mind's tendency to transform mental images and imprints of events, imaginatively embroidering on their narrative content. If we are to achieve full equality, we need more than the courage to remember or to heal. We also need the courage to imagine" (1999, 39). In Žižek's (2008) words, "a distinction needs to be made . . . between (factual) truth and truthfulness: what renders a report of a raped woman (or any other narrative of a trauma) truthful is its very factual unreliability, its confusions, its inconsistency. . . . the very factual deficiencies of the traumatised subject's report on her experience bear witness to the truthfulness of her report, since they signal that the reported content 'contaminated' the manner of reporting it" (4). Žižek does not expand on the transformative power of this unreliability, but his emphasis on truthfulness via inconsistencies opens the door to the potential for such imaginative regeneration.

In other words, the focus is on the potential for the invention of the self that this word-shaped reality entails rather than the excavation of a core center. Rape is a reality that feels anything but real to the victim, yet this very same unreality can become the basis of a representation the speaker can manipulate and gain control of, that can command an audience's attention and be made intelligible in other than the available cultural terms. Empowerment in this respect is about accessing one's life as material rather than about depth. In other words, while I agree with Wendy Brown that empowerment as a substitute for the discourse of freedom is a vacuous move if it signifies "an oddly adaptive and harmonious relationship with domination" and locates "an individual's sense of worth and capacity in the register of individual feelings" (1995, 22), I disagree with her contention that consciousness raising and speak-outs are sites where such personalizing moves occur.

It is unclear that the consciousness-raising of the late 1960s functioned, as Brown contends, as a site where experience was unproblematically taken up as the basis of feminist epistemology. According to Jean Curthoys, for example, such a feminist reliance on experience as the end-all of analysis is in fact a distorted representation of second-wave feminism or of consciousness-raising. Curthoys casts quite a different light on the relationship of second-wave feminists to the category experience. In contrast to MacKinnon, who identifies consciousness-raising as the epistemological practice from which her social theory of gender (as sexuality) derived, Curthoys (1997) argues that the early women's liberationists never relied on experience "epistemologically, as a justification for a theory" but as "the immediate object of the theory" (166).

Postmodernists regularly remind us that feminist discourse often contributes to maintaining the very same unequal relations it seeks to undermine. We are told, for instance, that in representing women as victims, radical feminists often entrench powerlessness as an identity. Their emphasis on victimization denies women's agency and reinscribes a problematic victim/agent opposition. There are two problems with this critique. First, it is self-contradictory. If the point of emphasizing women's agency is to help them not to be victims and to suppress the conditions (psychic or otherwise) that allegedly lead to their victimization, then agency continues to preclude victimization since one cannot both have it and be a victim. As such, the two concepts continue to exist in a dichotomous relationship to one another. Postmodern feminists denounce a focus on women's victimization on the grounds that such focus denies women's agency. Yet in focusing on agency as a solution to women's prevalent victimization in our culture, they keep the binary intact by assuming that agency equals an absence of victimization (which itself equals passivity).

Secondly, this postmodern mantra has now rendered any discussion of women's victimization automatically suspect while ironically leaving the category of "victim" fixed and unscrutinized. Whether critics are using the term "victim" or criticizing its use, they use the category without ever questioning what it encompasses and how it operates historically. Whether the condition it refers to is seen as a result of masculinist dominance or, as is more often the case now, of feminist discursive practices, the concept immediately invokes a form of passive suffering and interiority. It assumes an obviousness that obscures its historicity and the theoretical difficulties it presents. Critics use the term but fail to look at the processes through which cultures count or discredit people as victims and at how victimization has been defined by historically changing conditions of intelligibility.[18] Such a genealogical investigation would necessarily take us back to the political correctness debates of the 1990s when the devaluing of victim became the tool of choice in the race to undermine minority rights. How we make sense of victimization today may be more an extension of the ideologically loaded culture wars of the previous decade than of a useful exposition of ideology.

3 • "BIRTH RAPE"

Laboring Women, Coaching Men, and Natural Childbirth in the Hospital Setting

> In American hotel rooms you can decide whether or not to turn on the air conditioning (that is *your* business), but you cannot open the window.
> —Mary McCarthy, *Vietnam*

In 2010, debates surrounding "birth rape," a controversial phrase, which had previously circulated on midwife and childbirth blogs, was vigorously discussed anew on the worldwide web. "Birth rape" refers to the violating experiences laboring women incur in the hospital setting. The blog Birthtalk.org defines it in the following way:

> A vulnerable woman, who is powerless to leave the situation, is at times held down against her will, has strangers looking & touching at private parts of her body, perhaps without appropriate measures being taken to acknowledge her ownership of her body or to preserve her comfort levels. Perhaps she has fingers or instruments inserted without her consent, and sometimes against her consent, invading and crossing decent boundaries. She is fearful of what is happening to her and perhaps for the wellbeing of her baby, and receives no reassurance that either she or her child are ok. That is a violation, no matter how you look at it. Even IF this treatment is given with no malice and [with] the intent of attempting to assist her with birthing her child, there is NEVER a reason to forgo common decencies that will enable her to maintain a role in the birth, some autonomy over her body, to be involved in the decision-making, to be informed about what they want to do BEFORE they do it. (Birthtalk.org 2010)

While some find the use of the term "rape" as a metaphor for "birth trauma" justified, others think it inappropriate because they do not want the profound experience of giving birth to a baby to be associated with the trauma of rape. The phrase also upsets those who see its use in the context of childbirth as insulting to women who are subjected to forced sexual contact (see Faulkner 2012).

Rather than immediately take sides in the debate about whether rape is a legitimate metaphor for hospital birth, I suggest that we suspend the desire for such moral judgment in favor of an analysis of the terms that would allow us to make that judgment in the first place. In other words, instead of determining whether the notion of a sexualized form of violence should or not be applied to hospital birth, let's consider how childbirth can illuminate the attendant questions of agency and consent that define rape. The answer to these questions would then make us better equipped to assess the legitimacy of what is to some a literal and to others a metaphorical reference to rape. What is more, refusing to consider the ramifications of the association between rape and childbirth assumes that unlike childbirth, rape refers to an experience that is not itself subject to contestation, which is far from the truth, as the debates concerning date rape in particular have amply shown. In fact, the idea that "birth rape" may just be an attempted natural birth gone awry is strongly reminiscent of conservative reframings of rape on campus as "bad sex."

I argue that we should scrutinize the two models of agency that the understanding of "birth rape" as either metaphor or reality makes possible. Representations of hospital birth as antithetical to rape evoke a liberal model of agency whereby the individual subject is the "author" of his or her destiny and choices, while more postmodern views that align childbirth with the rape experience emphasize the subordination of the subject to the institutional structures of ideology, power, and language that define masculinized medicine. The fact that hospitalized childbirth can be experienced as "birth rape" at all is one of the most salient examples one can provide of the untenability of the opposition between metaphorical and referential that typically characterize discussions of rape.

The health care industry today has adopted a rhetoric of family-centered maternity care that offers a plethora of choices to expectant parents in the hospital setting (natural childbirth, epidural, narcotics, personal birth plans, etc.). This rhetoric echoes the liberal model of choice and agency. However, I will show how the very approach that emphasizes the subject's will and decision-making power ultimately works to compound and obscure women's disempowered status in relation to the birth experience. Through the staging of a normative form of masculinity in the delivery room, the husband as "coach," or the Bradley method, this individualist and interpersonal model makes the expectant parents responsible for the disappointments and violations they experience during childbirth. I argue that instead of serving as evidence of U.S. culture's endorsement of a woman-centered approach, this model's widespread popularity is evidence of the health care industry's appropriation of "natural" childbirth as a site for the production and reproduction of patriarchal and capitalist power. It also fails to account for the ways actors can be thoroughly constituted by their social context while acting as agents. This chapter exposes how the gendered power-dynamics that underlie the practices of hospital delivery and its liberal model of agency reinforce a form of victimization that is all the more pernicious for being veiled by a rhetoric of choice.

Feminists have written extensively about how reproductive technologies turn the natural process of conception, pregnancy, and birth into disempowering experiences for women.[1] Paradoxically, this medicalization of birth is taking place at the same time that hospitals are increasingly adopting a rhetoric of "natural" childbirth and family-centered maternity care. Medical institutions across the country are now sponsoring childbirth classes that draw on alternative models of childbirth (the Lamaze and Bradley methods) and encourage couples to become participants in "natural" childbirth rather than passive recipients of the health care industry's drug-induced intervention. Yet despite the time, resources, and energy that are spent representing "natural" childbirth as the ideal form of delivery, couple after couple enter the labor room determined to have a natural childbirth and leave it after having (begged for) an epidural. As Naomi Wolf (2001) points out, "What most parents-to-be don't realize until it is too late is how little effect on pain [natural childbirth techniques] are likely to have in a hospital setting: such ... techniques were not designed for high-tech hospitals that place time limits on labor and seek to speed up contractions" (88).

Works such as Wolf's *(Mis)conceptions* (2001) elucidate the contextual reasons for the failure of the "natural" childbirth model in the institutional setting of the hospital. What they do not explain, however, is why the institution itself is not taken to task for the lack of success of the model it so uniformly and warmly espouses. Since hospitals encourage "natural" childbirth and an extremely high percentage of couples give up on it during labor, why isn't the mainstream holding these institutions responsible for this high rate of failure? Instead of giving up trying to have a natural childbirth *in the hospital setting*, expectant mothers are increasingly giving up on natural childbirth altogether. Why aren't more couples turning away from hospital delivery, given its disempowering effects? The potential failure of the natural childbirth model outside the hospital setting is immediately used to discredit home birth and its proponents. Why such a double standard?

I argue that what explains the health care industry's lack of accountability for the waves of failure and disappointment couples experience when they attempt natural childbirth in the institutional environment of the hospital is the deployment of masculinity through childbirth education. Childbirth classes have predominantly adopted the husband-as-coach model of childbirth as standard practice. They thus stage a hegemonic form of masculinity (the man as leader) that paradoxically flounders when an inexperienced and poorly trained coach fails to live up to the expectations raised in childbirth class. It is unrealistic to think that a six-week course could possibly provide an expectant couple with the experience and competence needed to cope with the pains of labor. That the health care industry nonetheless continues to sponsor these classes suggests that far from being costly to the institution, the failure of the "natural" husband-coached model of childbirth might in fact be serving its purpose. By integrating men as coaches in the labor room, industry shifts responsibility for the failure of the natural childbirth model onto the couple, thus effectively obscuring how the highly clinical and profit-driven environment of the hospital is necessarily implicated in such a failure. Because power is rhetorically and performatively located in the husband's masculinity,[2] it eclipses the power of institutionalized delivery as hospitals rush through birthing practices to save and make more money. As a result, a highly institutional relationship is displaced and personalized. In a striking reversal of the usual ruse of capitalism, health care's touchy-feely "feminist patriarchy" is thus substituting unpaid labor (the husband-coach) for (under)paid female labor (the doula or professional labor assistant), thus destabilizing norms of masculinity for its own purposes. This chapter examines the costs and implications of this reversal for the laboring woman.

Throughout this chapter, I use my own experience as a template for my analysis of childbirth education. I do so not because my experience speaks for itself but precisely because it failed to do so when I most needed to make sense of it. It is only with hindsight that I could put it in its proper institutional and ideological context and explain my own conflicted feelings during the birthing process. I therefore appeal to experience not as incontrovertible and transparent evidence that forgoes scrutiny but as the very element that requires analysis in an investigation of childbirth education. Specifically, the anecdotal weight I bring to the argument seeks to illustrate the degree to which childbirth practices today personalize and obscure ideological discourses and their effects. It also serves to show the continuing relevance of the category of experience for feminist politics and philosophy and to challenge the experience/theory opposition that continues to inform much of feminist inquiry in the twenty-first century. As Susan Bordo (1997) reminds us, "Discourses impinge on us as fleshly bodies, often in ways that cannot be determined from a study of representations alone. To make such determinations, we need to get down and dirty with the body at the level of its practices. . . . Keeping track of the practical life of our bodies is important to keeping us intellectually honest" (183–184).

During my first pregnancy, my husband and I did what all first-time parents are expected to do; we enrolled in the childbirth class sponsored by the hospital where we were slated to deliver. The course took place once a week from seven to nine P.M. and was six weeks long. There were five expectant couples in the class, all heterosexual, and, except for one couple who dropped out after two weeks because of a scheduling conflict, we were all faithful attendees and conscientious students. My husband and I were extremely pleased that the partners of pregnant women were not only welcome but were in fact encouraged and expected to attend and participate in the course and in childbirth. We would not have had it any other way, and it was a relief to know that we would not have to seek another source of "live" support and information when it came to preparing for childbirth together. Like most pregnant women, I could visualize sharing the experience of my child's birth with no one but my partner, and he was the person I wanted as my sidekick during the whole process. Neither he nor I believed that a female presence would or could provide better labor support by virtue of her gender or personal experience of motherhood. Years of activism in the feminist movement had disabused me of the belief that gender identity alone could provide the grounds for the kind of bonding and solidarity identity politics proclaimed. The only kind of closeness I now valued was based on choice and actions, not on biological or social destinies people happened to share by virtue of their gender. The kind of women-only ritual that childbirth education and childbirth itself had been in the context of second-wave feminism represented the separatist feminism I had long disavowed, so I was all the more willing and eager to embrace the husband-as-coach method.

The hospital course we attended was an eclectic mix of various methods. Our childbirth instructor, Diane, soon identified herself as a Lamaze instructor. At the same time, she drew on Bradley method terminology since she foregrounded husband-assisted births as an inherent part of natural birthing. In fact, she spent (too) much energy trying to put the men at ease, thanking them for their presence and highlighting the importance of their role during but also before and after delivery. The Bradley method was named after the man who designed it, Robert A. Bradley, a U.S. obstetrician from Kansas. In 1965, Bradley published *Husband-Coached Childbirth*, in which he explained that women could give birth naturally and successfully by relying on the help of their husband (after he had been trained as a coach) and by following six principles. These were the need for darkness and solitude, the need for quiet, physical comfort during the first stage of labor, physical relaxation, controlled breathing, and closed eyes and the appearance of sleep.[3] The Bradley method strongly echoes the Lamaze method, the most popular method of labor and delivery today, which first became known in 1959 with the publication of Marjorie Karmel's *Thank You, Dr. Lamaze* (1959). Lamaze too relies first and foremost on relaxation as a way of alleviating anxiety and minimizing pain during labor.[4]

When we joined the childbirth class, we naively assumed that the integration of the husband-as-coach model of childbirth into the standard care of pregnant women was based on the experience of a significant number of women who had deemed it the most effective kind of support during birth. If, as we were being taught in childbirth class, relaxation was what we should strive for during labor, it made sense that a loving spouse/partner who was absolutely committed to being his lover's helper during labor would be a better source of support than a well-meaning but nonetheless intruding stranger. Furthermore, like many feminists of my generation, I thought that the patriarchal envelope in which my relationship to my husband was being packaged through childbirth education would not affect our experience of childbirth or the egalitarian relationship to which we were both committed. We could both read through and hence ignore how the husband-assisted model reinscribes hegemonic masculinity and the father's status as head of the family in the feminine space of labor.

Needless to say, the very choice of "husband" rather than "partner" illustrates the heterosexism that has traditionally characterized the institution of motherhood and that continues to define hospitals' co-optation of alternative childbirth education. Bradley, a product of the conservative 1950s, was very heterosexist in his conception of the birthing team, and the institutional appropriation of the Bradley rhetoric perpetuates this heterosexism. In the alternative birthing scene, however, Bradley has changed with the times: there is no assumption, for instance, that the coach will be one's husband or partner. The course is a ten- to twelve-week marathon where the couple spends more time lying on blankets side by side working on pain exercises than listening to lectures. The exercises involve touching, massaging. The coach is taught to be entirely focused on the needs of the laboring woman and the assumption is that s/he will be as exhausted as the mother by the end of the birth. However, this new and improved Bradley method is still a very fringe movement that most health insurances do not cover.

In addition, using the term "coach" to name the activity of the partner also says a lot about what kind of gender roles the parents are expected to play in the delivery room. Tellingly, when the supporting cast is someone other than the husband, they are designated as *doulas* or *assistants* rather than as coaches (Sears and Sears 1993, 23–24). In other words, when the support person is more likely to be female, her role is described as more passive and subordinate. The role of coach is reserved for the male partner, who is perceived not as taking orders but as giving instruction, training, and direction. The association of the term "coach" with sports is yet another way the husband-as-coach model tries to ensure that the man's conventional role as the site of authority is not threatened by his presence in the unknown and feminine space of labor. By indirectly framing labor as a sporting event, the language of coaching represents the woman's sweaty and straining body as one whose activity and level of pain can and should be directed by her partner. It ultimately turns the alienating experience of labor into a familiar site where a masculinized form of power seeks to reassert itself through the figure of the husband. As a feminist involved with a feminist, I knew that my husband and I would not be perpetuating such conventional norms of masculinity and femininity. This was a script we knew not to follow. What we were not aware of, however, is the extent to which we remained mere pawns in a play even though the hierarchical gender structure underlying the husband-assisted method did come undone (and only marginally through conditions of our own making).

What often unfolds in the labor and delivery room is anything but the successful coaching scenario for which childbirth classes prepare expectant couples. The reality is in fact radically different from the scenarios depicted in childbirth education (whose worst cases, in retrospect, do not look bad at all). When our much-awaited day finally arrived, for instance, my husband was extremely intimidated by the role of "expert" he was supposed to play and not surprisingly, he could only perform it as the amateur that he inevitably was—that is, with a complete lack of self-confidence. He was as far from fulfilling the part of a directing coach as one could imagine. His desperate attempts to help were just the confused gestures of a person who felt completely out of his depth in the face of so much pain. I knew him too well not to read through the façade, through the periodic smile or nod with which he sought to appease me. Neither he nor I could focus or relax, nor could we go on automatic pilot and do the breathing exercises effectively when they were most needed. My pain was so upsetting to him that he would have done anything to put a stop to it. When I asked for an epidural, he immediately acquiesced even though his job was to guide me through natural childbirth. And when I was not given the epidural, his despair at finding out that it was too late clearly equaled mine. Despite the weekly classes we had attended and the copious readings we had done, neither of us were prepared for the amount of pain delivery entailed. As Wolf (2001) points out, one of the things childbirth class does not explain effectively is "the pain of childbirth and what to do about it other than breathe helplessly in its grips or take major drugs simply to cut off sensation" (91). She also draws attention to the fact that the educational birth videos shown in childbirth classes represent passive and emotionally detached births where no one yells, grunts, or pants and where no one is stroked or kissed during labor. It certainly did not help us to know that childbirth had all been scripted ahead, classified, described, and explained and that millions had experienced this before. It did not help that the nurses and medical staff around us had all-knowing faces. They were too busy attending to their duties and assumed an understandingly blasé attitude. The nurses have neither the time nor the energy to attend to and manage the expectant mother's fluctuating emotions and needs. And after all, isn't that the husband's role as coach?

While the model of husband as coach is supposedly put into place to provide the laboring woman with continued support, it typically fails to provide the kind of expert guidance she needs to achieve relaxation and calm. One can then only wonder why health care continues to sponsor a model of normative masculinity (the husband as coach, the man in charge) that flounders again and again and fails to provide the kind of guiding and benevolent patriarchal direction it is supposed to represent. What function, then, can an ineffectual coach possibly play in labor? Why is there such institutional commitment to staging a gender performance that almost always results in gender trouble?

In her influential books *Gender Trouble* (1990) and *Bodies That Matter* (1993), Judith Butler advocates a cultural politics that works to expose the constructedness of gender identity. Gender, she argues, is a performance, a show we repeatedly put on (through dress codes, behaviors, etc.) that "congeals over time to produce the appearance of substance, of a natural sort of being" (1990, 33). Nevertheless, the very repetition on which the naturalization of gender identity depends also opens up the potential for performative subversion. Repetition always introduces the possibility of failed repetition, and full conformity to these norms is ultimately impossible. In other words, the system itself guarantees its own subversion. Unlike Michel Foucault (1978), who tends to regard such processes of resignification as a ruse of power, Butler is more willing to investigate their destabilizing force, even though they are contingent, hence her much-contested celebration of drag in *Gender Trouble*. For Butler, "in imitating gender, drag implicitly reveals the imitative structure of gender itself—as well as its contingency" (1990, 137).

Ironically, the repetitive staging of heterosexual structures of gender and power in the husband-as-coach model of childbirth also subverts those structures, since over and over again the coach is unable to live up to the norms of controlling masculinity. While drag highlights the unexpected identifications and sexual practices that reveal the arbitrariness of conventional gender distinctions, the model of "natural" childbirth sponsored by hospitals today exposes the constructedness of gender even as it stages it in conventional and heterosexist terms. In fact, the quotation marks I use throughout the chapter to qualify "natural" are meant to emphasize the fact that hospitals appropriate the term but do not adhere to the drug-free, vaginal delivery it implies. The myth of a "natural" childbirth in the hospital setting is then maintained, I argue, through the yoking of the practice with a gendered division of labor (pun intended). Because the supposedly "natural" model of childbirth hospitals have endorsed is based on traditional gender roles, the understanding of gender as a resistant variety of natural difference constructs the illusion of naturalness even as delivery is medicalized.

Through childbirth education, men and women are taught a script on how to perform their proper masculine and feminine roles within the heterosexual matrix of the labor room. That roles that would not have to be taught were they indeed "natural" have to be assigned and learned reveals how unnatural "natural" childbirth actually is. When the couple then fails to convincingly act out the script of "natural" childbirth, the performativity of gender is further exposed. The coach is feminized as his inexperience and incompetence render him passive, while the laboring woman's anger defeminizes her. Far from working to subvert institutional practices, this denaturalizing of gender categories through the feminizing of the coach functions as a ruse of power. The performativity of gender thus highlighted is not a by-product of a system otherwise invested in maintaining the sex binary so much as it is a crucial aspect of the system's deployment of the gender script. The couple's inability to carry out the assigned script in the labor room, in other words, ultimately serves the ends of the birthing industry even as it threatens the naturalness of gender.

The laboring partners are so busy sorting out their ambivalent positions in relation to each other, their gender roles, and the birthing experience that they are unable to recognize that their contradictory feelings have less to do with the personalities involved than with the environment in which they find themselves. The alienating effects of the hospital setting are obscured by the vicissitudes of the husband-assisted model. What this script fails to prepare the birthing mother for is the parade of nurses, residents, and medical students with whom she has to interact during labor and the highly stressful and medicalized context of birth in which she is operating. I, for one, was so focused on the ramifications of the coaching partnership and my husband's ineffectualness that much more disturbing issues hardly fazed me: since my partner was to be my continuing source of support throughout labor, I did not think twice about the fact that the only member of the medical staff I knew and trusted personally in this whole process, namely my OB/GYN, would not appear until the very last stage of delivery; neither did I express any uneasiness when a medical student came in to ask questions I had already answered or when a second one tried to pass as a doctor (while her shocking inability to make sense of the discrepancies in heartbeat picked up by the electronic monitoring device made us extremely anxious). I was too discombobulated by my husband's own confusion to object to the resident who came to examine me before her shift ended and whose replacement insisted on engaging me in intellectual conversations about English literature even as he was examining me vaginally again. I did not say anything when the labor nurse whom I liked but whose shift ended just as my contractions were picking up was replaced by a nurse who did not take my pain seriously because my contractions were still irregular ("It is your first child; you have at least twelve more hours to go"). As it happens, my contractions never became regular, so that the crowning of the baby's head literally took the medical staff by surprise. The nurse had to pull a doctor out of surgery to deliver the baby because there was not enough time for my OB/GYN, who was on call, to make it to the hospital.[5]

My way of coming to terms with my feelings of powerlessness was through anger. Faced with a busy and hence indifferent medical staff, I resented my husband's frightened and hesitant ways. I distinctly remember his attempts to relax me by rubbing my hands and the glares I directed at him any time he persisted in touching me. I kept shaking my head from side to side and he kept turning to the nurse with beseeching eyes. When the contraction subsided, we were both so shaken by what had just transpired that we could hardly concentrate on what was coming next. In fact, the more my husband tried to help me refocus, the more irritated I got. I knew he was uncomfortable, I could feel his despair and confusion, and that too made me impatient. The feeling was overwhelming and inexplicable, all the more so since he was desperately trying to comfort and help me through my ordeal.[6]

Fortunately for both of us, labor was unusually short for a first delivery and the bad vibes gave way to joy and relief at the sight of our healthy and vigorous son. I would probably never have revisited the issue had I not come across the "birth rape" debate online or heard similar testimonies from other happily married couples. These women too were overcome by anger, resenting either the emotional distance their partner assumed to perform the role of coach or how his sense of powerlessness reflected their own.[7] Some of them also spent most of their delivery worrying about their partner's feelings of inadequacy and fright instead of focusing on their own needs. In keeping with common lore, these women believed that their often-explosive resentment during childbirth was just a psychological side effect of "natural" childbirth or an inevitable extension of a male-female dynamic à la Camille Paglia (1990). Like models that, eager to celebrate gender subversion, examine it in isolation from other categories of power, this understanding of women's anger in childbirth solely in relation to the male/female dynamic ignores the larger institutional background against which this relationship plays itself out. It assumes that men and women are already constituted as sexual subjects prior to their entry into the arena of social relations. By contrast, I argue that the institutional context cannot be examined after the fact as if it exists outside the relation of women with men. While it is true that at a psychological level resentment allows the laboring woman to cope with her feelings of disempowerment, these feelings do not ultimately result from her partner's inexperience. They derive from the stressful setting in which natural childbirth techniques are in fact almost automatically destined to fail.

By incorporating alternative models of childbirth into their delivery practices, hospitals ensure that the responsibility for the failure of "natural" childbirth gets shifted onto the couple's shoulders. Childbirth education trains the laboring partners to think of the coach as the source of comfort and support, so much so that they then automatically attribute the birthing mother's disempowerment and inability to relax during labor to the coach's poor skills. When the responsibility for making labor woman-centered is thus shifted, it is the man and the woman's relationship that is at stake rather than the clients' relationship to the hospital. By foregrounding the traditional structure of masculinity and femininity that governs the domestic sphere, the husband-assisted method thus privatizes what is primarily an institutional relationship. The expectant couple that was given the illusion of autonomy in decision-making through childbirth education simply internalizes their incompetence as personal failure. It must be their fault if labor becomes so overwhelming that they cannot take charge of it. They should have paid closer attention in childbirth class, they should have meditated more, or they should have honed the relaxation techniques by longer practice. Never mind that nothing in the high-tech and high-traffic delivery room is conducive to relaxation. Never mind that neither the laboring woman nor her coach could possibly feel like participants in the context of the aggressive labor and birth management style that continues to characterize hospitals today.[8] Never mind that "in the United States, . . . it has become increasingly clear that what parents learn in childbirth classes does not prepare them adequately to deal with the highly medicalized environment and crisis atmosphere in the hospital" (Kitzinger 1995, 88).

Childbirth classes teach the laboring woman "to see her proper role in childbirth as providing a prompt, docile response to a series of medical interventions and instructions, and [guide] her husband or partner to comply as well" (Wolf 2001, 94). In fact, the coach's inexperience turns the hospital's way of delivering babies into a most welcome and reassuring intervention, while the hospital's high-tech methods highlight the neophyte's incompetence. The interpersonal conflicts that ensue between the partners as a result of unfulfilled and unrealistic expectations raised in childbirth class further contribute to giving the hospital an aura of neutrality and competent mastery. Despite its alienating effects, the institution is left off the hook because it becomes the backdrop against which the male/female dynamic is acted out. It simply assumes the role of a neutral arbitrating force that is ready to intervene when, for instance, the husband fails to perform his role. That this scenario perpetuates itself no matter how many couples find the model flawed has a lot to do, I suspect, with the participants' unwillingness to draw attention to what might be perceived as the coaching partner's incompetence.

Thus, what is ironic about the health care industry's apparent reliance on a patriarchal form of power is that whether or not the model of hegemonic masculinity it propounds lives up to its norms (which it mostly fails to do) is insignificant to the success of corporate profit-making. That hegemonic masculinity may be destabilized in the unfamiliar realm of labor does not ultimately hamper the effectivity of its ideological function for capitalist gain. Economic interests in this context are dependent not on the maintenance of a gendered hierarchy but on the deployment of masculinity. As long as the focus remains on the performance of the partner (where it cannot help but remain), hospital procedures assume an aura of neutrality and the capitalistic venture of the birth industry in the United States can continue, veiled and unhindered.

The deployment of hegemonic masculinity by a profit-driven health care industry thus requires a consideration of the imbrication of both capitalism and patriarchy in our analyses of childbirth practices in the United States. This two-pronged dynamic immediately evokes a feminist dual-systems theory. Throughout its history, socialist feminism has attended to the intersection of patriarchy and capitalism by looking at how patriarchal relations help preserve and reproduce the social relations of capitalism and how capitalist interests play a role in constructions of gender (by maintaining, for instance, a low-paid female workforce in certain industries or by consolidating the dominant modes of femininity and masculinity). Both approaches are important because they bring an economic perspective to bear on gender relations, but they are also problematic because they almost automatically approach capitalism and patriarchy as two systems that are neatly overlaid on top of one another. Socialist feminists have too often assumed that capitalism is either necessarily invested in reproducing traditional patriarchal relations or dependent on hegemonic norms of masculinity and femininity that reproduce, for instance, the binaries of male/female, active/passive, mind/body, culture/nature, and so forth.[9] Economic motives are thus seen as determining gender structures that are invariable and predictably hierarchical (whereby the right side of these binaries is always subordinated to the left side). By contrast, institutionally sponsored "natural" childbirth reveals how late capitalism has learned to deploy postmodern forms of gender fragmentation and instability in its relentless race for profit. As the childbirth industry reveals, gender-bending practices are as effective a tool for minimizing cost and liability exposures as are conventional gender roles.

In effect, her partner's presence gives the expectant woman the illusion of adequate support in the form of one whose ineffectiveness she will retroactively be less likely to question, anxious as she often is to avoid highlighting his incompetence or hurting his feelings. As second-wave feminists were keen to point out, "what we bring to childbirth is nothing else than our entire socialization as women" (Rich 1976, 178), and it is unrealistic to assume that "the mother [will] easily come to childbirth a changed woman after a few classes in natural childbirth or a heavy dose of Women's Liberation" (Arms 1975, 22). Just as my intense resentment during childbirth cannot ultimately be made sense of without accounting for an investment in normative masculinity (he failed to be the man in charge), the laboring woman's unwillingness to draw attention to the model's failure (and hence to her partner's incompetence) or to the hospital's violating practices also implies a reenactment of conventional gender roles as she often worries less about herself or her OB/GYN than about her spouse. She feels guilty about her inexplicable anger instead of focusing on her own needs and body.

Women's sense of alienation from their own bodies during childbirth is no new phenomenon. Childbirth has historically been an experience during which women have "felt out of control, at the mercy of biology, fate, or chance" (Rich 1976, 178). Feminists have written at length about how this disempowerment exponentially increased when obstetrics transformed from a female into a male province with the growth of an elite medical profession. As Suzanne Arms (1975) points out, one of the major differences between the midwives and obstetricians traditionally has been that midwives respond to labor pains by assisting the laboring woman and reassuring her that this is supposed to happen, while the obstetrician's impulse is to intervene, stop the pain, and do it for her. In this scenario, the husband-coach, who is often too stressed and inexperienced to provide the direction and advocacy he was barely trained to give, is only too happy to step back and let the nurses and doctors "do it for him." As a result, "mothers and babies are delivered from each other in a mechanical maneuver performed by professionals" (Reid 1997, 18). This medicalized delivery takes place at the hospital, a space that was decisive in associating childbirth with the male medical establishment. As the site of birth, the hospital is all the more problematic because it links birth to disease. In its antiseptic and clinical setting, labor necessarily becomes something to be gotten through rather than a process over which the laboring woman can or even would want to take charge: "From being subjects of the birth experience, active agents, the primary participants in the event—active together, laboring together, mothers and babies have been reduced to objects of medical treatment, incapacitated into passive recipients of 'care,' to which the women at most give their 'consent'" (ibid.).

Unless the expectant woman and her partner educate themselves about the choices they have during labor and delivery and make specific requests, they will most likely not be offered any of these options at the hospital. Instead, the nurses and physicians follow a routine whose main raison d'être is expediency and whose modification they rarely welcome. In childbirth class, couples are encouraged to put their requests down in writing if they want the hospital routine to be changed. They have to let the staff know, for instance, if they want to gaze into their baby's eyes before his or her vision gets blurred by the antibiotic ointment that is immediately administered after birth (Sears and Sears 1993, 45, 55). The mother has to explicitly decline having an episiotomy, a surgically planned incision on the perineum and the posterior vaginal wall, which is otherwise automatically performed to "facilitate" delivery. In fact, the procedure is performed on 80 to 90 percent of first-time mothers during delivery (Bruce 2001, 54; Davis-Floyd 1998, 15; Sears and Sears 1993, 27; Wolf 2001, 172). According to Sheila Kitzinger, "It is the only surgery likely to be performed without her consent on the body of a healthy woman in Western society" (1995, 1), even though there is no evidence to suggest that babies arrive healthier because they emerged faster due to an episiotomy (Wolf 2001, 173).[10]

When we went to the hospital to deliver, we had a birth plan and were both determined to be participants in rather than mere observers of the birthing experience. Unwilling to take risks, we chose the hospital over home birth. We actually believed that we would be able to combine the best of both worlds; that is, enjoy the safety of the technological world of the hospital while preserving the kind of intimacy and nurture associated with home birth. We thought that with my husband's continued support throughout labor, we could create a safe haven of intimacy in which our active participation in childbirth would transcend the alienating aspects of my environment. I had convinced myself that the fact that I would become a laboring mother in an invisible assembly line of other expectant women would only help us create a parallel universe that would be meaningful to the soon-to-be three of us. The nurses and doctors would do their job and my husband and I ours. We would make the requests we had come prepared to make and ask, for instance, to be left alone with the baby after birth. We would periodically unplug the electronic fetal monitoring device that keeps women flat in bed to avoid disturbing the monitor tracings and simply walk around and put into practice the physiologic positioning we had been taught in childbirth class. Like a flâneur who succeeds in being alone in the midst of a crowd, we would manage to preserve a self-contained familial unit in the midst of the institutionalized turmoil of the delivery room. Like many other women of my generation, I thought that because I was an enlightened and educated person who had assimilated feminism's lessons, I was somehow less likely to be affected by the structures of power that surrounded me. I believed that my enlightenment in fact allowed me some measure of distance and control vis-à-vis potentially disempowering situations. I had knowingly chosen a more impersonal and clinical setting for delivery, and I was determined not to let the environment in which I was to give birth have any bearing on my relationship to the birthing experience or to my husband. Their script, I thought, would not affect ours.

Little did I know, however, how meaningless our script would become in the contexts of labor and hospital practices. It was not that the medical staff was unwilling to accommodate our wishes but that our wishes quickly sounded hollow and trivial in the institutionalized context of the hospital where only systematic procedures appear reasonable and acceptable. Faced with insufferable labor pains and blasé nurses, we were quickly overwhelmed, and the pseudo-authority with which my husband was laden as coach only highlighted our feelings of disempowerment. In fact, we felt like asynchronous hippies every time we made a request that deviated from standard practices.[11] I could not help but feel guilty when I unplugged the fetal monitoring device to move around, so much so that eventually even going to the bathroom felt like a dereliction of my duty as a mother. By the end of the day, we were more invested than the nurses on call in following and interpreting the needle's movement on the monitor. After the birth, we were allowed to spend two hours with our son in the delivery room before he was taken away to the nursery, but that was only because the delivery that was slated to follow mine had been postponed. The room was not going to be needed right away, so I was not rushed into a recovery room after birth. We had of course been made aware that we had the "choice" (provided we could afford it) to opt for a single room should we wish to keep the baby by our bedside during the hospital stay. Considering our financial situation, we chose not to take advantage of the rooming-in option. So for the following two days, I made endless trips to the nursery to fetch my son and nurse him. My request that he be exclusively breastfed did not stop well-meaning maternity nurses from bottle-feeding him while he was in the nursery. As Sears and Sears point out in *The Baby Book*, "kind nurses will often 'spare' the mother a feeding and go ahead and feed baby a bottle during the night" (1993, 48).

In light of such experiences, the medical institution's openness to the husband-as-coach method can hardly be read as a sign of protofeminist consciousness. Far from representing an increased sensitivity to women's needs or to egalitarian family structures, what accounts for this smooth corporate endorsement of the Bradley method is the fact that it is the least likely to affect the delivery routines and time pressures under which hospitals operate today. Husbands who are bound to be intimidated by their wife's excruciating pain during labor are more likely to defer to the authority of medical experts in the delivery room. They become as invested as the professional staff in having the birthing process be over as soon as possible, and they contribute to a climate that sacrifices the mother's autonomy and authority by giving the birth experience away to technology, anesthesiologists, and nurseries. In an environment that by its very nature defines birth as illness and labor pains as symptoms of a disease, the expectant couple is in fact often relieved to see the process taken out of their hands. The birth experience thus becomes anything but an occasion for the expectant woman and her partner to have responsibility and control over the basic life event that the birth of a family represents.

The forceful feminist critiques of institutionalized childbirth need to be extended to account for the incorporation of the husband-as-coach into the feminized space of labor and for its radical (mis)appropriation of the male-female dynamic during delivery. Far from providing the kind of advocacy and support the laboring woman needs, the husband-as-coach model only ensures that the role of supporting cast will not be filled by a doula or professional labor assistant who might, from the medical profession's perspective, interfere, slow down, or challenge the high-tech processes hospitals follow today. By virtue of their experience and practice, doulas are less likely to be intimidated by the physicians and nurses' authority or by their client's labor pains. Their primary concern is to make sure that the laboring woman's emotional and physical needs are met so that she can approach the birth experience with the right frame of mind. They know that slowing down labor and delivery is part of the relaxation techniques hospitals advocate in theory but not in practice. Where the husband-coach hesitates and defers, doulas inform and advocate. Where the husband-coach might control, doulas provide encouragement and guidance. They assist instead of directing and empower instead of taking over. In fact, studies have shown that when a doula is present to guide the couple and model supportive behaviors, fathers tend to offer more adequate support to their partners as well (Simkin 1999, 22).

Effective continued labor support has been shown to lower cesarean rates, requests for epidurals, and maternity care costs in general (Kennell et al. 1991, 2197; Simkin 1999, 23). By virtue of their training and experience, doulas are necessarily more likely to provide effective labor support than the husband-as-coach model promoted by the Bradley method and facilitated by hospitals today. Nevertheless, medical institutions have remained invested in the husband-as-coach model, downloading the costs incurred by bad support onto other entities—the parents, the child, and so on. Their rational calculation of costs and potential liability lies at the very inception of the ambivalent forms gendered authority takes in the delivery room. Normative masculinity is deployed so that health care can be produced at minimum cost. This imbrication of patriarchy and capitalism is particularly evident when the exclusion of a supporting cast who would interfere with the doctor's absolute power is paradoxically combined with the absence of doctors (who only briefly appear at the end of labor). Until economic motives override patriarchal allegiances and the costs incurred as a result of poor labor practices are shown to be significantly higher than the costs of hiring adequate support for the laboring woman, this state of things will not change. Only then will the doula become a staple of childbirth education and replace the misguided role husbands are now playing during labor. For this to happen, however, doulas would have to be remunerated in an adequate manner. Today, they still receive no third-party reimbursement and are underpaid for their work.

Although the contradictory deployment of normative masculinity in delivery practices enhances capitalist profit by disempowering women, this is not to say that we should advocate a blind endorsement of the doula or professional labor assistant as an alternative model. Some formulations of this alternative childbirth model are as likely to maintain unequal power relations as the health care industry's co-optation of the Bradley method. William Sears and his wife Martha Sears are, respectively, a pediatrician and a nurse whose books on childbirth and childrearing are bound to be recommended to expectant couples at one point or another during pregnancy. The Searses' expertise is based on years of parenting experience (they have raised eight children, some of whom were adopted) and on thousands of hours of counseling pregnant couples and confused parents during twenty years of pediatric practice. They are probably the most well-known proponents of "attachment parenting" today, a style of parenting that consists of connecting with the baby as soon, as unconditionally, and as thoroughly as possible. The major components of attachment parenting are responding to the baby's cues, breastfeeding (on demand), wearing the baby (slings are highly recommended), and co-sleeping with the child. Their *Baby Book* (1993) in particular, a book that emphasizes the importance for both mother and father of sharing the nurturing role in childrearing practices, has been one of the twenty-first century's bibles of pregnancy and baby care.

Sears and Sears firmly discourage men from being the primary source of support to their expectant partner during labor and delivery. In fact, they identify the coaching husband as a thing of the 1980s. This role, they claim, was no doubt an improvement on the previous era, when fathers were banished from the clinical and sterile hospital environment where birth occurred. It is nonetheless not a role, they argue, that compares to the kind of "division of labor" that should characterize contemporary approaches to delivery. In the more relaxed, intimate, and humane environment of the contemporary birthing room, "the pressure is off father to perform as coach" (Sears and Sears 1993, 20). The supporting cast is instead the professional labor support person, or PLA (professional labor assistant), someone the couple has previously met and trusts and who is trained to assist the laboring woman. The PLA is, as it were, a personal trainer whose job is to make sure that labor is progressing comfortably and efficiently. She attends to all of the laboring women's mental and physical needs and "helps the mother move through labor in harmony with her body" (23). She serves as a liaison between the medical staff and the laboring couple.

The Searses' suggestion that the expectant couple hire a PLA for delivery is problematic, however, because it ultimately promotes a separate-spheres ideology that says more about their preconceptions about gender difference than about women's needs in labor. The Searses themselves hired a labor support assistant for the birth of their last four babies, and according to Bill Sears, "she and Martha spoke a woman-to-woman, mother-to-mother language of labor that [he] did not understand but [has] grown to respect" (23). In other words, men are from Mars and women from Venus, and they are inherently so rather than through circumstance or social intervention.[12] For the Searses, gender differences should be accepted as dictates of nature rather than interrogated as effects of power. The mother bonds with her child because she cannot help but do so: "The biological signals of the baby trigger a biological response in the mother.... Because she is there and physically attuned to baby, [mother] immediately picks up and feeds her infant. . . . Her milk-ejection reflex functions smoothly, and mother and infant as in biological harmony" (49).

Differences between men and women in *The Baby Book* are grounded in biology, and this is what, we are led to believe, ultimately makes the PLA a better labor support than the male partner: "The labor support person does not replace the father; rather she frees him up to do what a man does best—love his wife. Men seldom relate empathetically to the emotional and physical challenges of the laboring woman. It is usually better for the father to leave the technical matters to a labor support person while he embraces his wife, rubs her back, walks with her, gives her ice chips and fluids, and guards against commotion" (23). The term "empathetically" is significant because it implies that the PLA should not only necessarily be a woman but that she should herself have undergone the pains of labor before becoming a certified PLA. This privileging of biology embodies a mystique of birth that is hardly generalizable when it comes to women's relation to the experience. Many women who have had children would not relate empathetically to another woman's laboring needs or pain. They might not in fact have related to their own. In foregrounding empathy, the Searses also undermine the importance of expertise and training in the making of a good PLA, thus contributing to a climate that does not adequately remunerate doulas for their work. It is difficult to value the activity as work if all that goes into providing adequate labor support is empathy based on biology.

Furthermore, while I certainly agree that what "a man" should do during delivery is love "his wife,"[13] Dr. Sears's investment in preserving clear demarcations between the roles of the husband and the PLA also says more about his own investment in safeguarding a dominant notion of masculinity than about the laboring woman's best interests. It is quite unrealistic to imagine that the roles of two people striving to attend to the woman's emotional and physical needs during delivery will not overlap. If the husband is to love his wife and support her emotionally, then what part of the emotional support is he to leave to the PLA? What are the "emotional challenges" that, according to Sears, require professional intervention and not the loving spouse's? And how would he know the difference? Similarly, need the PLA restrain herself so as not to step on the man's loving toes? The Searses postulate a "division of labor" during delivery, but the working out of the details of such a scenario reveals the vacuousness of attempts to demarcate these roles. For instance, they delegate to the PLA the role of liaison between the couple and everyone else while charging the husband with the responsibility of guarding against commotion. How are these two responsibilities to be kept distinct? And most importantly, why should they be? Is helping the laboring woman breathe by modeling the breathing techniques merely a technical matter? Should the husband refrain from joining in? And what if, after all, both the doula and the husband overlap in their supporting roles? What would be so bad about duplicating efforts in the service of a laboring woman?

While it is true that the Searses assign a nurturing role to men throughout their book, they never do so at the risk of challenging gender distinctions. Even when they assign a quality usually associated with femininity to men, they ensure that nurturing does not constitute a threat to dominant masculinity. Throughout the book, they reaffirm a Victorian ideology of separate spheres that reinscribes male authority (disguised as benevolent detachment) and female subordination (disguised as instinctual motherhood). That women's reproductive functions and bodily differences provide the foundation of gender difference is so taken for granted that even male forays into feminine roles cannot challenge the binary opposition that underpins the Searses' conception of gender. The male/female and mind/body dualisms are left intact as fathers learn their nurturing role from scratch while mothers only have to listen to their built-in response mechanism to cater to baby's needs: "A father's nurturant responses are a little less automatic and a little slower to unfold than a mother's" (Sears and Sears 1993, 44).

As Chris Weedon (1993) explains, "The effect of privileging certain ideas of difference—for example women's natural and intrinsic mothering nature—has been to limit women's value, whatever their individual circumstances, to discourses of motherhood with which most women did not fully or even partly identify" (12). Childbirth education needs to move beyond the normative dualisms that maintain existing social relations if the structural power relations that govern women's lives are to change. This is not to say, as my analysis of institutionalized childbirth education demonstrates, that the subversion of gender roles will automatically contribute to empowering women. As the corporate co-optation of the Bradley method in today's delivery practices reveals, whether the model of hegemonic masculinity that the health care industry propounds lives up to its norms or flounders is insignificant to the success of corporate profit-making. Its presence is all that is required to contribute to capitalist gain.

Since the 1980s, hospitals have done much to adopt the rhetoric of family-centered maternity care. In fact, as Celeste Phillips (1999) points out, "For a hospital to admit that family-centered maternity care is not a priority is to commit economic suicide" (11). The incorporation of what was once considered an alternative model of childbirth into delivery practices is part of an institutional effort to give the appearance of being woman-centered. But as I have shown, even changes that first appear as a concession to a protofeminist agenda can be and are often appropriated as tools for capitalist profit-making. The institutional control over women's bodies is paradoxically consolidated even as HMOs are sponsoring a model of "natural" childbirth they claim will reempower the laboring woman. A transformative feminist analysis of childbirth must therefore necessarily attend to the political economy of patriarchy if it is to contribute to a feminist struggle for transformative change. It needs to emphasize a perspective on social relations that does not merely link capital's drive to accumulate to the construction or consolidation of sexual difference but also accounts for how the destabilization of gender may also serve the health care industry's profiteering ends. It also needs to discuss labor and childbirth in relation to both femininity and masculinity. While feminist analyses such as Wolf's (2001) focus on the facts and figures surrounding the conveyor-belt philosophy of maternity wards, I have sought to add an important personal dimension to the story, namely the impact of birthing on the couple rather than exclusively on mother and child. Before both mother and father can experience the birthing process as empowered participants rather than, respectively, as passive object and performing monkey, hospitals will have to abide by the values of the natural childbirth rhetoric they have co-opted. That would entail employing adequately remunerated professional support personnel in a truly relaxing setting or reconfiguring home birth as a "natural" choice that may or may not lead to hospital birth.

I am well aware that hospitalized childbirth began in the early twentieth century in the hope that it would reduce morbidity and mortality. However, while hospitals have a part to play in the care of women with serious medical conditions and women who develop a problem during labor, it is safe to say that "the supporters of hospital births have never been able to produce a single valid statistic which shows that hospital birth is safer for all women than home births" (Beech 2000, 1). Marjorie Tew's (1986) work on birth outcomes in Britain and the Netherlands even shows that in all risk groups, hospital birth produced higher mortality rates. According to Tew, one of the reasons some studies show the mortality rate at home to be higher is because they include women who had unplanned home birth and often no prenatal care. Even after taking unplanned transfers to the hospital into account, Tew concluded that home birth is safer than hospital birth (see Tew 1986, 1990; Tew and Damstra-Wijmenga 1991). Rona Campbell and Alison McFarlane (1986), and Howe (1988) similarly demonstrate that there is no evidence to suggest that hospital birth is safer for women than home birth, and that in fact, the perinatal morbidity rate may be higher in hospitals. Mark Durand (1992) and Ole Olsen (1997) determined that there were no significant differences in perinatal morbidity rates between planned home births and planned hospital births. Both studies deemed home births to be a safe alternative to hospital delivery and one that leads to fewer interventions (also see Johanson, Newburn, and Macfarlane 2002; Lothian 1995; and Wickham 1999).

More recent sources focusing on countries such as Holland, where 30 percent of women give birth at home, support these findings (see de Jonge et al. 2009; and Stand and Deliver 2009). The three key elements that contribute to the overall safety of home births in Holland are access to well-trained midwives, a good transportation system for home birth transfers, and a referral system that allows midwives to collaborate and/or refer to specialists when indicated. In many states in the United States, women who desire home births do not have access to least one or two of these key elements. I certainly felt like I did not when I was expecting my second child four years later.

As soon as I knew I was pregnant again, I inquired about my options regarding home birth, only to discover that my current insurance refused to cover midwives and that the deadline for "the health insurance option transfer period" was past. I also met parents who, after attempting home birth and going to the hospital for follow-up care, were shamed by hospital staff for having done something so "foolish and irresponsible." Both our insurance policies and general societal attitudes and expectations regarding home birth quickly dissuaded us from "choosing" that option. For reasons of cost, insurance, and closeness, we even "chose" the same hospital for delivery (not to mention that my current OB/GYN delivered in no other location). My husband and I realized that we had neither the energy nor the time to face the uphill financial and social battle that having a home birth entailed, and we were not about to turn another pregnancy into a site of traumatic ideological awakening or social analysis. At least, for all its foibles, the repeat scenario of hospital delivery had the advantage of being familiar, and we would be going into it all-knowing and prepared this time. We resigned ourselves and checked into the same hospital, only to experience a nontraumatic but remarkably similar version of my son's birth.

If, as trauma theorists have argued, trauma is the state of being unprepared for and at the mercy of what has, in fact, already happened, my husband and I were no longer unprepared for the series of predictable violations that occurred again and again during the delivery of our second child: medical students kept being sent into the delivery room despite our request that none be allowed, the nurses expressed their disapproval every time I rose and unplugged the monitor, and so forth. The main differences were that we probably rolled our eyes as much as did the staff (who were flabbergasted by our requests) and that a particularly accommodating nurse made me almost forget about all the other mishaps and violating incidents that so strongly echoed my first labor experience.

At the risk of extending the rape metaphor to include the repeat occurrence to which date-rape victims subject themselves in *I Never Called It Rape* (Warshaw [1988] 1994), this reference to my second delivery aims to highlight a situation in which I "chose" to subordinate myself again to a scenario that was now familiar and that I thought I knew and could now control. According to the liberal model of agency that defines both rape and dominant representations of hospital birth, I got what I asked for. However, this chapter suggests that rather than hold people accountable for the limited choices that are set for them, we need to challenge the rhetoric of choice itself. Agency and choice have become the predominant ways citizens today are blamed for the potentially violating paths that unfold in front of them. What should prevail in our discussions of both rape and childbirth should not be the degree of individual responsibility for one choice over the other but the limited and limiting choices we are offered, for which we settle, and whose outcomes ultimately benefit a system that is too eager to shift accountability to the very subjects it subjectifies. To echo Mary McCarthy's words again, we should be able to open the window whether air conditioners are available or not (1967, 102).

The take-it-or-leave-it approach we have adopted in relation to occurrences that imply consent has obscured the fact that choices need not be limited to either/or, nor do they have to be exclusionary. Hospital and home birth are now defined oppositionally in ways that benefit the profit-making agenda of the health care industry rather than the needs of delivering parents. It is time for us to reframe our understanding of agency to include not just what we choose individually but what limited and limiting choices we are collectively offered in the first place. Laboring mothers should be able to see their options for delivery expanded without being infantilized for their choices. The "I told you so" response they get when complications turn a planned home birth into a hospital birth obscures the fact that such logical development should not discredit their original choice any more than infant mortality in the hospital setting discredits hospital care.

Choosing a hospital birth does not mean that women are consenting to being stripped of their power of self-determination. The conflation of choice and consent in this instance is part of how the health care industry is exonerated of any wrongdoing when it comes to labor. Because the manipulations that take place in the delivery room are institutionally scripted, endorsed, and carried out, the violations that women experience as such will never legally be recognized as "rape." Although this fact has made these violations legal, it does not make them legitimate. Nor does lowering one's expectations to the point of willingly compromising one's rights as I did during my second delivery, a déjà-vu experience that threw new light on what I "never called [birth] rape."

4 · PRISON RAPE, MASCULINITY, AND THE MISSED ALLIANCES OF HOLLYWOOD CINEMA

According to a report released in 2007 by the Bureau of Justice Statistics, 4.5 percent of state and federal prisoners surveyed reported sexual victimization in the previous twelve months (Beck and Harrison 2007). This would mean that in one year alone, between 70,000 and 100,000 prisoners were sexually abused. Put another way, nearly one in twenty inmates are raped or sexually abused in prison. For incarcerated women in particular, sexual assault, particularly guard-on-prisoner sexual assault, is simply a fact of life. It can vary from institution to institution, but in the worst prison facilities, one in four female inmates is sexually abused (Naughton 2009; Struckman-Johnson and Struckman-Johnson 2006; Summer 2008). Victims of sexual violence behind bars sometimes contract HIV and other sexually transmitted diseases, and they always suffer severe psychological harm.[1] In 2001, the first national study of male prisoner sexual assault published by Human Rights Watch and a number of mainstream media reports about male sexual abuse in prisons led to national outcry and a call for reform (see Mariner 2001). This was followed by a historic piece of legislation in 2003, the Prison Rape Elimination Act (PREA), which called for zero tolerance for sexual abuse in jail. Two years later, California enacted a similar law, the Sexual Abuse in Detention Elimination Act, which required the California Department of Corrections and Rehabilitation to prevent and respond to sexual abuse in its prisons. Like the Human Rights Watch study, the nationwide call to end the "cruel and usual punishment" of prison rape was focused on the treatment of male prisoners in correctional institutions. This is so much the case that today the gender-neutral phrase "prison rape" automatically evokes male prison rape, to the exclusion of the rape of female inmates.

The sociological context of the introduction of laws to combat (male) prisoner rape was driven by a public outrage that contrasts with the normalization of the victimization of female inmates. The public discourse of institutionalized male rape has overshadowed sexual violence against women, in part because men are seen as victims of homosexual rape and hence as "undeserving" victims of sexual violence. By contrast, views of rape of women prisoners subscribe to heteronormative understandings of women as somehow deserving of rape.

This chapter juxtaposes a discussion of prison rape with an analysis of Hollywood cinema's representation of male victimization in the context of the legacies of the 1990s political correctness movement. This juxtaposition helps expose how the phenomenon (male rape) that should have led to an alliance with feminists and women led instead to the reinforcement of the gap between masculinity and femininity (and men and women) in the name of a damaged and threatened masculinity. After all, since feminism was the movement that brought rape to public attention in the 1970s, it would have been logical to expect the renewed public interest in male prison rape to be aligned with the goals of the group whose intervention removed rape from its association with the private, the domestic, and the personal. Instead, my study of the ideological messages inherent in anti-prison-rape literature and in Hollywood cinema reveals that the issue of male victimization has led to a separatist rhetoric that isolates male from female prison rape and male from female victims and continues to blame feminists and victims themselves for the woes that befall the victims of sexualized violence in culture.

Sexual violence in the U.S. penal system is mediated by neoconservative configurations of victimization that obscure the gendered and racialized dimension of violence against women in prison. Indeed, as I showed in chapter 1, the meanings of the term "victim" over the last decade have undergone significant rhetorical and ideological developments that affect imprisoned women along gendered and racialized lines. The renewed sociocultural shift toward neoconservatism initiated in the 1980s has entrenched the view that the United States has been emasculated and has led to calls for the remasculinization of U.S. culture. In this discursive space, victimhood is no longer a political category that can effectively be used as a basis for calls for policy and law reforms and is recast instead as a sign of moral weakness, personal failure, and lifestyle choice (Paglia 1990; Roiphe 1993; Sommers 1994). It is in this context that we need to consider the lack of attention to sexual violence inside women's prisons despite national efforts to address the prevalence of (male) prisoner rape. I suggest that the issue of the rape of women in prison is obscured in large part due to an antifeminist backlash.

The dominant cultural meanings surrounding victimization are encoded in the language of both conservative popular writings and influential feminist discussions. Juxtaposing an analysis of this data with an analysis of the ideology of anti-prison-rape projects and national studies published by the Bureau of Justice Statistics and Human Rights Watch further reveals how widespread anti-victimist conceptions of oppression have become. This approach not only helps highlight the shifting meanings of "victim"—a term that is paradoxically discussed as a fixed "identity"—but also extracts the ideological messages inherent in representations of gender, race, and class in anti-prison-rape literature. This allows for a careful analysis of the cultural intersections and rhetorical dynamics at play in representations of male victimization. As Stuart Hall (1980b) has argued, cultural texts and representations produce meanings in society that are imprinted with the workings of the dominant culture. The qualitative textual analysis I am offering here uses a feminist and cultural studies perspective to show how cultural meanings surrounding victimization transmit ideologies of race, gender, and class that expose men's but normalize incarcerated women's sexual violation.

Antifeminist conservative ideology in U.S. culture at large has generated a gendered view of victimization that aligns with a binary conceptualization of passive (and feminized) victimhood and resistant agency (masculine self-sufficiency). This binary configuration also defines the response to sexual violence. Along with a number of other feminist legal theorists, Martha Mahoney (1994) has shown that the dichotomous understanding of agency and victimhood is so entrenched that any exhibition of women's agency actually diminishes their status as victim and the severity of the abuse in the eyes of the law (see also Abrams 1995, 361; Connell 1997, 118; Mahoney 1994, 63; Picart 2003, 97–98). Mahoney predicted that this "all-agent or all-victim conceptual dichotomy will not be easy to escape or transform" (1964, 64), a prediction that turned out to be correct, since the binary persists today. Alyson Convery (2011) has shown that today, this opposition between agency and victimhood paradoxically defines antifeminist commentaries and feminist theory alike. A notable exception is Megan Sweeney (2004), who emphasizes the "active, resilient efforts [of incarcerated women] to give shape and name to . . . experiences [of victimization]" and thus sees claiming victimhood as a manifestation of agency rather than its denial (478).

To fully understand the ramifications of the regulating discourses of victimhood in prison culture, it is thus important to see "victim" as a dynamic and rhetorical term whose meanings are shifting rather than fixed. We need to be attentive to the contingent ways preconceived notions about who is or is not a "victim" in jail reinscribes normative power relations based on race, gender, and class. Such a cultural analysis produces a more complex and nuanced understanding of the gendered and racial dimensions of victim subjectivities in the prison context.

Feminist academics and activists who have made clear the links between victimization, criminalization, and incarceration now have to contend with the repercussions of this victim/agent binary (Richie 1996; Sudbury 2005). The prison industrial complex has expanded as prisoner populations have swollen to unprecedented levels, and conditions of disorder and sexual violence plague underresourced yet highly securitized prisons.[2] From 1980 to 2008, women's rate of incarceration increased twice as fast as that of men; as a result, the number of women imprisoned in the United States has tripled in the period 1995 to 2008 (NOW 2010). According to research conducted by the Pew Center on the States (2008), 1 in every 279 Black women is incarcerated, compared with 1 in every 1,064 white women and 1 in every 658 Latinos. One in every 100 black women aged 35 to 39 is in jail or prison—the highest proportion of any female group. Women prisoners are thus disproportionately women of color: African American women constitute 46 percent of the population nationwide, white women constitute 36 percent, and Hispanic women constitute 14 percent. Paula C. Johnson (2003) similarly points out that the incarceration rates of African American women have historically increased even when crime is at an unusually low level. Statistical data reveals far higher incarceration rates for women of color, who constitute nearly two-thirds of the female population in state and federal institutions (Kruttschnitt and Gartner 2003). This disparity is in large part a result of the strengthening of federal drug laws, which has had devastating consequences for minority women and their families (Johnson 2003).

Study of the growing phenomenon of incarcerated women has allowed a profile of the typical woman prisoner to emerge. Nancy Kurshan (2006) notes that the typical woman prisoner is "a young, single mother with few marketable job skills, a high school drop-out who lives below the poverty level" and that "seventy-five percent are between the ages of twenty-five and thirty-four, are mothers of dependent children, and were unemployed at the time of arrest." She continues, "Many left home early and have experienced sexual and physical abuse. Ninety percent have a drug or alcohol-related history" (2). This profile indicates that the circumstances of poverty, interpersonal and familial violence, and dependency often shape and determine a woman's fate. As both Nancy Kurshan and Brittney Mazza highlight, the imprisonment of women thus takes place against a backdrop of patriarchal relationships that remain undetected when the focus is a decontextualized context of criminality (Kurshan 2006, 1; Mazza 2006, 80).

Instead of benefiting from informed prevention and treatment, black women are labeled as "drug mothers" or "crack mothers" who need to be punished for victimizing their unborn children (Mazza 2006, 81). They are thus reframed as abusers themselves. Such racist portrayals also consistently evoke the stereotype of the "welfare queen" who allegedly abuses the system for personal gain and has multiple pregnancies during which she unashamedly uses drugs (Irving 2007, 74; Mazza 2006, 82). Again and again, these representations recast the victims of racialized poverty, the root cause of drug offenses, as perpetrators who deserve to be disciplined and punished (for victimizing their own unborn children and abusing social service and health care systems). Women in prison have experienced the negative consequences of this sociocultural shift toward blaming victims. These women have been criminalized for drug-related offenses, welfare fraud, and prostitution and thus are seen as crossing the boundaries of normative heterofemininity, especially expectations about mothering, family life, and moral character. In large part because of their criminal(ized) background, women in prison are not considered victims, even though ample empirical evidence exists of the prevalence of sexual and physical victimization, poverty, drug addiction, and mental illness in their lives before and in prison.

Once someone is criminalized, conceiving of that person as a "worthy" victim demands a deconstruction of binaries such as perpetrator/victim that have been naturalized in U.S. culture. A more nuanced understanding of the concept of victimization has been obscured by today's homogenizing representations of victimhood. What is more, victims are people whose status as victims is seen as preceding and extending beyond their victimization and whose agency is at least heavily suppressed, if not altogether nonexistent. Victim and agency, in other words, are now ineluctably defined as exclusive categories of identification: "victim" appears as one unambiguous end of the spectrum and "agency" as its uncritically valorized and infinitely nuanced opposite at the other end.

The conditions of confinement to which women are subjected in prison are typically assumed to be necessitated by their criminal histories. Penal control of women prisoners functions as gendered violence whose ideological nature is obscured by appeals to notions of deterrence and justice. As Chandan Reddy argues in *Freedom with Violence* (2011), the modern liberal nation-state's claim that it provides freedom from violence is actually a form of freedom with violence, since it relies on the systematic deployment of violence against people who are perceived as non-normative. For Reddy, liberal modernity not only authorizes state violence, its very promise of freedom from violence depends on the violence it deploys against nonnormative racialized subjects. Institutionalized violence, she explains, has become the condition of possibility for liberal rights and citizenship.

Today, any claim of victimization on behalf of criminalized women is considered suspect, all the more so since women in prison do not "live up" to the stereotype of the proper, feminized, white victim who has historically mobilized the sympathy of the U.S. public. As Maria Bevacqua (2000) has shown, since the nineteenth century, "victims" have typically been configured as white women who are violated by black men. This dominant narrative of rape has continued to frame sexual violence in racialized and racist terms. Incarcerated women do not look, behave, talk, or live like the ideal of passive and proper (white) femininity that continues to haunt and determine our gendered social arrangements. As a result, there is a lack of attention to the history of sexual violence women suffer in prisons and an underreporting of prison rape that stems directly from the treatment of rape victims by police and the courts. A raped woman struggles against rape myths that attack her credibility and character and deem her to be either sexually promiscuous or a lying slut (Stewart, Dobbon, and Gatowski 1996). What then can we expect of the state's treatment of women prisoners who are sexually assaulted by prison guards and staff?

SEXUAL VIOLENCE IN THE PRISON CONTEXT

While the policy actions that followed the public outcry against prison rape over the last decade or so were certainly important and welcome, their focus on men inadvertently served to obscure the fact that incarcerated women are statistically and proportionally more likely than incarcerated men to be sexually assaulted by male prison staff. In one study, researchers found that although male prisoners were more likely to be victims of inmate-perpetrated rape than women (21 percent versus 19 percent), 41 percent of women prisoners reported being sexually assaulted by prison staff (Struckman-Johnson and Struckman-Johnson 2006, 1601).

In their study of strip-searching in women's prisons in Australia and Northern Ireland, McCulloch and George (2009) assert that sexual violence exists along a continuum of "forced nudity and sexual humiliation in the form of routine strip searches" and constitutes "an official, deliberate and gendered strategy aimed at breaking down prisoners, particularly women prisoners" (108). Thus, security and control in women's prisons relies on sexual(ized) violence; it affects women inmates in ways that are often obscured because of the normalization of the subordination of femininity to the masculine position in culture. Expectations of what constitutes a "proper" victim in particular explain why female inmates' experiences of sexual violence are often denied, naturalized as consensual, or recast as "deserved." According to Beck and Harrison (2007), inmates with a sexual orientation other than heterosexual also report significantly higher rates of sexual victimization: "An estimated 2.7 percent of heterosexual inmates alleged an incident, compared to 18.5 percent of homosexual inmates, and 9.8 percent of bisexual inmates or inmates indicating 'other' as an orientation." Similarly, a Human Rights Watch report on the sexual abuse of women in U.S. state prisons revealed that sexual misconduct by prison guards was more likely to be directed against lesbian and transgendered prisoners (Human Rights Watch Women's Rights Project 1996). Young or mentally ill prisoners were also shown to be particularly vulnerable to abuse, as were prisoners who had in some way challenged an officer. Yet the custodial violence to which inmates are subjected is mostly seen as a means of restoring control in what is otherwise an inherently violent environment and not as a regulating mechanism that seeks to reinscribe normative boundaries of identity and a masculinist order at all costs—that is, at the expense of human rights. The studies expose how in the context of incarceration, sex and violence can no longer be strictly distinguished from one another, as both are used as tools for the imposition of masculinist and racial hierarchies.

According to Toni Irving (2007), "For black women, in particular, gender, race, and sexual relations collude in a dense matrix of social regulation that still condition[s] the terms of their existence" (69). She argues that the construction of the normative white, propertied, and masculine citizen as the universal subject is made possible by the construction of the hypersexualized and particularized black female body. Indeed, since slavery, the image of black women as promiscuous has deflected attention from the racialized and sexualized violence to which they have been subjected and has made sure that, as Joy James (1996) points out, black women's sexual victimization remains utterly invisible. Because of this racist narrative, black women's experiences of violence in jail are either obscured or interpreted as effects of their own stereotyped hypersexuality.

Today, women of color are the fastest-growing incarcerated population in the United States (Glaze and Maruschak 2008; Young 1990). Sexual violence in prison, which is not unlike the plantation world, works to perpetuate hierarchical relations of gender and race. Black women's transgressions of the boundaries of "proper" femininity mark them as unrapeable, since the story of rape demands an "innocent" victim who enacts an "innocence" that can only be performed through highly gendered, racial, and class characteristics and behaviors.

Scholars have written at length on the ways that alterity functions as a marker of criminality in U.S. society: whites may commit crimes, but blacks are criminals.[3] In fact, the racist apparatus that grounds this discursive sleight of hand is so pervasive that one concept now automatically implies the other: blackness evokes criminality, while criminality leads to the racialization of the person accused of a crime. Scholars such as Khalil Muhammed (2010) have shown not only that the idea of the black criminal was key to the making of modern urban America but that it continues to function as a form of social policy that sustains and justifies racial inequality. Today, black oppression is consistently recast as an extension of black criminality rather than as a crime that requires intervention. The two terms are so intricately linked in the national imaginary that racial and gendered identities are often seen to fluctuate to reflect and reify that interdependence. As a result, the metaphorical, rhetorical, and ideological dimensions of the dynamic at play between race and crime make it all the more difficult to address the sexualized and racial victimization that black women in particular endure in prison. The racialized and sexualized system of mass incarceration and violence functions as a regulatory system that works to put non-normative individuals back "in their place."[4] It is a system that is all the more invidious because it is buttressed by the victim-blaming rhetoric that I have been outlining in earlier chapters and that also defines penal cultures.

VICTIM BLAMING AND PRISON CULTURE

Among inmates, female victims of sexual violence are subjected to the same assumptions about the diminished character of the victim as rape victims in the culture at large. They too are perceived as morally and psychologically weak and lacking in agency and power, people who wear a "mask" of victim that singles them out as different. They are inherent "victims" rather than "normal" individuals who happen to be victimized by prison assaults. The perception, then is that what victimizes them is their inner failings that are reflected in their appearance rather than the deplorable or criminal outside forces that lead to their victimization. While victims' social position and difficult circumstances may make them more vulnerable to victimization, it is ultimately their inner failings that are seen as responsible for the assaults to which they are subjected. For example, a report prepared for the National Institute of Justice shows that even though the sexual worldview of prison culture condemns prison rapists and prison rape, it also paradoxically tends to subscribe to a "blame the victim" attitude toward those who suffer sexual violence, reproducing mainstream assumptions about victimization as an inherent form of weakness on the part of the victim (Fleisher and Krienert 2006, 144). The authors quote a woman inmate who maintained that "it's like [victims] wear a sign on their head that says 'we're a victim.' There's something about them that's different. Every pedophile will say they look for children who are vulnerable. Rapists too. They just know who to get. It's like victims wear a mask rapists see" (159). According to the report,

> Men's and women's prison culture share common perceptions of the consequences of sexual victimization. Inmate culture presumes that no one needs to be raped; rape can be prevented; and that if rape occurs, fault lies with the victim. Inmate culture condemns sexual victims as manipulators or liars [who are] largely responsible for their own victimization. First, victims may have staged their own sexual victimization to garner attention from inmates or staff. Second, they may have staged assault to falsely blame an inmate or staff member. Third, they may have owed canteen or drug debts and thus set the stage for sexual assault. Fourth, they may have sexually enticed a woman by flirting and then failed to fulfill a silent promise of a sexual affair. The reasons for sexual victimization matter not: sexual victims are always social outcasts. (178)

In other words, rape myths that blame victims operate in prison cultures: prisoners often perceive a sexual assailant as entitled to commit sexual violence because of preconceived attitudes about sexual violence. As Fleisher and Krienert explain, "Entitlement to commit sexual assault emerges in more than a fringe percentage of both men and women inmates. Inmates' perceptions of sexual assault as a form of entitlement are instigated by a victim's physical or mental weakness or by a victim's violation of inmate behavior protocols" (172).

This victim-blaming attitude is all the more remarkable since recent studies conducted by the federal Bureau of Justice Statistics have shown that those responsible for the sexual abuse of female prisoners are usually correctional officers (Kaiser and Stannow 2010, 37). In 1999, the UN Special Rapporteur on Violence Against Women, Its Causes and Consequences reported that only two U.S. states had inmate grievance procedures that relied on outside monitoring.[5] Most grievances are addressed within the institution, and wardens have a great deal of discretion in assessing cases. Many grievances are dealt with through informal counseling by the prison staff with the assistance of the warden: "Most of the inmates said that they had no faith in internal grievance procedures. They were also afraid of retaliation. If someone brings a charge of sexual misconduct against an officer, she is usually removed to administrative segregation or solitary confinement, allegedly 'for her own protection.' Such segregation is experienced as punitive. Additionally, many inmates reported that staff in the administrative segregation, out of loyalty to the accused officer, are often abusive to the inmate who has complained. It is for reasons such as this that outside review should be an essential part of the monitoring of inmates' complaints" (United Nations 1999).

According to a 2005 study conducted by the Quaker United Nations Offices on violence against women and girls in prison, women in jail who are imprisoned in mixed-sex detention facilities are at greatest risk of violence, and the hierarchical nature of the relationship between guards and prisoners only exacerbates that risk. Human Rights Watch has documented that in fact all sexual interaction between staff and inmates is necessarily coercive because the inherent power inequality between them precludes consent (Human Rights Watch Women's Rights Project 1996). Even though the UN's Standard Minimum Rules for the Treatment of Prisoners stipulates that "women prisoners shall be attended and supervised only by women officers," Amnesty International (1996) and Human Rights Watch (2007) have found that 70 percent of guards in federal women's correctional facilities in the U.S. are men, and often the men hold "contact positions" vis-à-vis female prisoners.[6] Sexual misconduct is more pervasive when women prisoners are guarded by male correctional staff. Records show that correctional officials subject female inmates to various forms of sexual assault, sexual extortion, and improper touching during body searches (Amnesty International 1999; Human Rights Watch Women's Rights Project 1996; Smith 1998). For instance, as a way of silencing their victims, correctional officers have been known to threaten to withdraw visitation rights or to issue infraction tickets that extend the prison stay (Amnesty International USA 2005). Sometimes interactions between guards and inmates involve the use of direct physical force, but most often guards rely on indirect force based on the prisoners' total reliance on them for basic necessities. Some women are forced into sex in exchange for favors such as extra food or personal hygiene products or to prevent the withholding of privileges (Amnesty International 1999; Human Rights Watch Women's Rights Project 1996; B. Smith 1998).

Prison officers who are convicted or suspected of such crimes often do not suffer the consequences of their actions. Prison employees who are found guilty of sexual assault are often simply transferred ("walked off the yard") to another facility. Sometimes the inmate is transferred as well. In 1997, according to the U.S Justice Department, only ten prison employees in the entire federal system were disciplined, and only seven were prosecuted (Amnesty International 2005). Kaiser and Stannow (2010) note this trend continues today: even in confirmed cases of the sexual abuse of juveniles, fewer than half of corrections officers are referred for prosecution, while almost none are punished. One-quarter of all known staff predators in state youth facilities are permitted to keep their jobs (ibid.). In women's prisons, less overtly violent acts such as improper touching are simply tolerated as "sanctioned sexual harassment" (United Nations 1999). This acceptance of sexualized violence is compounded by the fact that inmates themselves subscribe to an understanding of sexual victimization that tends to place the blame for sexual assault on the victim. Female inmates' experiences of sexual violence are denied, naturalized as consensual, or recast as "deserved" while the shifting meanings of victimization, masculinity, and femininity obscure the operations of power. In other words, victim blaming and self-blame are the reasons why prisoners themselves are less likely to link it to the inequity of the penal system, despite the fact that the sexual victimization of women inmates occurs in such ubiquitous ways. Inmates blame themselves and each other, thus displacing the responsibility for the crime from its real perpetrators onto its victims. In this climate, it is not surprising that few perpetrators of violence against inmates are held accountable for their crimes.

This lack of accountability is exacerbated by the fact that prison complexes are becoming privatized at an alarming rate. On 8 October 2010, the Southern Poverty Law Center (SPLC) filed a federal suit again the state-funded, for-profit, Thompson Academy juvenile prison in Broward County, Florida, a state where 80 percent of prison beds are privately operated and where children are imprisoned at nearly twice the national rate. The suit was filed on behalf of children who had been subjected to horrific physical and sexual abuse by the correctional officers at the facility and had been intimidated by staff from reporting the abuses (Southern Poverty Law Center 2010).

The discursive and ideological processes involved in demarcating "good" and "bad" victims in U.S. culture work in the prison environment to reinforce hierarchical relations based on race, gendered, and class power. Penal power operates at the intersection of race, class, and gender, excluding the issue of the rape of women prisoners from official policy response, such as the implementation of the Prison Rape Elimination Act. The rape of women prisoners, most often by staff, is redefined by rape myths of the undeserving victim: women who are black, poor, drug addicted, mentally ill, or prostitutes. In stark contrast, male prisoner rape is reported to be a serious problem that requires surveillance and denunciation. Perhaps the social and political condemnation of male rape in prisons is part of a broader sociocultural antifeminism that has challenged the violence against women movement as political correctness.

The prison complex is a space of sexualized violence because women's bodies are watched and managed by men in positions of power. Despite the flow of evidence that has exposed the high incidence and debilitating effects of sexualized violence in prison, this egregious abuse of power continues unabated. I have suggested that "commonsensical" understandings of the term "victim" may very well be at fault for the lack of intervention and the absence of public outcry about rape in prison. The gendered power dynamics that underlie the meanings of victimization and criminalization are reinscribed and exacerbated in women's prisons, where the masculinization of certain female inmates works to obscure their victimization and the racialization of others marks them as inviolable. "Criminal," like "victim," is viewed as an inherent trait/flaw that defines incarcerated women and one that they cannot escape. As Michael Pinard's (2010) research shows, the consequences of incarceration are more pervasive in the United States than in other countries and prevent incarcerated individuals from moving past their critical records. These consequences include ineligibility for housing and employment, for instance, and curtailment of some citizenship rights. In this victim-blaming society, race and gender function as signifiers whose shifting meanings are deployed to anchor the concepts of "victim" and "criminal" as fixed rather than finite identities, identities that inmates should be assisted in overcoming.

MALE PRISON RAPE IN FILM

Hollywood cinema's representation of male prison rape provides a particularly useful source for exposing the double standards that have characterized cultural responses to male prison rape and female prison rape. In the rest of this chapter, I will focus on two movies that were released in 1996, in the midst of the raging political correctness debates, one on prison rape and one on the social dynamics surrounding a noncoerced threat to the hero's masculinity. The 1990s was also the decade when, as Susan Jeffords (1994) notes, Hollywood film began introducing more nuanced representations of male behavior and psychology, including qualities such as feelings, sensitivity, and attentiveness that are stereotypically associated with female characters. This development elicited a "feminizing" of social identity that, ironically, Hollywood cinema simultaneously worked to contain. It is in the context of this containment strategy that representations of male vulnerability in film are significant. I focus on how the films *Sleepers* and *Jerry Maguire* avoid the "pitfalls" of feminizing their male protagonists and threatening their "male" supremacy by resorting to stereotypical images of feminism and femininity. I argue that despite the films' negotiation of hard and soft masculinity, they succeed in reinstating a hegemonic opposition between threateningly blurred identities (masculine and feminine, black and white, working and middle class) by introducing stereotypes of "radical" feminism whenever the hero's masculinity is vulnerable and needs to be redefined. This dynamic reveals the changes that have shaken the representation of the white American male from hard to soft masculinity since the 1980s has ultimately less to do with "a creative revisioning of masculinity" than with the updating of "a masculinity defined primarily in terms of aggression and competition" (Hunter 2003, 72). Here I demonstrate the extent to which masculinity operates in relation to femininity in a configuration of crisscrossing differences (of race, gender, class, nationality, etc.) that demand that we be attuned to the interdependence of identity categories in our discussions of structural masculinity.

As Susan Jeffords's book *Hard Bodies* chronicles, following the waves of hard bodies and hegemonic masculinities of the 1980s,[7] Hollywood movies began to introduce more sensitive male heroes. Kinder, gentler, new-age guys who combined the hard body with the role of family man increasingly supplanted the energetic and invincible masculine body of horseback-riding cowboys such as Ronald Reagan. Whereas 1980s cinema relied on muscular prowess and hardness to obscure the crisis of masculine identity, 1990s film highlighted and dramatized that crisis. In the 1990s, heroic identity was no longer assumed as a natural identity but was exposed as a construction. This trend is epitomized in the "office movies" that took over the big screen during this decade. As Latham Hunter points out, movies such as *Falling Down* (1993), *In the Company of Men* (1997), *Very Bad Things* (1998), *American Beauty* (1999), *Being John Malkovich* (1999), *Office Space* (1999), and *Fight Club* (2000) were all part of a "male disempowerment awareness campaign, each highlighting the self-estrangement and repressed anger of men lost in the alienating ranks of management culture and cubicle grids" (2003, 72). The crisis of masculinity attendant on this development is exemplified by heroes whose own alter ego, for instance, is their rival for the romantic affections of the women in their lives. The women protagonists invariably prefer Superman, Batman, and Spiderman over the superheroes' real-life equivalents, Clark Kent, Bruce Wayne, and Peter Parker.[8]

Rather than assume that the softened or bonded masculinity in movies such as *Sleepers* and *Jerry Maguire* undermines dominant gendered configurations, I will show that the softened masculinity in such movies has less to do with a revamped gendered binary than with the continued role the feminine plays in the consolidation and negotiation of hierarchies that define the structurally masculine position. Such an approach (which Eve Sedgwick's groundbreaking *Between Men* instigated) is important because it "shifts the methodological framework of feminist research by demonstrating that gender works to adjudicate the relations of domination and subordination not just between men and women, but among men themselves" (Wiegman 1995, 12). It also reveals how the structural relation between femininity and masculinity works to negotiate, contest, or (more often) reinstate and reinforce other categories of identity (such as race, sexuality, or class) with which it intersects. Indeed, as Judith Butler argues in *Bodies That Matter*, the importance of looking at the imbrication of identities and their meanings cannot be overestimated: "Though there are good historical reasons for keeping 'race' and 'sexuality' and 'sexual difference' as separate analytic spheres, there are also quite pressing and significant historical reasons for asking how and where we might not only read their convergence, but the sites at which the one cannot be constituted without the other" (1993, 168).

Sleepers (1996), a film directed by Barry Levinson that stars Brad Pitt, Dustin Hoffman, Jason Patric, and Robert De Niro, is a *Bildungsfilm* about four boys who live in Hell's Kitchen, New York, in the late 1960s. Their childhood games lead to the accidental death of a hotdog vendor and their subsequent incarceration. Like many of Barry Levinson's films, the movie focuses on male bonds in the specific context of working-class and white ethnic urban communities. In jail, the boys are subjected to years of humiliation and sexual violation. The title *Sleepers* refers to anyone who has spent time in a juvenile facility and suggests that the juvenile victims of rape are invariably patient about avenging themselves.

It is significant that the sexual assaults that provide the basis for the film's revenge plot take place in the late 1960s, in the heyday of a feminist movement to which the narrator in *Sleepers* makes a passing but telling reference. The sexual violence portrayed in the film could and probably should have generated a site of alliance with the feminist activism that was raging at the time and that was instrumental in raising consciousness about sexual violence as a social problem. One would expect victims to turn to the very movement that has taken a pro-victim stance in relation to sexualized violence. However, because the culture codes rape as a gendered crime that is perpetuated against women, the film resists what it clearly represents as a softening of the "hard" masculinities typically associated with working-class gang life.

Sleepers represents the women's movement as a kind of mass-mediated spectacle of symbolic middle-class protest and resorts to a militant antifeminism in order to reinstate the gendered and heteronormative authority of its male working-class heroes. Indeed, in a crucial scene, one of the heroes is shown watching a demonstration by radical feminists on TV. As it is often the case with props and mise-en-scène elements in movies, this cameo appearance by radical feminism plays a crucial ideological role, namely that of qualifying and reifying a working-class masculinity that is in danger of losing its authority because of the same-sex rape to which the heroes are subjected. No matter how similar their experience is to the women and feminists who "broke the silence" in the late 1960s, the movie represents that relationship in terms of a contrast rather than a parallel between the two. It stages a "revenge fantasy" instead of an alliance with feminists. *Sleepers* celebrates the heroes' mob-oriented values and brotherhood by opposing their avenging masculinity to the misled and misleading activism of radical feminists.

Before the accident that leads to the end of innocence, the boy narrator relates what life was like in the late 1960s in Hell's Kitchen, an insular neighborhood far out of the mainstream rush of late 1960s and early 1970s America, a closed world where "few mothers worked and all had trouble with the men they married. . . . Yet, there was no divorce and few separations. The will of the Church was forceful." Domestic violence, the narrator emphasizes, "was a cottage industry in Hell's Kitchen. For a marriage to end, someone usually had to die." Yet instead of making the obvious connection that links his father's violence to the motivations of the radical feminist demonstrations that placed the issue on the public agenda, the film gives way to feminist bashing. Images of antiwar and feminist protestors on the nightly news show a group of women assembled around a huge barrel, throwing in items we automatically assume are bras (in keeping with mainstream stereotypes of radical feminism). The narrator comments over this image:

> Outside events meant little. In a society changing radically by the hour, we watched the images scatter nightly across the TV screen. . . . We viewed with skepticism the faces on television, those protected by money and upper-middle-class standing. A growing army of feminists marched across the country demanding equality. Yet our mothers still cooked and cared for men who abused them mentally and physically. For me and my friends, these developments carried no weight. They might as well have occurred in another country, in another century.

In other words, feminists and their bra-burning antics were as remote from the concerns of real victims as they could have been. The second wave of the late

1960s is thus briefly mentioned and summarily dismissed in the film despite the fact that many of the demonstrations were about raising public awareness about battery and rape as social problems.

Sleepers represents domestic violence as an individualized and private issue that cannot be adequately addressed by feminist political action. It works to distinguish between the retribution that the boys exact and the long-standing abuse the women in the film suffer. The narrator qualifies his indictment of domestic violence by adding that "despite the harshness of life, Hell's Kitchen offered the kids on the street a safety net enjoyed by few other neighborhoods." Domestic violence is thus so woven into the fabric of life that its existence does not preclude "feeling safe"—the norm for men. Besides thus erasing women's subjectivity altogether, the film represents children as inexplicably unaffected by and spared the violence to which their mothers are subjected. Since one of the ways feminists have tried to mobilize a desensitized mainstream is by emphasizing how children also suffer from the domestic violence directed at their mothers, the film's portrayal naturalizes gendered violence as an expected, contained, and socially accepted practice. Women are shown as participants in their own subjection. Although the Church is identified as the source of women's indoctrination into accepting their fate, it also represents through the character of Father Bobby (played by De Niro) the only moral pole in the boys' lives. The film thus both deplores and naturalizes hegemonic culture's condoning and reinforcement of gendered violence. It does so precisely because it is trying to negotiate the vexed relationship between working-class masculinity and middle-class authority and does so through a misogynist agenda.

Life might be tough in Hell's Kitchen, but it is well worth it (for working-class boys) because the kind of loyalty and closeness such toughness produces is unparalleled. In fact, it is as if the "safety" net that the boys enjoy would not have been possible without the violence to which their mothers are subjected. The softened masculinity that underlies the rhetoric of closeness, loyalty, relationality, and nurture that the narrator celebrates presupposes women's victimization as a necessary condition. In identifying feminism as merely a source of middle-class propaganda rather than as a gendered intervention, it creates a new style of working-class masculinity that, although different from masculinity in its "hegemonic" form, reproduces its misogynistic overtones. Their softened masculinity notwithstanding, the protagonists naturalize the source of violence in their community instead of identifying with other oppressed groups.

The function of the scenes depicting domestic violence and feminist activism is to distinguish between the "real" suffering of the boys in Hell's Kitchen and the pseudo-oppression represented by the demonstrators on TV. Not surprisingly, the film takes the same stance toward antiwar protesters: "Young protesters spoke about how they were going to change our lives and fix the world. But while they shouted their slogans, my friends and I went to funeral services of the young men in Hell's Kitchen who came back from Vietnam in body bags." The kind of collective action represented by the antiwar or the women's movements should not, in other words, be conflated with the kind of brotherhood based on notions of working-class masculinity and national character the boys represent and that is constituted through its opposition to other forms of solidarity such as feminism.

The representation of the kind of masculinity associated with working-class gang life in the movie is radically threatened when the boys are subjected to prison rape. At the point in the film when they are at their most vulnerable, their brotherhood and solidarity runs the risk of being folded into the very feminized form of collective resistance the film stereotypically represents, one that highlights the homosocial bond that unites them rather than an individualist and working-class masculinist ethos. This is why the film needs a victim-blaming portrayal of domestic violence and a stereotypical representation of radical feminism: the male protagonists' closeness and interdependence, their mutual support for each other must not be read as their feminization and potential "queering." The contrast between the solidarity that unites the boys and the solidarity that underpins radical feminism (a movement that almost automatically evokes lesbianism in the public mind) ensures that their masculinist heteronormativity remains unthreatened. The protagonists' explicit opposition to the feminine and the feminist in the film remasculinizes their closeness and the qualities that are otherwise associated with the "feminine" as a working-class rather than a non-normative site of difference. In other words, precisely at the moment when the intersection between the fate of the heroes and the fate of other oppressed groups is most visible, the movie chooses to highlight the gap between the two in order to reconstitute a heteronormative agenda that sends them on their avenging path. In this context, the voiceover narration functions to instruct the audience about how to reinterpret and reify the protagonists' compromised masculinity. It is an additional strategy to steer us away from seeing the men as feminized or queer, one that directly uses images of feminism and women to promote working-class masculinity. Significantly, Carol (Minnie Driver), the one female and extremely feminine friend among the group of boys, similarly works to reinforce the hegemonic masculinity of the boys.

That threatened "white" masculinity depends on the subjection of structural femininity to reinstate itself as the norm is evident in another 1996 movie, *Jerry Maguire*. The movie, directed by Cameron Crowe and starring Renee Zellwegger and Tom Cruise, hit such a nerve in the U.S. public's psyche that it catapulted a series of recognizable quotes and expressions into the public consciousness. Phrases such as "Show me the money" or "You had me at hello" continue to appear in the media to this day.[9] Here too, stereotypical representations of minority subjectivities reinstate the threatened "white" masculinity of the middle-class protagonist, Jerry Maguire (played by Tom Cruise).

After an uncharacteristic attack of conscience one night, Jerry, a sports super-agent, writes a mission statement about how everyone involved in the business world could be doing their jobs more honestly and ethically and distributes to all the members of his firm. He is instantly fired for having attempted to instill some conscience into the profit-driven corporate world where he had previously been thriving. Jerry's challenge to the aggressive and competitive individualism to which "hard" men aspire lands him in a relationship with two other marginalized characters, Dorothy Byrde, a single mother (played by Renee Zellweger) who patiently waits for him to fall in love with her, and Ron Tidwell, the only athlete (played by Cuba Gooding Jr.) who remains loyal to him after his firing. Significantly, these two mavericks are a white women and a black man, and they powerfully exemplify the inextricable imbrication of categories of race and gender in the narrative. The dominant subject's relationship to each of these individuals is mediated by his relationship to the other, so much so that Jerry's gender identity itself is exposed as constituted and reconstituted through its articulation with both racialized and feminine difference.

Jerry, who was once the embodiment of white middle-class entitlement, is now in the uncomfortable position of having to test his own mission statement's philosophy as an independent sports agent. In the process, he finds himself holding on to the bottom rung of the social ladder in the company of a desperate black male athlete and a paradoxically idealist single mother. Rod Tidwell, a swaggering and endearingly boastful receiver for the Arizona Cardinals, knows he has at most five years left in his career and not enough money to provide for the family he adores. He has a third-rate reputation and no product endorsements other than for a local waterbed company. In other words, he needs an agent as much as Jerry needs a client, although in choosing Jerry over a corporate-backed agent, he incomprehensibly risks his family's well-being in the name of a puzzling sense of loyalty. Dorothy Boyd, previously Jerry's co-worker at Sports Management International, follows him out of the corporate offices to express her solidarity with his revisionist mission statement. In doing so, she gives up her and her son's only source of income in exchange for a career of starry-eyed gazing at her new love interest. Indeed, while her ethical and political stance is initially what motivates her to quit her job, these are soon overridden by a blind loyalty to a man whose own commitment to the ideals he put to paper is shaky rather than principled. Her love interest supplants her political ideals as she becomes preoccupied with Jerry's feelings for her. While her relationship with him takes the shape of a conventional romance plot, Jerry's relationship with Rod reveals the extent to which the once-privileged white hero seeks not to overhaul the corporate system so much as to infuse it with a softened sensibility.

Significantly, Jerry's uncharacteristically impulsive bout of compassion and disinterestedness leads him into a dangerously feminized space from which his masculinity is unlikely to emerge unscathed. He moves in with Dorothy, her five-year-old son (Jonathan Lipnicki), and her protective and sharp-tongued older sister (Bonnie Hunt). The living room of this household seems perpetually occupied by a group of divorced women who meet weekly to engage in consciousness-raising. While such gatherings provided the means through which second-wave feminists came to realize how "the personal is the political," they are represented here as sites where embittered women are falsely trying to pass off their personal as the universal experience of women. Roger Ebert's review of the movie sums up the movie's stance: "the kvetching self-help group for divorced women, who spend all of their time talking about men. Someone should tell them that resentment is just a way of letting someone else use your mind rent-free" (Ebert 1996). Through mise-en-scène and sound elements, these women literally provide the background to the development of the narrative, thus structurally reinforcing the idea that they are seething in their own culture of complaint. They are stuck endlessly recycling their own "resentments" while life is passing them by (life being of course incarnated by the two protagonists who are shown walking back and forth in the foreground).

As in *Sleepers*, feminism is represented as internalized propaganda whose collective forms of apathetic reaction rule out the kind of individualized and self-determining response the film advocates as the only viable one. It is striking, for instance, that neither Jerry nor Dorothy seems to be aware of the existence of, let alone seek to surround themselves with, like-minded individuals. Dorothy clings to Jerry as if he was the only other survivor on the desert island of corporatism. The only option open to these two idealistic characters is to change the system from within.

Instead of leading to a search for and establishment of alternative and socially responsible business practices, Jerry's anticorporatism ironically becomes a symptom not of his communitarian ideals but of his individualist ethos. This is why the movie distances itself from politicized gatherings and support groups, so that even the possibility it introduces of a socially responsible management system paradoxically becomes a symbol of the individual(ist)'s capitalist and competitive drive. The movie provides a stereotypical notion of collectivity and solidarity that, through contrast, shores up masculinist individualism by grounding it in the white female protagonist's submission and the black male's subordination. The alternative community constituted by the divorcees is represented as tainted by a self-defeating and psychologized source of resentment rather than as motivated by genuine alternative, ethical, or communitarian ideals. And similarly, while the alternative community Rod's African American family embodies is certainly endearing, it is also one that is intended to elicit the audience's smiles as the infantilized male head of the household clowns around and is literally mothered by his assertive wife Marcee.

In both *Sleepers* and *Jerry Maguire*, second-wave feminism and its legacies constitute the narrative's ideological hinge because the films' seemingly innocuous representation of feminism indirectly works to condemn any form of alternative social arrangement to existing structures. As a result, the practice of consciousness-raising and the expression and analysis of women's experiences for which it provided a forum is the target of criticism and scorn (thus linking such conservative representations of feminism in Hollywood cinema to the postmodern feminists I discuss in chapter 2): it is represented as resentful, circular, destructive, and irrelevant, all the things that the male hero cannot and the female heroine should not be. As in Wendy Brown's assessment of consciousness-raising, feminism is represented as endowed with a "slave morality" that recalls the Nietzschean logic of *ressentiment* that "reiterates impotence, a substitute for action, for power, for self-affirmation that reinscribes incapacity, powerlessness, rejection" (Brown 1995, 69). Consequently, feminist moral claims are reinscribed as a symptom of weakness, of incapacity to action, and of a thwarted "will to power" that leads to toxic resentments and makes women react to pain emotionally. This alignment of a feminist practice with the logic of resentment applies to a political movement a Nietzschean trait, which, by personalizing and psychologizing feminist politics in this way, effectively neutralizes its radical critique.[10]

The women's circle and their sentimental pop-therapeutics of "recovery" and mutual support function as a contrasting prop that is meant to throw a positive light on the heroine's unrelenting, devoted, determined yet self-effacing and selfless efforts to earn the protagonist's love (the kind of ultra-feminine qualities that are needed to reify the hero's authoritative masculinity). In distinguishing between the complaining divorcees and the accepting heroine, between a flawed feminist reaction to power relations and the hero's reaction to such relations, the film succeeds in reinscribing the feminine/masculine opposition that the sensitizing of the male hero initially threatened.

Most important, however, this male/female dynamic cannot be fully accounted for outside the racial context that structures the narrative. The meanings of gender are inextricably linked to the configurations of race in the film, as the male/female relationship is determined by the homosocial bond that defines the white hero's relationship to his black counterpart. Indeed, as a result of his firing, Jerry finds himself in the extraordinary position (for a white middle-class man) of having to pander to a black man, literally begging the latter to keep him on as agent. He then goes on to become the black athlete's sidekick, as it were, and until Jerry's standing in the corporate game is restored through his client's athletic antics, the two men's relationship apparently reverses a centuries-old social and racial hierarchy. Instead of endorsing the challenge it seemingly levels against such social arrangements, however, the movie works to redress this power reversal through its articulation of gender and race. On the one hand, *Jerry Maguire* exposes the extent to which the restitution and maintenance of the white man's standing in corporate America depends on the black man's physical prowess, while on the other hand, it obscures the disturbing ramifications of such dependence for white hegemonic masculinity by reinscribing a gendered hierarchy vis-à-vis the white woman. The white hero might temporarily be dependent on the black man because of a loss in social status, but because Dorothy is a docile and rather submissive partner, he exudes and exerts more authority than the black man whose wife so ostentatiously dominates the household. In distinguishing between Dorothy's acquiescent adoration of Jerry and Marcee's matriarchal domination of Rod, the film reifies the black/white opposition that Jerry's fall from grace threatened. Without Marcee, Rod would be lost, while without Jerry, it is Dorothy who would be less of a person. The power dynamic is reversed in the white couple, thus preserving the white man's authority over both the white woman and the black man.

The equivalence this dynamic establishes between the black man and the white woman (in relation to the straight white man) reproduces the typical historical convergence of "blacks and women" that has been such a defining feature of the cultural and philosophical discourses of modernity. Indeed, the now-familiar coupling of "blacks and women" (most recently in affirmative action discourse) has a questionable history, since it goes back to the race-based pseudo-science of the nineteenth century that focused on brain size and sexual organs to draw conclusions about the perversely developed sexuality of black and female bodies. This "science" read and established the difference of the black body through sexual difference, thus demonstrating the interimplications of sexual and racial categories.[11] In aligning the representation of its black male character with that of the white female protagonist, *Jerry Maguire* reproduces this highly questionable formula of "blacks and women" as a means of consolidating the hegemonic identity and authority of the white masculine subject. As Wiegman (1995) argues, "In aligning representations of black men with the constructed position of women, dominant discourses routinely neutralized black male images" (14). Wiegman thus echoes Richard Dyer's thesis, that "the treatment of black men ... constantly puts them into 'feminine' positions, that is, places them structurally ... in the same positions as women typically occupy," so that this enforced passivity can allow "the fantasy of power over them to be exercised ... justify[ing] their subordination ideologically" (Dyer quoted in ibid.) "and averting as well the possibilities of change" (ibid.).

Even as the film seems to challenges racial hierarchies on the one hand, it reinscribes them through gender on the other. Gender functions as race's double to maintain the white straight hero's racial superiority in times when his dominant status as a white man is in question. Jerry regains the authority he temporarily lost through the articulation of race and gender. The female protagonist's role is confined to serving as the link between men whose homosocial and interracial interdependency needs to be contained to preserve hegemonic social structures.

Both *Sleepers* and *Jerry Maguire* resort to images of politicized or radical women to generate a contrasting prop. Through this contrast, the shifting processes of gendering and racialization the protagonists undergo are congealed back into normative social identities. In each movie, the threat to the social hierarchy is contained because challenging the existing structure would align one with a collectivity whose common cause for complaint is exposed as a culture of complaint. Detached from the contexts of oppression that brought them together, the radicalized women who meet in the films appear mired in bitterness and spitefulness rather than actively involved in a movement for social change. The source of their discontent is decontextualized and as a result, they are represented as the cause of their own problems, as fixated on a collective self-perpetuating resentment rather than as legitimate victims of injury and injustice. They represent the condition the movie's individualizing and individualist rhetoric rejects, and their othering produces the renewed sense of self-reliance and courage the protagonists can, by contrast, embody.

In both movies, the male characters' compromised normative masculinity (working class in one instance, middle class in the other) is revalorized because neither they nor their female partners are in the state of arrested development that characterizes the groups of women and minorities that are stereotyped in both films. Where less manly men and less womanly women turn to collectivities to seek solace and find solutions to social problems, the protagonists' refusal to recognize the social nature of their oppression is precisely what helps revalorize their destabilized normative masculinity.

The representation of male victimization in *Sleepers* in particular echoes my analysis of the ideology of anti-prison-rape literature because it reveals U.S. culture's resistance to seeing male-on-male rape as an extension of the rape of women. In the cultural response to prison rape in both instances, male victimization is treated as a form of violence that sets men apart instead of putting them on the same continuum as female victims. It is what ultimately reinforces hegemonic masculinity instead of revealing the position of structural femininity the male protagonists occupy along with female victims of violence. In *Jerry Maguire*, the vulnerability of the male protagonist is similarly remedied through an articulation of gendered and race dynamics that reproduce the singularity of the hegemonic masculine subject instead of a site of compassionate solidarity. The opportunity for alliance is foregone in favor of a neoliberal individualist ethos that reconstitutes itself on the back of a debased feminism and femininity.

Juxtaposing the way each film seeks to redress the masculine subject's unambivalent position through a process of differentiation that rejects feminism and subordinates femininity highlights how heroic masculinity prevails through the same structural processes of differentiation and discrimination as violating masculinities. It is because normative subjectivity depends on the subordination of nonnormative subjectivities that Western culture naturalizes sexual violence. As long as this structural process is represented, reproduced, understood, and celebrated in its infinite variations, sexualized violence will continue to thrive as a mode of self-making. And ironically, when postmodern feminism joins the fray by ascribing a logic of *"ressentiment"* to the political interventions of anti-rape feminists, it too becomes complicit with an ideological machinery that reifies dominant masculinity.

Redeployments of dominant masculinity in the mainstream also demonstrate over and over again that configurations of difference work as doubles for each other. In other words, it is impossible to get a sense of gender in isolation from other categories of identity. The workings of one identity (such as class in *Sleepers*, for instance) cannot be adequately understood without accounting for the ways in which, as Sedgwick (1993) points out, "race, ethnicity, postcolonial nationality criss-cross with [gender and sexuality] *and other* identity-constituting, identity-fracturing discourses" (8–9). Tropes of racial, sexual, and class difference are inextricably articulated with one another in a way that exposes the ideological process through which the structural relationality of masculinity and femininity gets fixed in discourse. In the next and final chapter of this book, I turn to representations of sexual violence that expose rather than fix the workings of such relational paradigm.

5 · RAPE BY PROXY IN CONTEMPORARY DIASPORIC WOMEN'S FICTION

As critics and historians have shown, the intersection of rape and racism has a long and inextricable history, and no representation of slavery or its legacies would be complete without a consideration of how sexual violence has worked to perpetuate hierarchical relations of gender and race in the plantation world. The rape of black women by white men has historically been the underside of white rule. As a result, a large number of works of African American fiction, for instance, has been consistently informed by the presence of male-on-female rape and its relation to racism in black women's lives (Hesford 2001, 40; Kubitschek 1988, 45–48).[1] By contrast, while it is true that members of a more recent generation of writers from the African Diaspora have over the last few decades rediscovered slavery and begun to tackle it head on in their fiction (Ledent 1997, 271),[2] their unorthodox representations of sexual violence sometimes seems to reproduce rather than expose stereotypes of black female sexuality in fiction. This is particularly true of the third generation of diasporic Caribbean writers, those born in the 1960s and after. This younger generation followed the second wave of Caribbean immigrants who, unlike the first wave of mostly male and "Oxbridge-educated" writers who moved to England to publish, set the trend of moving to a new neocolonial setting, namely the United States.[3]

In novels such as Haitian American Edwidge Danticat's *Breath, Eyes, Memory* (1994), Dominican American Loida Maritza Perez's *Geographies of Home* (2000), and Antiguan American Marie-Elena John's *Unburnable: A Novel* (2006), women are raped not by male representatives of any colonial or neocolonial power but by other heterosexual women. Instead of a typical narrative of a dominating masculinity that subdues and violates a "black(ened)" womanhood, it is paradoxically the unorthodox representation of women sexually assaulting women that makes the reader take stock of the violent legacies of slavery. Similarly, in South African novelist Yvette Christiansë's *Unconfessed* (2007) and Antiguan American Jamaica Kincaid's *The Autobiography of My Mother* (1996), the scenes of sexual violation undo the usual oppositions of consent and coercion, agency and passivity, trauma and healing through which we usually make sense of rape. In reframing the significant and recurring trope of colonial/patriarchal domination that rape is, these writers urge us to rethink the neoliberal paradigm of choice, agency, and consciousness that continue to mobilize contemporary responses to sexualized violence. While marketability and novelty may certainly be elements of the choices these authors made, this "sensationalistic" trend in fiction does not preclude analytical complexity. It presents a complicated take on feminist politics that aims not so much at mere polemic as at its reappropriation.

I have argued earlier that for the last few decades, Western cultural responses to rape have individualized and decontextualized the issue of rape instead of extending the type of politicized analyses offered by transnational feminists or even by the feminists of the second wave of the women's movement (albeit within a more limited framework of white middle-class femininity). Why does consideration of the imbrication of the discourses of nation and rape seem to be restricted either to the non-West or to the pre-twentieth-century past in the United States? In non-Western war-torn settings, rape has long been discussed as inseparable from issues of nationalism and citizenship. In "Feminism, Rape, and War," for instance, Mia Bloom (2005) discusses how rape is often applied methodically as an efficient "war tool" to demoralize civilians in a war zone. In ethnic wars and especially during stalemates, systematic rape targets women as bearers of a society's culture and identity in order to implode that society from within.[4] By contrast, the West's inability to think of gendered violence in systemic terms and its advocacy of individualized deterrence as a prevention model may be one of the reasons why the most recent generation of immigrant U.S.-based women writers has looked for new ways to mobilize its Western audience's consciousness about the issue.

An engagement with history, the political, and postcoloniality has traditionally always been an integral part of diasporic women writers' most personalized narratives.[5] In light of the ways the West has reinterpreted sexual violence as an issue of interiorized passivity rather than social inequality, its representative strategies necessarily fail to undermine the personal/political and memory/history binaries diasporic African women authors have always been keen to expose through their fiction. It is therefore not surprising that what has become a decontextualized trope of personal failure in the national imaginary should be radically revised in the fiction of authors who are particularly invested in exposing the legacies of slavery's past.

Alternatively, it could be that the representation of rape as an extension of male domination suffers from the kind of unraveling that Vivian Gornick (1997) identified as the source of the declension of feminist politics after the galvanizing fervor of the 1970s: "Conversations [began] to bore, ideas to repeat themselves" (66–67). Rape has been such a consistent trope of female oppression since the second wave and has so often been used as a metaphor for colonial relations in literature that it may be too clichéd a trope for a new generation of migrant writers who are as invested in commercial success as they are in literary success.[6] Along with their desire to move beyond old configurations, these writers' straddling if not dismantling of the high/low culture divide through fiction may very well be the reason why the few sustained representations of sexual violence in their novels have taken the unorthodox and seemingly sensationalistic forms of women raping women or of women who seem to be complicit in their own rapes. It is this "sensationalistic" turn in recent novels by migrant women that I will place in context and analyze in this chapter.

In her rigorous study of the trope of rape in U.S. fiction, Sabine Sielke (2002) elaborates on how rape and race have been inextricably tied historically. In fact, our understanding of sexual violence today derives from the cultural register developed during the interracial conflicts of the nineteenth century, in the context of slavery and postslavery societies. These societies were defined by strict hierarchies of class and race in which the whites constituted the most powerful segment of the population that ruled over the black majority. Black women in slave societies were seen as mere commodities that were forced to procreate in order to supply hands for labor. And because they were constructed as sexually voracious, the forcible ways through which they were made to bear children or engage in sexual acts were hardly ever defined as "rape" or even as violence. The image of black women as promiscuous not only deflected attention from the racialized and sexualized violence inflicted by white men but it has also made sure that, as Joy James (1996) points out, black women's victimization through sexual violence remained utterly invisible. In Jamaican writer Cliff's memorable words, "The past . . . has been bleached from her mind just as the rapes of her grandmothers [were] bleached from her skin" (1991, 45).

The historical link between rape and the construction of race affected other groups beyond black women, however, since in the post–Civil War era, the myth of the oversexed black male body also served to justify violence against black men, and fraudulent charges that black men had raped white women were routinely invoked as grounds for lynching. By the 1890s, rape was irremediably configured as the violation of white women by black men.[7] As Maria Bevacqua (2000) explains, the racism through which rape was brought to the public's attention in the nineteenth century also characterized the arrival of rape on the public agenda in the 1970s. Indeed, the tough-on-crime rape policies that emerged then were primarily adopted to protect the nation's white women against black criminality. In *At the Dark End of the Street*, Danielle McGuire also recounts the brutal and systematic torture, sexual abuse, and rape committed by white men on black women during the civil rights era. McGuire shows how "sexual violence and interracial rape to became the battleground upon which African Americans sought to destroy white supremacy and gain personal and political autonomy" (2010, 47). This consistent projection of rape into interracial contexts across history is what grounds the kind of generalized statement about the defining role of sexual violence in African diasporic cultures that we may find in African American writings: "We is a nation of raped children . . . the black man in America today is the product of rape" (Sapphire 1997, 70–71).

In light of this historical legacy, it is not surprising that the fiction of the earlier generation of diasporic African writers (who were born in the 1930s and 1940s and achieved notoriety in the 1970s and 1980s) is strewn with references to this sexual history of colonization. Writers such as Elizabeth Nunez (2006), Austin Clarke (2004), Jamaica Kincaid (1996), and Maryse Condé (1994) have exposed how rape has historically been configured as sexual aggression between classes and races and how victims and perpetrators have consistently been distinguished from one another on the basis of other categories of identity than gender. For instance, Maryse Condé alludes to the rape of black female slaves in *I, Tituba, Black Witch of Salem* (1994); Tituba was conceived when an English sailor raped an Ashanti captive on the slave ship *Christ the King*.

As critics such as Sielke (2002) and Projansky (2001) have shown, rape is not just a sociological fact but a rhetorical and narrative device that continues to regulate our collective thinking about race, nationality, social class, and sexuality. This is the kind of displaced rhetoric, for instance, that Canadian Trinidadian Elizabeth Nunez evokes in her 2006 novel *Prospero's Daughter*, a retelling of Shakespeare's *The Tempest* set in the 1960s. The narrative begins with an accusation of rape leveled against a mixed-race boy who is involved with the daughter of a white British man, Dr. Gardner. The latter is enraged by the thought of a sexual union between his daughter and the dark-skinned man, and when the case is investigated, he is revealed as the real criminal in a story that dramatically exposes the historical intersection of rape and race. The figure of the racialized "rapist" other is thus revealed as a trope of power in a postslavery society that continues to distinguish between victim and violator on the basis of race and ethnicity and in so doing reinscribes threatened social hierarchies.

Another much-acclaimed Caribbean Canadian detective story, Barbadian Austin Clarke's *The Polished Hoe* (2004), further illustrates how the still-lingering plantation system in former slavery societies "naturalizes" sexual violence "into seemingly consensual views on gender, sexuality, and the world at large" (Sielke 2002, 6). The narrative takes place on a sugar plantation in colonial Barbados (Bimshire) right after World War II and showcases the tripartite social system through which the mulatto heroine paradoxically experiences both material privilege and personal degradation, social elevation and sexual subordination. Mary Gertrude Mathilda was a thirteen-year-old field worker when she caught the eye of the white plantation manager, Mr. Bellfeels, and was in essence offered to him by her mother, who was his previous mistress. Mary becomes one of the most respected women on the island and gives the plantation manager his only son, Wilberforce (now the town's most respected doctor). After thirty-eight years of a life of loveless "fooping" in what has become her "home-prison," Mary Mathilda uses the hoe the title refers to take a gruesome revenge on her "master" and on the ritualized life that has kept her isolated from both poles of the social spectrum, her own people as well as the white elite. The novel takes the shape of her 24-hour confession to Sergeant Percy Stuart, a black member of the police force, about her childhood and her relationship with Bellfeels but also about the island's colonial history, music, and U.S. politics, among other things. To a readership accustomed to equating material success with personal and moral satisfaction, such a tale of murder and delayed retaliation requires a readjustment if not a complete overhaul of conventional social values and expectations. We are asked to understand how the seemingly incompatible experiences of violation and social elevation, despair and material comfort, victimization and agency can coexist and define one another.

The representation of rape in recent novels by the third wave of Caribbean women writers takes this blurring of the boundary between victim and agency to its extreme by turning rape's most likely victims—women—into its most sadistic perpetrators. In *Breath, Eyes, Memory* (Danticat 1994), *Geographies of Home* (Perez 2000), and *Unburnable: A Novel* (John 2006), it is paradoxically heterosexual women who sexually assault the vulnerable bodies of their daughters and "sisters" with fingers, fists, and broken glass bottles. Instead of a typical narrative of a man raping a "black(ened)" woman, it is the representation of women raping women that symbolizes the violent legacies of slavery.

The reader's expectations about sexual violence and gender are dramatically put to the test, for instance, in Loida Maritza Perez's *Geographies of Home* (2000), a novel that explores the realities of emotional and physical suffering in an immigrant Dominican American family. The novel's protagonist Iliana is a young student returning home from college to help her struggling and dysfunctional family. Most notable is the deterioration of her sister Marina, a schizophrenic whose mental breakdown was brought about by the violent rape she had experienced in the Dominican Republic and that ironically turns her into a sexual predator herself. In one horrifying scene at night, Marina attacks Iliana sexually not once but twice, "with her hand curled into a fist, crash[ing] against [Iliana's] womb.... Iliana freed her hands to claw at her sister, but her nails were short and Marina's skin rubbery and thick. She clenched her fingers into fists and aimed, but it was as if Marina had merged with darkness and could see clearly enough to avoid the blows.... Her sister's hand tore into her. The pain, when it shot through her, was incisive as a blade" (284). In "her determination to defy fear" (285), Iliana sends her brother away by claiming that "nothing happened.... I'm fine" (286) but is subjected to another attack when "her sister leap[s] from behind the closet door to knock her back onto her bed" (289). Significantly, the description of the reenacted rape undermines the reader's inclination to read Marina's attack as a sign of "temporary insanity" on the part of a mentally ill character. Instead, the narrator repeatedly draws attention to the hatred and awareness that characterizes Marina's actions: "Hatred was visible in Marina's eyes: raw, unadulterated hatred that confirmed those times Iliana had detected glimmers of it but had dismissed it.... Hatred that now conveyed: *You think you're so special, so goddamn smart and cute! Let's see what you think of yourself after I'm through!* This hatred paralyzed Iliana as the blankets were again stripped from her body, her legs violently pried apart. This hatred pierced her infinitely deeper than the hand thrust between her thighs" (289). After her parents emerge on the scene, Iliana again points out that "her sister knew. Her sister knew precisely what it was she'd done. She knew and was pleased that no one else would ever detect what it was she had destroyed. She knew and depended on shame to silence Iliana and to efface whatever self she'd been" (290). The victim-turned-perpetrator in the novel is neither a sympathetic character nor an exonerated one. Her knowledge of the effects of the pain she is inflicting is highlighted so the reader cannot simply absolve her of responsibility because of her mental illness.

In Haitian American Edwidge Danticat's first novel, *Breath, Eyes, Memory* (1994), the violation perpetrated against the protagonist Sophie's body by her own mother consists of "testing," a cultural practice that consists of probing the vagina to check that the hymen is still intact. It is traditionally performed by mothers who want to ensure that their daughters' chastity is preserved before marriage. Not surprisingly, by blurring the distinction between maternal nurture and torture, it also leaves Sophie with indelible emotional and psychological scars. This aspect of the "virginity cult" is passed on "like heirlooms" (233) through the generations of women who perform it on their own daughters, even though they have suffered from it intensely themselves. Martine, for instance, does it to her daughter even though her own testing was such a source of self-loathing and shame to her that she could not help but see a later traumatic rape experience by a Tonton Macoute as a nightmare that freed her from it. Testing is so deeply damaging to Sophie that she finds herself unable to have a healthy sexual relationship with her husband. When, years later, she confronts her mother about the practice, Martine simply retorts "because my mother had done it to me. I have no other excuse" (170). As in Perez's narrative, it is not lack of awareness that motivates the character. Grandma's response is no less frustrating: "You must know that everything a mother does, she does for her child's own good.... My heart, it weeps like a river ... for the pain we have caused you" (157). The boundaries between pain and compassion, love and torture, violation and convention dissolve and render the protagonist's journey toward self-individuation all the more complex for lacking the usual benchmarks on which characters rely to make sense of their self-development.

By contrast, in Antiguan American Marie-Elena John's *Unburnable: A Novel* (2006), it is anxiety surrounding threatened class rather than gender hierarchies that naturalizes and legitimizes sexual violence against women, including a rape perpetrated by women themselves. The novel recounts the story and genealogy of Lillian Baptiste, a Dominican woman who leaves her island of origin at fourteen after discovering that she is the daughter of the half-crazy and infamous prostitute Iris and the granddaughter of the convicted murderer and obeah priestess Matilda, both of whom have become the legendary subjects of *chanté mas* songs ("Bottle of Coke" and "Matilda Swinging") that are sung during Carnival and on school grounds. After twenty years away, Lillian returns to Dominica to face the demons of her past, and the novel interweaves the three women's stories in a way that powerfully illustrates the transgenerational workings of trauma. The sadistic rape in the novel is carried out by an outraged white upper-class creole mother-turned-avenger after Iris confronts and publicly humiliates her daughter Cecile in broad daylight. Mrs. Richard enlists the help of two black washerwomen on the plantation to "placate the gods of social order" and help restrain Iris: "There would need to be a bloodletting, a sacrifice. Mrs. Richard had chosen blood, and it was her prerogative" (117). In a brutal act that everyone involved (including Iris) interprets and accepts as an inevitable and necessary reinstatement of threatened class and race boundaries, the older woman repeatedly rapes Iris with a broken Coca-Cola bottle that she leaves lodged far inside the victim's vagina. Significantly, while the interests and experiences of the black washerwomen link them to Iris, the interconnectedness of oppression with the very woman to which their racial and social identity points does not prevent them from holding her down during the gruesome rape. Instead, they ally themselves with the upper-class woman with whom they incidentally "shared the same great grandfather—a parentage which [both washerwomen] advertised widely" (118). They even follow her without a word "to save her the indignity of having to seek them out, of appearing to need them" (118).

In other words, although the novel brings to light the differential structures of power that are inscribed on the population, it also challenges a politics that anchors political opposition and alliance in racial or class difference and assumes that one's identity and social position will determine how one acts. As Lawrence Grossberg (1992) points out, the problem with identity politics is its rationalist assumption that "people act based on a calculation of their interests, which are rooted in their experiences, which are determined by their identity, which is an expression or representation of their place within a system of social differences" (376). This model "effectively erases affective subjectivity" (379). By contrast, these novels scrutinize but do not fetishize categories of race and gender, and instead of a politics of solidarity based on essential identities, we are shown a world where personal and political affinities constantly violate and expose the ideological boundaries set between races, genders, and classes. In *Unburnable*, the transgression of class is rectified through a form of sexualized violence that puts Iris back in her place, while the inextricable imbrication of class, race, and gender is dramatized through the containment of one form of transgression (class) through another (gender).

These instances of violent rape are bound to function as exceptions to the statistical gender imbalance that has traditionally defined the narrative of rape. They constitute "extraordinary" instances that may be and are often perceived as challenges to the "ordinary" story of men raping women in disproportionate numbers. Yet what may appear as an exception to the rule in fiction by the younger generation of Caribbean women writers is instead, I argue, the exception that confirms the rule. This representation reinforces rather than challenges the role sexual violence plays in generating an ideal but unattainable masculinity as the normative form of selfhood. The "extraordinary," in other words, functions as an extension of the ordinary rather than as its opposite and recasts gender as a contingent identity that is anchored in constructed rather than biological difference. That women's subordination is legitimated by a female character reveals the extent to which masculinity and femininity work through their relation to one another rather than to a pre-given biological identity to reinstate the dominant form of selfhood as normative. What we have, then, is representations of "rape by proxy" that consolidate rather than weaken the thesis of a gendered and racialized culture of sexualized violence. The sensational/predictable and extraordinary/ordinary oppositions that unorthodox instances of women raping women initially evoke are exploded in favor of a model that places them on a continuum with traditional representations of rape.

In *After the Lovedeath: Sexual Violence and the Making of Culture* (2000), Lawrence Kramer argues that rape is not an unfortunate byproduct of Western culture but a practice that is fundamental to it: "The tendency to sexual violence seems lodged in the very core of ordinary subjectivity like a bone in the throat" (2). The way we make sense of ourselves as gendered beings through a system of gender polarities ultimately depends on the threat of sexual violence to maintain its rigid mandate. Indeed, as Kramer further explains, normative forms of heterosexual subjectivity promote a form of unambivalent masculinity to which alternative subject positions are subordinated and that legitimizes violence and more specifically violence against women and trans/intersex subjects as the basis of its cultural authority. The threat of violence is thus built into the "very structure of identity" (8), all the more so since the subject position of absolute masculinity is a fictitious notion of unambivalent self-possession and embodied autonomy that no one—not even men—can hold but that the norm nonetheless promotes and performs endlessly. Women too can support and promote the unambivalent subject position of masculinity, whether it is, like Mrs. Richard in *Unburnable*, by punishing the transgressor of social norms or, as in *Breath, Eyes, Memory*, by "protecting" their offspring's chastity. The system thus extends its workings to encompass both male and female agents and male and female victims, although women disproportionately bear the burden of maintaining the fiction of gender polarity. The forms of selfhood that are promoted as normal in Western culture rationalize violence against women or rather against the structurally feminine because they are grounded in a heterosexual gender identity that is constructed in opposition to certain forms of femininity and racial identity.

In the recent fiction by the Caribbean women writers I have examined here, the representation of female rapists may look like mere sensationalist polemics at first but is actually presented as an extension of the more predictable forms of violence men perpetrate against women. That female rapists are manifestations of the same economy of class, race, and gender domination as male rapists becomes evident when the female-on-female rapes in the novels are examined in relation to the male-inflicted forms of violence that frame them. Indeed, forms of sexual violence perpetrated by women are consistently juxtaposed in these novels with instances of male violence without being either contrasted or opposed to them.

It is no coincidence, for instance, that the female perpetrators in *Breath, Eyes, Memory* and *Geographies of Home* are both prototypical rape victims who are haunted by the memory of their own violation. Both Martine, the mother in Danticat's novel, and Marina, Iliana's sister in Perez's tale, were victims of brutal rapes by unknown men in their native islands and continue to suffer from the debilitating effects of these attacks in the United States. Traumatized by an event they could not prevent, they go on displacing their own vulnerability on others (in this case, their next of kin) in a way that resonates with one of Heathcliff's most provocative statements in *Wuthering Heights*: "The tyrant grinds down his slaves and they don't turn against him; they crush those beneath them" (Brontë 1847/1992, 111). The traumatized women ironically both go on to assume the role of monitors of the very gendered conventions that ground their own violation, seeking to regain the control they lost by reestablishing the parameters of patriarchal authority. Sensing that their violation stemmed from the need to contain their transgression of gender norms, they seek either to prevent this from happening to their loved one (as in Martine's insistence on keeping her daughter "chaste" and "pure") or to punish a similar transgression in others, as Marina does with her sister Iliana whom she perceives to be too manly.

Whereas Martine's anxiety that Sophie remain a virgin until marriage is an extension of her desire to protect her daughter by acting as a guardian of norms, Marina takes on a punitive role in relation to her sister's crossing of gender boundaries. On the one hand, we are constantly reminded of the intense emotional damage she still suffers as a result of the gruesome rape she experienced in the Dominican Republic: "Her instinct was to run. Yet she could barely breathe, much less move. And she knew that if she screamed, her parents would claim that she was crazy, that no one else was there.... Now there it stood: the embodiment of her worst fears. She had known it would arrive. But not so soon, not for her, not as the man who'd raped her. She recognized the shape of his body and its stench—an odor of rotting greens she had been incapable of forgetting" (Perez 2000, 16). She constantly burns imagined spiders off the walls and replays the rape in her mind, "remembering the teeth marks that had lingered on her breasts after she was raped" (119), even as she can make sense of the experience only by reproducing the dominant racist cultural register that has defined our understanding of sexual violence since the nineteenth century: "No flat-nosed, wide-lipped nigger would claim her soul. No savage with beads dangling from his neck" (17). On the other hand, she attacks her sister sexually to expose and stomp out the latter's transgressive gender behavior. "The width of her sister's shoulders, the prominence of her forehead, the impudent curve of her full lips ... the hair pulled austerely into a ponytail like Ed's and the baggy sweater more appropriate for a man ... her hips narrow as a boy's ... the exaggerated walk of a man imitating a woman" (276) are all traits that confirm Marina's conviction that Iliana is actually transgendered. The ensuing rape is explicitly framed as an attempt to reify the incontrovertible "truth" of the gender binary: "'I almost had it!' Marina shrieked, yanking her hand out from between her sister's thighs. 'I almost had it in my hand!'" (284).

The experience of rape in the novel is structurally followed not by Iliana's confrontation of the sister, "who knew precisely what it was she'd done," (290) but by a scene of sexist catcalling on the street. After a violated Iliana leaves the house to "walk aimlessly in the park ... to reconcile her to all that had occurred" (306), three men—"solicited by the provocative movement of her hips" and by her lack of response—cry out: "That's why bitches like you get raped!" (308). That these men's verbal and stereotypical abuse would echo Marina's reaction to her sister's "exaggerated walk" underlines the convergence of forms of sexual violence men or women perpetrate in the service of a masculinist racist domination. Being a woman or a victim does not absolve Marina of thinking along the same lines as hegemonic discourse when it comes to race and gender. Her "extraordinary" act is contextualized both by the "ordinary" form of sexist name calling to which Iliana is subjected on the street and by the domestic violence that greets Iliana upon her return home that night. Unaware of what had transpired between the two sisters, her father Papito hits her for staying out unescorted after dark, calling her "hussy" and "whore" (312). Later, his apology consists of recalling and legitimating past instances of physical violence when he would beat a young Iliana because "it was my responsibility to teach you about danger and keep you safe" (318). His self-justificatory stance, however, soon narratologically turns into fragments of sentences that Iliana, the narrator of the last chapter, hardly heeds and that expose the limitations of the father she had once thought of as "the paradigm of perfection" (320) or, as Kramer (2002) would put it, of "stigma-free masculinity" (2). Papito's inability to question the legitimacy of his own violence also exposes the irony of his outraged response to the domestic violence his other daughter Rebecca suffers at the hands of Pasión. The novel thus reveals through the juxtaposition of sites of gendered violence that seamlessly flow into one another how violating out of protectiveness (as Martine and Papito do, albeit on a different scale) or out of indignant anger (as Marina or her rapist do) are two sides of the same coin irrespective of the gender of the agent behind the deed. Both instances serve the ideological interests of an impossible and unambivalent masculine subject position (or, to use a Lacanian concept, the interests of the phallus), the illusion of which they preserve by occupying or generating the visible feminine position masculinity defines itself against. In other words, whether it is men or women who perpetuate sexual violence and whether they do so as protectors of women or as guardians of the normative, such representations equally expose the extent to which "the basis of the cultural authority associated with the impossible position of the absolute masculinity is precisely the threat of violence" (Kramer 2000,7).

While biological women are usually the ones to occupy the structurally feminine position in relation to unambivalent (and impossible) masculinity, other members of the social body may bear that burden as well. Indeed, blacks, gays, "manly" women (Iliana in *Geographies of Home*; Perez 2000) or "unmanly" men (Harry/Harriet, the transgendered transvestite in Michelle Cliff's *No Telephone to Heaven* (1987), who is described as "the novel's lesbian in a sense: he's a man who wants to be a woman and he loves women" [Cliff quoted in Elia 2000, 352]), similarly threaten to expose the polarized distinction between the sexes that defines our notion of humanity and obscures the fictitiousness of the ideal masculine position. As Kramer puts it, "Racial, sexual and social polarities cut across gender polarity in complex ways and further deplete the position of entitlement. Black men, for example, still do not have the unquestioned right to claim masculine privilege in relation to white women, and they may find that this racial limitation undercuts their ability to claim the socially inferior version of that privilege available through black women" (Kramer 2000, 6). "The other against whom (or against which) the human is made" (Butler 2004b, 30) is thus both sexualized and racialized, so that the re-production of the human species is viewed as the re-production of racially "white" human bodies through a process that affirms and articulates a normative heterosexuality as it operates. In this process, both men and women may legitimate the subordination of this structurally feminine "other."

In cultural criticism today, the awareness that rape is a trope that mobilizes other dimensions of identity than gender is often taken to mean that an emphasis on the gendered dimensions of the crime obscures and is necessarily complicit with the ways the discourse of rape regulates our ideas about race, class, or nationality. By contrast, Rosemary Marangoly George (2007) reveals how a focus on rape as a trope for the cultural construction of other concerns such as national identity may also obscure the gendered dimensions of the problem. George examines the increased instances of violence against women that occurred during the Partition months in India. Indeed, rape and other forms of violence (abduction, mutilation, murder) rose to unprecedented levels at the time and "have mostly been read as metonymic of the violation of the land" (136). Partition violence against women has been interpreted "as part of an exceptional moment of insanity in which men went mad" (ibid.). Against this general consensus, George argues that the fiction written in Urdu and Hindi about Partition provides an alternative to the usual nationalist narrative that subsumes rape under a nationalist rhetoric of undivided India. She shows how these stories emphasize instead that the increased violence that Partition brought to women is similar to—albeit on a different scale than—the usual fare women are doled out in a patriarchal society. The extraordinary is exposed as very ordinary indeed.

Similarly, representations of rape in recent African diasporic fiction by women may at first appear as sensational interventions that challenge the statistically prevalent forms of sexual violence perpetrated by men against women, but they are actually revealed to be extensions of a model of dominant racialized masculinity and femininity. This binary model of thinking is exposed as the means through which social domination reasserts itself in the face of threatened social and racial boundaries and identities. In so doing, these narratives offer a powerful challenge to the way the West traditionally conceptualizes rape through facile oppositions such as male agency and female victimization, power and passivity, resistance and complicity, yet they also expose the cultural weight a binary conception of gender continues to have in U.S. society. Most important, they reveal the interplay between sexual violence and the complex ways we continue to define ourselves as gendered and social beings in the twenty-first century. By thus reframing our expectations about rape and gender, they force us to readjust our readings of social and racial relations. Rather than challenge a politicized understanding of sexual violence, the representation of women raping women in this immigrant fiction functions as a form of rape by proxy that reinforces hegemonic power relations and the means through which Western norms of selfhood reproduce themselves.

I conclude by highlighting how the reconceptualization of rape offered in diasporic women's fiction also generates a more capacious notion of agency than the limited ones to which much of contemporary anti-rape discourse appeals. For instance, in both Yvette Christiansë's *Unconfessed* and Jamaica Kincaid's *The Autobiography of My Mother*, the representation of the recurring sexual violence the black heroine suffers at the hands of a white man is paradoxically depicted in terms of a seemingly consenting complicity or passivity rather than in terms of resistance or violation.

In her novel, Kincaid compellingly registers the complexities attendant on representing rape in a postslavery context by challenging her readers' preconceived ideas about the role and scope of agency in situations pertaining to sexual violence. As with *The Polished Hoe*, in accounting for black women's invisible because "naturalized" victimization, *The Autobiography of My Mother* explodes the boundary between consent and passivity, choice and oppression. The Western reader who is trained to conceptualize agency as an embodied form of subjectivity that precludes victimization is at a loss when it comes to making sense of Xuela's first sexual experience. The scene is described as a site of both the heroine's excruciating suffering and her active participation. The fifteen-year-old Xuela, who is sent to live as a servant and companion to her father's brown middle-class associates, soon realizes that Madame LaBatte is preparing to deliver her sexually to her husband so that Xuela can bear him a child. As Rhonda Cobham (2002) explains in her insightful essay on the novel's sexual politics, the ensuing seduction scene dismantles our assumptions about both rape and sex because it turns the young girl into both victim and instrument of sexual subordination. The description of the sexual encounter in the novel creates the illusion of her sexual agency even as it stages a classic case of sexual trauma and abuse:

> The inevitable is no less a shock just because it is inevitable. I was sitting, late one day, in a small shaded area behind the house, where some flowers were planted, though this place could not be called a garden, for not much care was applied to it. The sun had not yet set completely; it was just at that moment when the creatures of the day are quiet but the creatures of the night have not quite found

their voice. It was that time of day when all you have lost is heaviest in your mind: your mother, if you have lost her; your home, if you have lost it. . . . Such feelings of longing and loss are heaviest just in that light. Day is almost over, night has almost begun. I did not wear undergarments anymore, I found them uncomfortable, and as I sat there I touched various parts of my body, sometimes absentmindedly, sometimes with a purpose in mind. I was running the fingers of my left hand through the small thick patch of hair between my legs and thinking of my life as I had lived it so far, fifteen years of it now, and I saw that Monsieur LaBatte was standing not far off from me, looking at me. He did not move away in embarrassment and I, too, did not run away in embarrassment. We held each other's gaze. . . . To each piercing that he made inside me I made a cry that was the same cry, a cry of sadness, for without making of it something it really was not I was not the same person I had been before. He was not a man of love, I did not need him to be. When he was through with me and I with him, he lay on top of me, breathing indifferently; his mind was on other things. On a small shelf at his back, I could see he had lined up many coins, their sides turned heads up; they bore the face of a king. (Kincaid 1996, 69–71)

Cobham points to the difficulty of making sense of the series of negations through which Xuela describes her experience so much so that "by the end of the encounter, it is no longer clear who has seduced whom" (Cobham 2002, 878). At the same time, the passage evokes the psychic process of doubling, with "the body split in two—part flesh and part shadow" (Danticat 1984, 156) through which Xuela emotionally dissociates herself from the pain she has to endure. This psychological coping mechanism appears in a number of Caribbean novels dealing with sexual trauma.[8] Its roots can be traced back to the notion of doubling in vodou, the Afro-Caribbean religion practice that sees the world as inhabited by Loa, or spirits, two of the most potent ones being the Marassa, the sacred twin spirits.

This contextualization of doubling as a cultural and spiritual practice establishes a sense of agency out of oppression. By having the narrator describe her body as if it were someone else's and by anticipating Mr. LaBatte's every move, Xuela "refuses to naturalize her oppression by acquiescing to the role of object" (Cobham 2002, 878), even as trauma is both highlighted and repressed in the passage. Yet the sense of loss, trauma, and "inevitable" violation (Kincaid 1996, 69) is no less intense and palpable for being mediated both descriptively and stylistically. Doubling is recast as a refusal to engage the violence at the level at which it seeks to subjugate; it denotes resistance rather than compliance and willed survival rather than the denial of violation.

A similar treatment of rape characterizes South African author Yvette Christiansë's *Unconfessed*, the narrative of a nineteenth-century black woman slave condemned for infanticide to a life sentence on the notorious Robben Island. Inspired by nineteenth-century court records, the story of Sila van den Kaap moves between her alternating memories of her childhood, her servitude, her trial, and her prison experiences in an expressive and poetic stream of consciousness. Even as she is breaking stones in the prison quarry for Cape Town's streets and walls, Sila recalls being ceaselessly raped by her owner, who is referred to by his surname, Van der Wat. The account of one particular episode of violation eerily evokes Xuela's distancing mechanisms in Kincaid's novel:

> On the night that she decided enough was enough, she was waiting outside, determined to say no, ready to be beaten. But she did not say no. In a heartbeat she knew what had to be done. She walked away from him toward the barn. She could have walked tall and proud, but that was not the time. She kept her heart tall and proud, but lowered her head as she entered the barn. It did not matter how rough he was, she had shifted the line between them and knowing this shifted it even more. She had understood something about this man and needed to hide what she knew. Filth, was what he was. And filth was what she called him. Vuilgoed. She reserved a part of herself for the barn. It made him excited and he could not stay away. . . . She could feel his mind circling around her and trying to cut her away from the rest of her time, reducing her to just those times in the barn. She kept herself from him in the day, cleaning, washing, scrubbing, in the house . . . She began to understand that this wanting was born of a thing that these two people who claimed that they owned her, like a cow or horse, feared. And so she told her body to bring forth some sign of her power. (Kincaid 1996, 29–30)

Like Xuela, Sila turns a scene of subjection into a form of subjectification. She asserts her agency by engaging the rapist's own means of torture, reenacting the overpowering act to maintain control and dignity, reclaiming her own subjectivity by preparing for, anticipating, and performing the encounter rather than merely subjecting herself to it. This renarrativizing of sexualized violence into a paradoxical form of resigned seduction and imagined resistance recalls the process of doubling Xuela enacts because it too entails a splitting of the self: "she kept a part of herself . . . she told her body" (Kincaid 1996, 29–30). It also sets the stage for a reclaiming of the self that enacts resistance through performativity rather than through opposition. By performing the role scripted for her by her oppressor's colonialist fantasies, she exposes the ideological molds that contain his world as strings that control him as much as they subjugate her. Far from "naturalizing" the sexualized encounter, her apparent complicity exposes the rape as a scene in a play of power whose arbitrary rules she can perform again and again and from which she thus learns to distance herself.

In Shani Mootoo's *Cereus Blooms at Night*, the protagonist Mala Ramchandin resorts to a similar process of doubling to cope with the repeated rapes to which her father subjects her:

> Clutching a handful of hair at the back of her head, he shoved the bowl into her face again, twisting it back and forth. Her nose began to bleed. She concentrated on the sensation of enamel against her face, as though taking notes on an experiment. With every clockwise twist he slammed his pelvis into her, banging her against the counter of the sink. She felt no pain. She tapped her tongue against the roof of her mouth, checking the stew for seasoning. She tasted blood, she focused her eyes on the half-moon-shaped, chicken pox scar on her father's forehead. He let the bowl drop and leaned against Mala, resting his forehead on hers. The smell of his alcoholic body and breath agitated her more than the injuries he had just then inflicted. She slipped her tongue out of her mouth and licked the stew on her face. The taste of garlic and anise erased his smell. (1999, 205)

Just like fifteen-year-old Xuela turns her attention to the coins that are lined up "on a small shelf at his back" during the sex act (Kincaid 1996, 69), Mala adopts a form of "strategic ignorance" to "'erase' [her father] from her reality and from her body" (May 2004, 121). The incest leads to a psychic split between Mala/Pohpoh and to her taking refuge in the Edenic garden surrounding her house. The garden is an alternate space that bypasses the sense of dispossession and violation Mala associates with the house. Significantly located at the center of the town of Paradise, it is chaotic and unruly to outsiders but a place of refuge to Mala, who interacts with insects, birds, snails, and reptiles as her companions (Mootoo 1999, 130).[9] According to Vivian May (2004), it is certainly conceivable to interpret Mala's flight into the garden as "simply evidence of a flight into 'madness,'" (120) as the townspeople do when they describe her as "mad as a brainless bird" (Mootoo 1999, 107). It is also possible, however, to understand Mala's split subjectivity as a form of "double consciousness" (May 2004, 120) and doubling that ensures self-protection and survival: "by refusing to bind or cure Mala's split subjectivity, Mootoo could be suggesting that there is subversive potential in interstitiality, in 'splittedness' or 'composite subjectivity'" (Ritchie quoted in ibid.).

From a Euro-American perspective, doubling—which is generally understood as the abandonment of one's self-identity during times of trauma—necessarily evokes resignation rather than resistance, crisis rather than its remedy, an inability to cope rather than the motivation to overcome. The crisis is experienced as so intense and intolerable that moving outside of one's body and abandoning the self becomes the only avenue available to the suffering victim. In postcolonial literature, doubling has consistently been represented as a process to which victims of abuse and violence resort as a way of coping with forms of oppression and violence. In J. M. Coetzee's *Disgrace*, for instance, when the protagonist/narrator imposes himself sexually on a young female student thirty years his junior, she reacted "as though she had decided to go slack, die within herself for the duration, like a rabbit when the jaws of the fox close on its neck. So that everything done to her might be done, as it were, far away" (1999, 25). Representations of doubling as a means of coping and survival abound in fiction of the new African diaspora.

This is precisely what interests me about this recurring trope, that it constitutes a site where the line between trauma and healing, crisis and survival, passivity and agency gets consistently blurred and reconfigured. Whereas Western notions of embodied and autonomous subjectivity derived from Enlightenment thinking prompt us to read doubling as a form of giving up or, worse, as implied consent ("not quite rape"; ibid.), contemporary immigrant women's writings teach us to contest the facile binaries of victim and agent through which sexual and racial relations are typically configured. Instead of being conceived as a form of passivity that in the Western imaginary is then recast as a form of unwitting acquiescence to the violence at hand, doubling is represented as a form of survival and strategizing (conscious or unconscious) that derives from cultural resistance rather than individualized resignation. As such, doubling functions as the site of "diaspora literacy," the term Vévé Clark coined to refer to the process whereby readers become attuned to the multilayered meanings of stories "from an informed indigenous perspective" (Clark 1990, 304).

This reading radically revises Western views of victimization as weakness, passivity, or madness, states that are framed as the opposite of agency and resistance. The writings I have examined here show us a way out of the agent/victim binary that has dominated discussions of sexual violence and trauma in the last few decades. Through a focus on doubling and double consciousness, they expose the Western logic whereby the recognition of agency has come to depend on the outcome of and deterrence of the violence. These writings instead create a hybrid form of subjection and subjectification, coping and healing that does not reinscribe trauma through representation but rather transforms it.

CONCLUSION

The 2004 movie *Stealing Sinatra* tells the story of the kidnapping of Frank Sinatra's son in 1963, an incident that, as the movie's credits make clear in a tongue-in-cheek manner, failed to be momentous: "1963, an event shook the nation. This isn't it." One particular scene in the film depicts an altercation between Sinatra's kidnapped son (who is a singer as well) and the bumbling small-time criminal Barry Keenan who masterminded the operation. In the scene, tensions converge around the implications of using the term "victim" and highlight the loaded set of ideological meanings the term has amassed over the years.

BARRY: I am not unfamiliar with the movie business.... What we are doing here can really be a boost for you. Have you considered that?
SINATRA JR.: Being a kidnapped victim is not good publicity.
BARRY: No one is calling you a victim.
SINATRA JR: What am I then?
BARRY: What do you want to be? A failure?
SINATRA JR.: A success.
BARRY: Me too. Well, how do I do that? Do I call myself a victim? No, I call myself a success. I am halfway home. Do you see the difference? So Frankie, how do we reach your father? I don't want to make a big deal of this but here is a gun. I have one and you don't.

Instead of offering a window onto the 1960s, this altercation betrays the time of production of the movie (2004) precisely because the term "victim" constitutes such an issue for both characters. What occurs between them is a debate about the negative implications of using the term and a powerful illustration of the problematic status victimhood has come to occupy in the contemporary United States. To the suggestion that this kidnapping might actually bring him the kind of fame he has been yearning for, Sinatra Jr. responds that being a victim will not constitute good publicity. Such a statement makes sense only in light of the negative publicity the term has received over the last few decades, a negative connotation that goes without saying today but would not have then. This development was so prevalent by 2004 that it overrode the commonsense knowledge that in the world of show business, all publicity is good publicity. The problem for both men is not that Sinatra Jr. was kidnapped and that the experience might affect him or his reputation negatively. The problem is the term, the designation, the representation of the event, not the event itself. Barry insists that although Sinatra Jr. had been kidnapped, he was not a victim, thus challenging the idea that being kidnapped makes one a victim. To Barry, calling oneself a victim amounts to being a failure, and this certitude requires no explanation. Audience and characters alike have a tacit understanding of the negativity the term entails.

In popular and academic circles alike, the reduction of the discourse of victimization to an agentless and feminized condition that preexists being held at gunpoint (or raped) has contributed to our changing perceptions of what constitutes a victim and to refashioning the feminist movement. Victimization is increasingly conflated with passivity, and identifying someone as a victim now leads to the kind of circular logic surrounding representational politics that is illustrated in this scene.

This conceptualization and feminization of victimization in culture, as I have shown, affects the treatment of rape as a woman's or man's problem. I have argued that anti-rape discourse often conflates passivity with powerlessness and weakness, choice with consent, and agency with power; it also implies that because passivity is a possible response to rape, then it must be its cause. By contrast, I call for a reconceptualization of rape as a problem of the relationship of structural masculinity to femininity rather than a problem of feminine comportment; the latter can only lead to the problematic "profiling" of victims. The diasporic writers whose fiction I analyze in my last chapter provide one illustration of the new paradigm I am calling for and provide a way out of the current impasse in the theorization of rape and agency in culture.

Whereas concepts such as democracy are routinely abused by various imperialist or class-based agendas but (rightly) persist as ideals in culture, the term victim today evokes not compassion but suspicion. There is a double standard at work in our culture, since some concepts maintain their idealistic dimension no matter what, while others—which happen to be associated with the marginalized—become tainted to the point of dismissal. I am not advocating an uncritical valorization of victimization but a critical awareness that vulnerability to others is a human condition that cannot be limited to psychology. It can therefore not be blamed on one's inner propensities. Rather than try and find a cure for our interdependence, we should be acknowledging that it constitutes us. Rather than blame victims, we should recognize that the crime of rape is the radical abuse of this fundamentally human condition. So is the way the West has defined selfhood, namely as the unambivalent able-bodied and whole subject position that defines itself against the structurally feminine. Rape as we know it is the radical extension of this dominant version of subjectivity, one that is based not on the recognition of our vulnerability but on its rejection.

It is ironic that in insisting that an exhortation to agency is the solution to victimization, anti-rape discourse has reinscribed the very victim/agent binary it claims to challenge. Indeed, both feminists and conservative commentators typically promote the recognition of a supposedly unrecognized agency as a means of driving victims to prevent their own victimization. It stands to reason, though, that if the presence of agency evacuates the possibility of victimization, if victimization is truly what one can avoid through the recognition of agency, then the two conditions are still in a binary relation to each other since the presence of one precludes the other.

One of the legacies of the second wave that still shapes counseling techniques is the practice of bringing victims to distinguish between two conditions, passivity and victimization, whose conflation inevitably translates into victim-blaming and self-blame. For instance, the counselor casts a new light on behaviors or actions (laughing, screaming, remaining silent) the victim would not otherwise have identified as signs of agency. The victim's agency is thus redefined as doing whatever she deemed necessary at the time to survive the attack, whether that entailed fighting back or submitting to the rapist. Seen from this angle, passivity itself becomes a defense mechanism that can no longer be opposed to agency unless it is reduced to an internal logic that is divorced from material considerations. This is also, I argue, the kind of reframing of agency offered by the diasporic women writers I analyze in chapter 5, since their fiction represents passivity and "doubling" as an extension of a cultural practice of resistance derived from voodoo.

Similarly, the second-wave feminists who brought rape to the public agenda believed that victims of sexual violence were more than the sum of their traumatic experiences. Their efforts to improve women's financial, legal, educational, and personal rights were successful because of their intense and sustained political action. While we take their accomplishments for granted, we would not have many rights today without their influence: anti-rape legislation; sexual harassment legislation; the extension of civil rights laws to cover employment discrimination against women; the establishment and enforcement of domestic violence laws; the recognition of economic value of women's role in the home; the elimination of discriminatory insurance laws; admission of women to professional schools of engineering, law, and medicine; Title IX of the Education Act, which gives girls equal access to athletic programs in public schools; the recognition of the authority of women's voices in history, anthropology, science, law, medicine, ecology and culture; women's health initiatives; greater roles for women in politics, law, business, and religion, the latter resulting in the first female rabbis, Episcopal priests, Protestant ministers, Catholic Eucharistic ministers, altar girls, and a new wave of activist religious women. It took many years of intense lobbying and law-writing, extensive efforts to establish and staff hotlines for victims of sex abuse, domestic violence, and employment and judicial discrimination; to identify and promote women-friendly lawyers, doctors, and therapists; to sue businesses for discriminatory salary, promotion, and hiring practices. Activists picketed on behalf of women's health and education and workers' rights, and advocates went to court with rape victims and taught women assertive behavior. Feminists ran consciousness-raising groups, demanded and established day care facilities, established and staffed shelters for women, forced the media to consider their concerns, and challenged sexist language, practice, and assumptions at every turn. While such political activities still occur, they have been dissociated from victims to the extent that the latter are now seen as the objects rather than the subjects of these movements. We are back to a model of nineteenth-century charity whereby privileged women are perceived as better equipped to help victims cope with and make sense of their experience. Victims are represented as irremediably and unidirectionally shaped by the traumatic experience of rape and hence incapable of dealing with anything but their own inner turmoil.

Both academic and popular anti-rape discourses claim to know which discourse represents victims' best interests, and both reinforce the gap between incapacitated and naive female victims on the one hand and indoctrinating feminists who speak for them on the other. Feminist postmodernists such as Sharon Marcus locate the source of women's continued oppression in their inability to distance themselves from restrictive social codes and argue that feminists are responsible for rape victims' lack of critical assessment. Others have questioned the "evidence of experience" so thoroughly and convincingly that the practice of making the experience of victimization visible is immediately deemed suspect and undertheorized. Consciousness-raising has become identified as a site of reinscription rather than demystification, and its emphasis on the concrete consequences of living in a gendered and racially structured world has become evidence of the victim's inability to account for the constructed nature of her own experience.[1] The "backlashers" go even further, suggesting that it is because victims simply assimilate deluded feminist assumptions that they experience "bad sex" (or the sex wars) as rape. Even mainstream representations that condemn sexual violence go out of their way to separate victims from feminist politics and turn rape into women's problem. Anti-rape politics today not only fails to accommodate victims' participation in the fight against violence but are actually based on the exclusion of victims.[2] Although questioning victims' perspective has been both salutary and important, it has also contributed to doing away with the very sites of self-fashioning and politicization that early feminist consciousness-raising and organizing provided.

Today, victims have been relegated to the backdrop of the movement, cast as a uniform group driven by an emotional and incapacitating response to their own experience.[3] The meaning of the term "victimization" has simultaneously changed from an external reality imposed on someone to a psychologized inner state that itself triggers crises. I have argued that the way out of this impasse is for feminist politics to reconceptualize the word "victimization" and to produce a more capacious notion of agency, one that does not conflate choice and consent, agency and power, victimization and passivity but rather locates resistance in the seemingly inexistent space between these terms.

I argue that focusing on female passivity as a site of change ultimately advances the causes of a culture that is too eager to locate the source of the problem and its solution in women's putative inability to take action. In contrast, a reframing of rape in terms of the structural positions of masculinity and femininity rather than of biologically male perpetrators and indoctrinated female victims recasts rape as a social issue rather than a women's issue. It also restores masculinity to the concept of gender; somehow "gender" has come to evoke exclusively women or femininity in culture.

We need to resist the facile opposition between passivity and agency that has motivated popular and academic discussions of sexual violence since the 1990s. As I pointed out earlier, victims' passivity is not necessarily tantamount to their compliance to a dominant social script of femininity. Such an assumption ignores the fact that both men and women enact scripts of femininity and masculinity at various times and in shifting and contingent ways that fluctuate according to the relations and contexts they enter. We need to stop thinking of rape as the enactment of a "script" of femininity that is supposedly enabling the act of rape and focus instead on normative masculinity's dependence on and production of a subordinate femininity through rape. Assuming otherwise infantilizes victims as a uniform group of docile women. It also discriminates by implicitly excluding victims who are male; for them, the automatic and sustained enactment of a preexisting script of femininity would be more difficult to ascertain or maintain.

Reframing rape in terms of a structural relation between positions of masculinity and femininity that are occupied by both men and women accounts for the different forms sexualized violence takes in U.S. culture. It also frees us from the victim-blaming implications of much anti-rape discourse today. Indeed, when victims do display the kind of strategic behavior that is typically associated with "agency," the likely outcome is the disciplining of the victim or dismissal of rape charges by legal authorities. In a much-publicized case in Florida in February 1999, a videotape of a stripper's attempts to deescalate the situation that led to her alleged rape through sarcasm, taunts, and belligerence resulted in her arrest for filing a false police report, notwithstanding the evidence of violence that corroborated her story.[4] Similarly, seventeen-year-old rape victim Savannah Dietrich's decision to tweet the names of her attackers led to contempt charges that were dismissed only after they occasioned national and international outrage (Riley 2012a).

We need a feminist politics that addresses the psychological and individual effects of victimization without locating the deterrence of rape and victimization in individual or psychological narratives. At a time when feminists agree that women's subordination should be understood in terms of a wider social system, it is unfortunate that this larger context fails to be highlighted as a site of transformative action. In *Ludic Feminism and After,* Teresa Ebert wonders why the dominant feminist theory in the postmodern present ("ludic feminism") disregards the relations between gender and patriarchal capitalism and between rape and "the systematic working of wage labor and capital and the way that such a system needs the superexploitation of women" (Ebert 1996, 20). Contemporary feminist theorists' response to rape in terms of women's (or feminism's) psychic and affective orientations might indeed be a symptom of this reluctance to engage systemic practices of power. This focus unfortunately corroborates the hegemonic discourse on victimization and reduces the political to the personal.

Over the last few decades, the gulf between rape victims and those who speak for them has widened. It will only continue to do so unless we begin questioning the emphasis on female interiority in approaches to sexual violence. We need to become more alert to how the sources of oppression in this country are constantly reframed and located within victims themselves rather than in the institutional, physical, and cultural practices that are deployed around them. We need to change the depoliticizing course that approaches to rape in particular and to violence in general have taken over the last few decades. We need to theorize and reconceptualize the contingent meanings surrounding categories such as "victim" and "experience" rather than merely participating in the backlash's bashing of feminism's key concepts. Instead of reframing sex as violence, as earlier feminists did, I argue for a reconfiguration of sexual violence as the paradigmatic form of a social violence whose own sexualized dynamics have heretofore been obscured by the conceptualization of rape as *the* sexual crime. This reframing entails a recasting of masculinity as a structural (rather than biological) position that encompasses race, class, and other categories of differences and is no longer posited as preexisting the operations of power that produces it. In other words, we do not live in a "rape culture" because our culture and its representations teach men to rape women. Rather, we live in culture that fails to recognize that its most normative assumptions about "being a man" and a citizen legitimize a structural form of domination that is predicated on the subordination of a feminine position to a dominant masculine one. This is, then, a culture of violence in which the always already sexualized dimension of violence is hidden in plain sight. Recognizing this dynamic is, I argue, how we will restore rape to public attention as the logical rather than the aberrant expression of our understanding of normative subjectivity. It is also how we will successfully account for how sexualized violence in all its manifestations is imbricated in the making of culture.

NOTES

INTRODUCTION

1. In her book *Rape: A History from 1860 to the Present*, Joanna Bourke reveals that although one rape in three ended in a conviction in 1970 Britain, by 2007 that rate had dropped to one in twenty (2008, 389).
2. In *Violence*, Žižek makes a distinction between directly "visible" subjective violence that is performed by a "clearly identifiable agent" and whose "fascinating lure" helps render "objective" violence invisible (2008, 1).
3. See Malinen (2007) for a discussion of lesbian-on-lesbian rape and the difficulties of making it intelligible through the frames we typically apply to sexual violence.
4. In *The Metastases of Enjoyment*, Žižek (1994) argues that anything at all can be sexualized. Also see *After the Lovedeath: Sexual Violence and the Making of Culture* (2000), in which Kramer argues that the systems of polarities that ground gender and define culture both promote and rationalize sexual violence.
5. In *Feminist Theory: From Margin to Center* (1984), bell hooks similarly argues that it is better to understand "rape culture" as part of an overarching culture of violence.
6. Friedman (2013) recognizes that ending the pandemic of rape will require "men [who are] willing to do the hard work of interrogating the ideas they were raised with," but the infelicitous phrase toxic masculinity, while catchy, implies that it is a subset of masculinity rather than normative masculinity.
7. Examples include journals such as *Men and Masculinities*, *Psychology of Men and Masculinity* and the *Journal of Men, Masculinities, and Spirituality* as well as anthologies such as Cohen's *Men and Masculinity: A Text Reader* (2001), Harper and Harris's *College Men and Masculinities* (2010), and Whitehead's *Men and Masculinities* (2006).
8. See Judith Halberstam's (1998) focus on what she calls "female masculinity" as a potential way of evacuating "masculinity" as a term that attaches to sexed bodies.
9. I would like to thank Professor Joseph Valente for this insight into the adoption of the script as a "terrorized" one.
10. According to Sara Suleri (1993), the trope of colonialism as rape "in which colonized territory is rendered dubiously coterminous with the stereotype of a precultural and female geography" is no longer "culturally liberating" because this metaphor obscures "the anxieties of empire" (16–17). See Sady Doyle (2009) for a discussion of the ways sexual assault has become the right wing's favorite metaphor.
11. See Abdullah-Khan's *Male Rape* (2008), Lew's *Victims No Longer* (2004), and Scarce's *Male on Male Rape* (2001).

CHAPTER 1: FRAMING THE VICTIM

1. *The Year of Magical Thinking* gets its title from the occasions when a grieving Didion "was incapable of thinking rationally" and "was thinking as small children think, as if my thoughts or wishes had the power to reverse the narrative, change the outcome" (2005, 35).

2. As such, Bryant would be epitomizing the "colorblindedness" that Aleinikoff defines as "in essence, not the absence of color, but rather monochromatism . . . when there is only one race—when blacks become white" (quoted in Shropshire 1996, 8).

3. Filipovic (2012) discusses how integral to the party such assertions were.

4. Ironically, the comment came as Greig was criticizing Todd Akin for his "forcible rape" comment. She told the *San Jose Mercury News*: "*That was an insensitive remark. I'm sure he regretted it. He should have come back and apologized*" (quoted in Harmon 2013).

5. Sharon Lamb's edited collection *New Versions of Victims* (1999) focuses on the constructed and shifting nature of victimization without resorting to victim blaming and a regressive turn in feminist politics. For instance, in her essay "Constructing the Victim," Lamb investigates the shifting meanings of the term "victim" in order to challenge the damaging association of the concept with extreme suffering and pathological mental states.

6. For evidence of the substitution of "survivor" for "victim," see Alcoff and Gray (1993, 261–262); Bahar (2003, 1025); Gunn (1998, 179). Usually the two terms are discussed in terms of a narrative of transition and progress from "victim" to "survivor," with the former appearing in quotation marks while the latter is used referentially (Convery 2011). Also see Dunn (2010).

7. After a particularly grueling day of listening to mothers weep over their lost children, the narrator claims: "Truth has become a woman. Everybody recognizes her, yet nobody knows her."

8. In *The Myth of Empowerment* (2005), Dana Becker gives examples of the ways women have traditionally been disempowered by their association with interiority and privacy. Indeed, normative femininity's association with the home, family, and inner propensities has traditionally worked to prevent and dissuade women from acquiring a public self (via property and rights) that has historically defined the constitution of the male subject. It is also no coincidence that professions such as counseling that are heavily dominated by women have been deprofessionalized. Becker explains that it is often in the name of this same interiority that women have been able to participate in the public sphere; examples include the female healers and preachers of the past and the psychotherapists of the present, many of whom are female.

9. According to Shirley Samuel, the Civil War is the historical event that marked the dramatic shift from identifying the U.S. nation as feminine to identifying it as masculine. See *Facing America: Iconography and the Civil War* (2004).

10. See Nicholson (1989) for another account of this conundrum and for ways feminists have mediated between the two paradigms since the 1990s.

11. This is not to say, however, that victims' participation in legal proceedings would have the same negative effects outside the ideological context of the Western juridical model I am examining here.

CHAPTER 2: RAPE AND VICTIMOLOGY IN FEMINIST THEORY

1. In her historical account of the development of anti-rape consciousness, *Rape on the Public Agenda*, Maria Bevacqua (2000) traces the appearance of the issue on the public agenda in the 1970s, although she is careful not to overlook the presence of a political understanding of rape in the work of earlier feminists.

2. "Subject of feeling" is a term I borrow from Lauren G. Berlant's important essay "The Subject of True Feeling" (2001).

3. One essay on sexual violence appeared in *Feminist Studies* in 1994: Viven Ng's "Sexual Abuse of Daughters-in-Law in Qing China: Cases from the Xing' An Huilan" focused on the material limits of the agency of women, and more specifically of daughters-in-law, in

nineteenth-century China. In summer 1996, *differences* devoted a special issue to violence and published Pamela Haag's "Putting Your Body on the Line," one of the few theoretical investigations of rape I came across. Haag's essay provides a genealogy of feminist thinking on violence from the beginning of the second wave through the 1980s. Of the six articles on rape that appeared in *Signs* in the 1990s, two share the kind of theoretical and speculative impulses I was looking for: In "Survivor Discourse," Alcoff and Gray (1993) argue that media representations of rape survivors disempower survivor speech and diminish its subversive potentials. Janice Haaken's "The Recovery of Memory, Fantasy, and Desire" (1996) surveys feminist approaches to sexual abuse and incest and critiques the narrow psychologizing sexual abuse undergoes in most analyses. The other four essays provide either traditional psychological accounts or sociological studies of the issue: Sherene Razack's "What Is Gained by Looking White People in the Eye?" (1994) exposes the imperialism and racism embedded in the legal system's response to violence against North American aboriginal women and women of color; Janet Liebman Jacobs's "Victimized Daughters" (1993) draws conclusions about the bonding between incest victim and perpetrator based on fifty interviews of incest survivors; Jacobs's "Reassessing Mother Blame in Incest" (1990) adopted a similar method and used clinical data from a support group project treating twelve girls to study the destruction of the mother-daughter bond in cases of incest. In both essays, her claims are grounded in the "reality of the child's subjective experience" (514). Last but not least, David Lisak's "Sexual Aggression, Masculinity, and Fathers" (1991) also follows a conventional psychological framework in its study of rapists and links male sexual aggression to father-distant child-rearing practices.

4. See, for instance, Leola Johnson's "Forum on Feminism and the Media" (1995); Julia Lesage's "Disarming Film Rape" (1978); Maaike Meijer's "Countering Textual Violence"; Jane Mills's "Screening Rape" (1995); and Suzanna Danuta Walters's introduction to her book *Material Girls* (1995).

5. For a review and critique of conservative feminist writers in the 1990s, see Elizabeth Kamarck Minnich's "Feminist Attacks on Feminisms: Patriarchy's Prodigal Daughters" (1998). Also see Melissa Deem's essay "Scandal, Heteronormative Culture, and the Disciplining of Feminism" (1999) for an excellent account of the ahistorical contemporary discourses about feminism in the popular media. Deem criticizes the media's "paramnesiac" containment of feminism whereby the complex history of the movement is represented through a cluster of reductive and recycled images and figures (feminism as dogma, as an acontextual and essentializing practice, etc.).

6. This observation is based on discussions of the backlash in women's studies classes and in the workshops and advocacy I did as a volunteer for Rape Crisis Services. In both contexts, participants openly shared their histories of victimization.

7. For an analysis that breaks down the opposition between victim and powerful woman, see Kathleen B. Jones's "The Politics of Responsibility and Perspectives on Violence against Women" (1997). Illustrating that "there is no unencumbered feminist explanation of violence against women" (14), the essay focuses on what would typically be considered an unlikely eventuality, namely the murder of an activist feminist student (trained in self-defense) by her boyfriend.

8. Like other postmodern feminists such as Heberle, Marcus relies on one source, the circumscribed empirical research by Pauline Bart and Patricia O'Brien (1985), to buttress the claim that women who respond in aggressive ways to their attackers are more likely to avoid rape. Alternative findings are neither cited nor entertained. This source is treated as the final word on the subject, which is ironic in light of postmodernism's challenge to empiricism.

9. See Sharon Lamb's chapter on "Victims" in her book *The Trouble with Blame: Victims, Perpetrators, and Responsibility* (1996, 22–56).

10. See Joanna Bourke's *Rape: A History from 1860 to the Present* (2008) for an example of scholarship that puts the rapist, not the victim, in the spotlight as it boldly envisions a future without sexual violence.

11. See, for instance, Milman's victim-blaming account of the Steubenville case, in which his focus remains on the victim's drinking and inability to remember, as well as CNN's breaking the news of a guilty verdict in the case by lamenting that the "promising" lives of the rapists had been ruined (both accounts in Edwards 2013).

12. Lamb no longer subscribes to this paradoxically victim-blaming standpoint model but emphasizes instead that "a subject might misrepresent herself" and "the spoken version of an event may be only one version, one narrative" (1999, 130). She analyzes the experience of two women to illustrate how their conceptualizations of their experiences are molded by the culture's expectations of victims.

13. Bordo originally published her critique of Butler's gender theory in "Postmodern Subjects, Postmodern Bodies" (1992), an essay that prompted Butler to acknowledge that the subversion of norms and the destabilizing power of parodic bodies could not be determined independent from the concrete (and often limiting) contexts in which they are situated. See psychologist Nicola Gavey's work for an example of a feminist theory that, while influenced by a postmodern perspective, does not ignore the materiality of the body in stressing the constitutive effects of the language of sexual victimization. As Gavey explains, "at any one point in time, we are some complex and fluid product of embodied-biography-in-cultural-history. We may be socially determined in some sense, but this does not imply we are blank spaces, able to be totally shaped by discrete discourses" (2005, 174).

14. The subject's potential for overcoming socially imposed limitations is an important aspect of later Foucault's analysis of power relations. In *The Use of Pleasure*, for instance, he advocates self-monitoring and self-discipline—that is, the reflexive examination of the self's imbrication with wider cultural dynamics—as the basis of individual autonomy. In stressing self-fashioning and self-mastery, he seeks to offer an alternative to the Christian tradition of self-renunciation. Foucault does not, however, simply transpose this model to conditions of "domination" like rape. At the same time that he promotes an ethics of the self, he emphasizes how the solidification of power relations into "domination" limits the practice of resistance and freedom. This distinction between domination and power is important if we are to acknowledge the role of physical violence—even when it is not directly exercised—in shaping the materiality of the body.

15. See my introduction for a discussion of "Confinement" (1988), where Foucault goes further to advocate desexualizing rape by decriminalizing it and treating it like any other civil offense such as a physical attack or a punch in the face. See Monique Plaza's "Our Costs and Their Benefits" (1980) for an account and critique of this position.

16. This argument was first made by Linda Alcoff and Laura Gray in their essay "Survivor Discourse" (1996).

17. The meanings attached to rape in the West have, however, changed over time. See, for instance, Vigarello's *The History of Rape* (2001) for an analysis of the shifting meanings of rape across the centuries in France. Through numerous case studies, Vigarello highlights how the relative tolerance toward sexual violence in early modern France gave way to changing legal attitudes at the end of the eighteenth century and the slow recognition in the nineteenth century of the role of moral violence in rape.

18. For an analysis of the contemporary meanings associated with victimization, see Lamb (1999).

CHAPTER 3: "BIRTH RAPE"

1. See Mary O'Brien's *The Politics of Reproduction* (1981), Barbara Duden's *Disembodying Women* (1993), and Emily Martin's *The Woman in the Body* (1987) for a radical critique of the disempowerment of pregnant women in the face of medical and state expertise about fetuses,

monitoring, health and hygiene. According to Michelle Stanworth, "New reproductive technologies are the vehicle that will turn men's illusions of reproductive power into a reality. By manipulating eggs and embryos, scientists will determine the sort of children who are born—will make themselves the fathers of humankind. By removing eggs and embryos from some women and implanting them in others, medical practitioners will gain control over motherhood itself" (1997, 483–484).

2. I use the term "masculinity" here to refer to the authority society invests in men through gender roles.

3. See Wallace (2000) for a fuller description of the method's components and history.

4. There is a clear distinction between Bradley and Lamaze: the former involves "natural breathing" rather than controlled breathing, for instance. Lamaze is also more flexible about medical interventions and is therefore more appreciated in the hospital setting. For a historical account of the childbirth movement since the 1920s, see Celeste Phillips, "Family Centered Maternity Care: Past, Present, Future" (1999); Doris Haire, "Focal Point on Childbirth Education: A History of Childbirth Education" (1999); and Richard Wertz and Dorothy Wertz, *Lying In* (1989).

5. See Wickham (1999) for the lack of continuity of care in hospital birth and the low levels of (sometimes very junior) medical staff.

6. See David Vernon's controversial edited anthology of birth experiences, *Men at Birth* (2011), which similarly argues that men are poorly prepared for birth and should not attend the birth of their child if that would make the birth more difficult for the woman. Also see White and White's *Men at Birth: Guide to a Successful Childbirth Experience* (2009), which similarly discusses men's inadequacy in handling pregnancy and childbirth.

7. Besides the numerous friends and acquaintances whose stories reflect my own, I also found further evidence of the gap between what men are prepared for and the reality of childbirth in much of the literature about birth. Barclay, Donovan, and Genovese (1996), Berry (1988), Donovan (1995), M. P. Johnson (2002), Simkin (1999), Steinberg, Kruckman, and Steinberg (2000), and Vahvilainen-Julkunen and Liukkonen (1998) report that men find the experience anxiety producing and fail as a result to provide effective labor support to their partner. In *(Mis)conceptions* (2001), Wolf also documents instances of what has now entered the common lore about delivery, namely women's anger directed at their partner.

8. See Midmer (1992) for a description of this management style and its effects.

9. See Weedon (1999) for an account of the development of Marxist and socialist feminisms.

10. For other routine procedures that occur without the laboring couple's consent, see Wolf (2001).

11. For other examples of the institution taking over, oblivious to the laboring woman's wishes or concerns, see Wolf (2001).

12. This is a reference to John Gray's best-selling book *Men Are from Mars, Women Are from Venus: A Practical Guide for Improving Communication and Getting What You Want in Your Relationships* (1993).

13. The formulation "a man" and "his wife," with its evocation of conventional marriage vows, says a lot about the Searses' gender allegiances.

CHAPTER 4: PRISON RAPE, MASCULINITY, AND THE
MISSED ALLIANCES OF HOLLYWOOD CINEMA

1. Studies of HIV in prison tend to focus on male prisoners (see Pinkerton, Galletly, and Seal 2007). For studies addressing the psychological impact of rape in prison, see Dumond and Dumond (2002). The most serious mental health concern after inmates are sexually assaulted has been suicide, which has been described as the "crisis behind bars" (Danto 1981). The

precise rate of suicide of incarcerated individuals is not clear, but estimates (calculated during 2006) range around 38 per 100,000, a rate several times higher than that of the general population (Hayes 2010, xiii).

2. See Scraton and McCulloch, eds., *The Violence of Incarceration* (2008), an international collection of writings on Iraq, Ireland, Australia, and the United States that examines the conditions of confinement after 9/11. The anthology powerfully exposes the link between state penal violence and state violence (in detainee military camps, for instance). This is the continuum that ultimately creates the conditions for the sexualized violence of men and women in prisons.

3. For a discussion of the racialized assumptions of criminality in the United States, also see Barak and Flavin (2010); Davis (1998), Gabiddon et al. (1998); Marable, Middlemass, and Steinberg (2007); Muhammed (2010).

4. See Irving (2007) for a discussion of how the universalism ascribed to certain bodies as unmarked, white, propertied, and male constitutes the ideal citizen. In *The Terror Dream* (2007), Faludi explains that the anxious response to 9/11 triggered the nation's return to a Puritan-derived myth of the brawny white male.

5. The Special Rapporteur on Violence Against Women, Its Causes and Consequences collects and analyzes data on in order to recommend measures to be taken at the national, regional, and international levels. This position was created in "Elimination of Violence against Women," Commission on Human Rights resolution 1977/44, http://www.unhchr.ch/Huridocda/Huridoca.nsf/TestFrame/08a61b451a2b743280256648004edcob?Opendocument.

6. The "Standard Minimum Rules for the Treatment of Prisoners" (1955) was adopted by the First United Nations Congress on the Prevention of Crime and the Treatment of Offenders, held at Geneva in 1955 and was approved by the Economic and Social Council by its resolutions 663 C (XXIV) of 31 July 1957 and 2076 (LXII) of 13 May 1977.

7. *Hard Bodies* shows that masculinity in the blockbuster films of the 1980s meant muscular heroes whose "hard bodies" and displays of explosive action were to restore faith in U.S. national power. According to Jeffords, the hypermasculinity of the Reagan era was a self-conscious reaction against the "soft body" of the Carter years and the crisis of masculinity for which the right wing blamed the feminism of the 1970s and the aftermath of the Vietnam War. 1980s Hollywood cinema "portrayed many of the same narratives of heroism, success, and achievement, toughness, strength, and 'good Americanness' that made the Reagan Revolution possible" (Jeffords 1994, 15). In fact, "the articulations of bodies constituted the imaginary of the Reagan agenda and the site of its materialization" (24), as the male heroes literally worked out Reaganite national and foreign policies through their own battles. *Rambo*, *Die Hard*, the Indiana Jones movies, *RoboCop*, and *Terminator* all came to embody the renewed national and international mastery that Reagan strove to embody. In the 1990s, however, with the transition from the Reagan to the Bush administration, the indefatigable masculine body gave way to a synthesis of 1970s softness and 1980s hardness. Jeffords highlights the evolution of movie masculinity in the Bush I years with their passive-aggressive new men in movies such as *Regarding Henry* (1991). While an elaborated account of this changing context for masculinity is not the focus of this chapter, it is also manifest in the difference between Reagan and the Clinton image (who was feminized through repeated references to his pudgy thighs, overeating, and pants-wearing wife), in the vision of a peacetime United States as it evolved with the end of the Cold War, in the rise of the "new economy," and in the development of Gen-X rhetoric.

8. See Abele's essay "Assuming a True Identity: Re-/De-constructing Hollywood Heroes" (2002) for a discussion of how Hollywood action movies "have called into question the naturalness of masculine roles and disrupted the influence of the male body" (448).

9. The hardcore band Bury Your Dead titled their 2002 debut full-length album *You Had Me at Hello* in reference to *Jerry Maguire*. In 2012, an article on maximizing shareholder values in *Forbes* was titled "Give Me the Money," and begins by explicitly identifying "the famous catch phrase from the movie *Jerry Maguire*" as its inspiration (Loftus 2012). In an article entitled "'You Had Me at Hello': Study Reveals Secrets of Memorable Movie Lines," Satran (2012) discusses a study conducted by computer science graduate students at Cornell University, who also singled out *Jerry Maguire*'s two famous lines to examine "the impact of language on the memorability of movie lines." The quotes "Show me the money!" and "You had me at 'hello'" also appeared on the American Film Institute's list of 100 Movie Quotes, ranked at #25 and #52, respectively (American Film Institute 2005).

10. Contrast the representation of consciousness-raising groups in Hollywood cinema with Spike Lee's portrayal of it in *Jungle Fever* (1991). Here, black women gather to debate their problems in a supportive and helpful way.

11. Wiegman's *American Anatomies* (1995) outlines how nineteenth-century pseudo-science produced a series of analogies between blackness and other forms of "visible" bodily differences to justify social hierarchies. Wiegman shows that "comparative anatomy read the African's difference through the twin registers of sexual difference: as both a stereotypically feminized category and the preeminently sexual" (44).

CHAPTER 5: RAPE BY PROXY IN CONTEMPORARY DIASPORIC WOMEN'S FICTION

1. Kubitschek singles out Harriet Jacobs's *Incidents in the Life of a Slave Girl*; Toni Morrison's *The Bluest Eye*; Zora Neale Hurston's *Their Eyes Were Watching God*; and Alice Walker's *The Color Purple* as examples of African American fiction that deals with the intersections of rape and racism in black women's lives. She contrasts the representation of rape in the literature of the African American tradition to its portrayal in Euro-American literature. Specifically, she shows that female victims in African American narratives survive the sexual violence and move on with their lives, whereas in Euro-American texts, which tellingly fail to represent the victim's point of view, they are either killed, commit suicide, or go mad while the rape itself is represented in ambiguous terms.

2. According to Ledent (1997), "up to the 1990s . . . the focus of major West Indian fiction was on the social, psychological, and ontological aftermath of what has been called 'the peculiar institution' or on the historical events preceding it, such as the European conquest or the Middle Passage, rather than on the material conditions of plantation life or the slavery system proper" (271). After the 1990s, Ledent argues, writers such as Caryl Phillips and Fred D'Aguiar, whose writings represent "the emerging tip of a body of historical fiction," reveal a "differently focused preoccupation" (272) with the past. Slavery is no longer just a pervasive presence in their fiction but an event they tackle "head-on" (271).

3. Critics such as Edmondson (1999) and Donnell (2005) have outlined the distinction between the first generation of mostly male Caribbean authors who left their islands for the metropole after World War II and the subsequent generation of mostly female immigrant authors who moved to the United States primarily for economic reasons and then began to write. What I am outlining here is the aesthetics peculiar to a third generation of writers born in the 1960s and thereafter.

4. Also see the documentary *Calling the Ghosts: A Story about Rape, War, and Women* (1996), a first-person account of two childhood friends and lawyers, Jadranka Cigelj and Nusreta Sivac, who were taken to the notorious Serb concentration camp of Omarska and were systematically tortured and raped by their Serb captors. The film allowed the two survivors to

successfully lobby to have rape included in the international lexicon of war crimes by the International Criminal Tribunal for the Former Yugoslavia at The Hague.

5. As Mark McWatt (1992) points out, history has exerted "an almost obsessive influence upon the creative imagination of the West Indian writer" (12). In her essay "The Island and the Creation of (Hi)Story," Florence Ramond Jurney (2006) argues that history is a recurrent theme in the writings of Michelle Cliff and Jamaica Kincaid, for instance. Both authors' works, she shows, include a pointed criticism of postcolonial times.

6. In an interview with Nealiegh Mitchell (2007), the author of *Unburnable*, Marie-Elena John, explained that her novel was an attempt to bridge this tension: "What I tried to do was to get away from something that is purely entertainment and something that is purely historical. I've read quite a few other Caribbean writers who try to do what I did but may not have done it in a way that is as engaging. And I really wanted this not to be a typical literary fiction which can be very slow. I am not saying I will never write a book that has a slower pace but it was almost deliberate that the plot is very very strong and very fast, and that is so that I don't bore those people who may not pick up a literary book. Yet I think I have managed to attract both, as evidenced by the emails I am getting from professors who will teach it as well as those regular folks who are saying I just couldn't put this book down." Similarly, in a personal correspondence, Edwidge Danticat, whose first novel was an Oprah Book of the Month, wrote that with *Breath, Eyes, Memory*, she mostly wanted to tell "a good story" that people would want to read. Also see Bongie's essay "Exiles on Main Stream" (2011), about the tension between postcolonial studies and cultural studies/popular culture. Bongie explains why postcolonial novels that are bestsellers (especially in the Caribbean) do not usually join the postcolonial academic canon.

7. See Lisa Lindquist Dorr's *White Women, Rape, and the Power of Race in Virginia* (2004) for an analysis of trial proceedings following charges of black-on-white rape in the South. Dorr shows that despite the prevalence of the "black beast rapist" trope, local contexts, and the reputation, character, and place in community of both blacks and whites influenced the outcome of each case of black-on-white rape.

8. Examples include Edwidge Danticat's *Breath, Eyes, Memory*, Marie-Elena John's *Unburnable*, and Shani Mootoo's *Cereus Blooms at Night*.

9. The image of the unkept and Edenic garden is a common trope in Caribbean literature. Beside Kincaid and Mootoo, it can also be found in the work of Jean Rhys, Dionne Brand, Olive Senior, and Lorna Goodson, who all thus engage and challenge the cliché of the Caribbean as a lost Eden.

CONCLUSION

1. Joan Scott and Wendy Brown both make passing disclaimers to the effect that we need not abandon the category of experience in our efforts to question and redefine it. Brown (1995) explains that "dispensing with the unified subject does not mean ceasing to be able to speak about our experiences as women, only that our words cannot be legitimately deployed or construed as larger or longer than the moments of the lives they speak from; they cannot be anointed as 'authentic' or 'true'" (40–41). Scott (1992) claims that "experience is not a word we can do without, although it is tempting, given its usage to essentialize identity and reify the subject, to abandon it altogether. But . . . given the ubiquity of the term, it seems to me more useful to work with it, to analyze its operations and to redefine its meaning" (37). In highlighting the essentializing gestures associated with its use, however, they have, along with Foucault, contributed to our wariness of the term in academia. Rather than asking what "truths" experience reveals, scholars are now increasingly studying the blindnesses

its invocation hides. This might explain why the analysis of the concrete experience of sexual assault fell out of favor with feminist theorists in the 1990s.

2. In claiming that victims today are spoken for in a way that they were not in the early women's movement, I am not arguing that the study of or advocacy for rape victims must be done by survivors alone. While I am advocating for a return to collective sites of democratic participation, I am not promoting a standpoint theory whereby the perspective of the oppressed is more valuable because of their "experience" of oppression. There is no guarantee that being raped makes an individual more sensitive to the workings of the discursive context through which experience is given meaning. Victims are as likely to reproduce "rape myths" as other members of society, and an individual who has not undergone a traumatic experience will not automatically be unaware of the dynamics of sexual violence. The perspectival and embodied location of a speaker has a bearing on the meaning they give to an event but does not determine it. See Linda Alcoff's essay "The Problem of Speaking for Others" (1992–1992) for an elaboration of how the meaning of an utterance or event is affected by the positionality of the speaker and by the discursive context.

3. Psychologist Nicola Gavey (1999) criticizes the positivism of empirical psychology research on these same grounds. She takes issue with the field's creation of "ready-made categories of victims" and its disregard for women's contradictory reactions. Similarly, in her essay "Trauma Talk in Feminist Clinical Practice," Jeanne Marecek (1999) reveals how the language practices of feminist therapists construct victims as "wounded" and "broken" and in the process turn therapy into a form of apolitical caregiving. Like Gavey, she concludes that "psychology's habits of authoritative expertise and its claim of privileged access to a single Truth, even when practiced in the name of feminism, should be received with skepticism" (180).

4. See Jennifer Baumgardner's article "What Does Rape Look Like?" (2000) for a detailed account of this case.

WORKS CITED

Abdullah-Khan, Noreen. 2008. *Male Rape: The Emergence of a Social and Legal Issue.* New York: Palgrave Macmillan.
Abele, Elizabeth. 2002. "Assuming a True Identity: Re-/De-Constructing Hollywood Heroes." *Journal of American and Comparative Cultures* 25.1–2: 447–455.
Abrams, Kathryn. 1995. "Sex Wars Redux: Agency and Coercion in Feminist Legal Theory." *Columbia Law Review* 95.2: 304–376.
Alcoff, Linda. 1991–1992. "The Problem of Speaking for Others." *Cultural Critique* 20 (Winter): 5–33.
———, and Laura Gray. 1993. "Survivor Discourse: Transgression or Recuperation?" *Signs: A Journal of Women in Culture and Society* 18.2: 260–291.
Amnesty International. 1999. "'Not Part of My Sentence': Violations of the Human Rights of Women in Custody.* New York: Amnesty International. http://amnestyusa.org/rightsforall/women/index.html.
Amnesty International USA. 2005. "Women in Prison: A Fact Sheet." http://www.amnestyusa.org/sites/default/files/pdfs/vaw_fact_sheet.pdf.
American Film Institute. 2005. "AFI's 100 Years . . . 100 Movie Quotes." American Film Institute Web site. http://www.afi.com/100years/quotes.aspx.
Arms, Suzanne. 1975. *Immaculate Deception: A New Look at Women and Childbirth in America.* Boston: Houghton Mifflin.
Armstrong, Nancy. 1987. *Desire and Domestic Fiction: A Political History of the Novel.* New York: Oxford University Press.
Associated Press. 2004. "Kobe's Lawyers Suggest Racism." *Fox News,* 24 January. http://www.foxnews.com/story/0,2933,109238,00.html.
Badinter, Elizabeth. *Dead End Feminism.* Trans. Julia Borossa. Malden, MA: Polity Press, 2006.
Bahar, Saba. 2003. "'If I'm One of the Victims, Who Survives?': Marilyn Hacker's Breast Cancer Texts." *Signs: A Journal of Women in Culture and Society* 28.4: 1025–1052.
Barak, G., P. Leighton, and J. Flavin. 2010. *Class, Race, Gender, and Crime: The Social Realities of Justice in America.* Lanham, MD: Rowman & Littlefield Publishers.
Barclay, Lesley, Jenny Donovan, and Ann Genovese. 1996. "Men's Experiences during Their Partner's First Pregnancy: A Grounded Theory Analysis." *Australian Journal of Advanced Nursing* 13.3: 12–24.
Bart, Pauline, and Patricia H. O'Brien. 1985. *Stopping Rape: Successful Survival Strategies.* New York: Pergamon.
Bartky, Sandra. 1988. "Foucault, Femininity, and the Modernization of Patriarchal Power." In *Feminism and Foucault: Reflections on Resistance,* ed. Irene Diamond and Lee Quinby, 61–86. Boston: Northeastern University Press.
Bassett, Laura. 2013. "New Mexico Bill Would Criminalize Abortions after Rape as 'Tampering with Evidence.'" *The Huffington Post,* 24 January. http://www.huffingtonpost.com/2013/01/24/new-mexico-abortion-bill_n_2541894.html.
Baumgardner, Jennifer. 2000. "What Does Rape Look Like?" *The Nation* 270.1 (3 January): 20–23.

Beck, Allen J., and Paige M. Harrison. 2007. "Sexual Victimization in State and Federal Prisons Reported by Inmates, 2007." Bureau of Justice Statistics Special Report, December. http://bjsdata.ojp.usdoj.gov/content/pub/pdf/svsfpri07.pdf.

Becker, Dana. 2005. *The Myth of Empowerment: Women and the Therapeutic Culture in America.* New York: New York University Press.

Becker, Maki, and Michael Beebe. 2009. *The Bike Path Killer.* New York: Pinnacle Books.

Beech, Beverley Lawrence. 2000. "The Safety of Hospital Birth: The Myth versus the Reality." *AIMS Journal* 11.4: 1–2.

Benhabib, Seyla. 1995. "Feminism and Postmodernism." In *Feminist Contentions: A Philosophical Exchange.* Ed. Seyla Benhabib, Judith Butler, Drucilla Cornell, and Nancy Fraser. 17–35. New York: Routledge.

Bennett, William. 2001. *Why We Fight: Moral Clarity and the War on Terrorism.* Washington, DC: Regnery Publishing.

Berlant, Lauren G. 2001. "The Subject of True Feeling: Pain, Privacy, and Politics." In *Feminist Consequences: Theory for the New Century,* ed. Elisabeth Bronfen and Misha Kavka, 126–160. New York: Columbia University Press.

———. 2008. *The Female Complaint: The Unfinished Business of Sentimentality in American Culture.* Durham, NC: Duke University Press.

Bernstein, Richard. 1990. "Ideas and Trends: The Rising Hegemony of the Politically Correct." *New York Times,* 28 October. http://www.nytimes.com/1990/10/28/weekinreview/ideas-trends-the-rising-hegemony-of-the-politically-correct.html?pagewanted=all.

Berry, Linda M. 1988. "Realistic Expectations of the Labor Coach." *Journal of Obstetric, Gynecologic, and Neonatal Nursing* 17.5: 354–355.

Bevacqua, Maria. 2000. *Rape on the Public Agenda: Feminism and the Politics of Sexual Assault.* Boston: Northeastern University Press.

Birthtalk.org. 2010. "When Birth Becomes a Violation." Birthtalk.org, 26 August. http://birthtraumatruths.wordpress.com/2010/08/26/when-birth-becomes-a-violation/.

Bloom, Mia. 2005. *Dying to Kill: The Allure of Suicide Terror.* New York: Columbia University Press.

Bongie, Chris. 2010. "Exiles on Main Stream: Valuing the Popularity of Postcolonial Literature." *Postmodern Culture* 14.1. http://pmc.iath.virginia.edu/issue.903/14.1bongie.html.

Bordo, Susan. 1992. "Postmodern Subjects, Postmodern Bodies." *Feminist Studies* 18.1: 159–176.

———. 1997. *Twilight Zones: The Hidden Life of Cultural Images from Plato to O. J.* Berkeley: University of California Press.

Bourke, Joanna. 2008. *Rape: A History from 1860 to the Present.* London: Virago.

Bradley, Robert. 1965. *Husband-Coached Childbirth.* New York: Harper & Row.

Brontë, Emily. 1847/1992. *Wuthering Heights.* Ed. Linda H. Peterson. Boston: Bedford Books of St. Martin's Press.

Brown, Wendy. 1995. *States of Injury: Power and Freedom in Late Modernity.* Princeton, NJ: Princeton University Press.

Bruce, Elizabeth. 2001. "Saying No to Episiotomy: Getting Through Labor and Delivery in One Piece." *Mothering* 104 (January–February). http://mothering.com/pregnancy-birth/saying-no-to-episiotomy.

Butler, Judith. 1990. *Gender Trouble: Feminism and the Subversion of Identity.* London: Routledge.

———. 1993. *Bodies That Matter: On the Discursive Limits of "Sex."* New York: Routledge.

———. 2004a. *Precarious Life: The Powers of Mourning and Violence.* London: Verso.

———. 2004b. *Undoing Gender.* New York: Routledge.

———, and Joan Scott. 1992. *Feminists Theorize the Political.* New York: Routledge.

Cahill, Ann. 2001. *Rethinking Rape.* Ithaca, NY: Cornell University Press.

Calling the Ghosts: A Story about Rape, War and Women. 1996. Dir. Mandy Jacobson and Karmen Jelincic. DVD. Women Make Movies.
Campbell, Rona, and Alison MacFarlane. 1986. "Place of Delivery: A Review." *British Journal of Obstetrics and Gynaecology* 93.7: 675–683.
Carle, Susan. 2005. "Theorizing Agency." *American University Law Review* 55: 307–388.
Christiansë, Yvette. 2007. *Unconfessed*. New York: Other Press.
Clark, Vévé. 1990. "Developing Diaspora Literacy: Allusion in Maryse Condé's *Hérémakon*." In *Out of the Kumba*, ed. Carole Boyce Davies and Elaine Savory Fida, 303–319. Trenton, NJ: Africa World Press.
Clarke, Austin. 2004. *The Polished Hoe: A Novel*. New York: Amistad.
Cliff, Michelle. 1987. *No Telephone to Heaven*. New York: E. P. Dutton.
———. 1991. "Caliban's Daughter: The Tempest and the Teapot." *Frontiers: A Journal of Women Studies* 12.2: 36–51.
Cobham, Rhonda. 2002. "'Mwen na rien, Msieu': Jamaica Kincaid and the Problem of Creole Gnosis.'" *Callaloo* 25.3: 868–884.
Coetzee, J. M. 1999. *Disgrace*. New York: Viking.
Cohen, Theodore F., ed. 2001. *Men and Masculinity: A Text Reader*. Belmont, CA: Wadsworth.
Cole, Alyson M. 2007. *The Cult of True Victimhood: From the War on Welfare to the War on Terror*. Stanford, CA: Stanford University Press.
———. 2008. "The Other V-Word: The Politics of Victimhood Fueling George W. Bush's War Machine." In *Feminism and War: Confronting US Imperialism*, ed. Chandra Talpade Mohanty, Minnie Bruce Pratt, and Robin L. Riley, 117–131. New York: Zed Books.
Collins, Patricia Hill. 1998. *Fighting Words: Black Women and Search for Justice*. Minneapolis: University of Minnesota Press.
Condé, Maryse. 1994. *I, Tituba, Black Witch of Salem*. New York: Ballantine Books.
Connell, Patricia. 1997. "Understanding Victimization and Agency: Consideration of Race, Class, and Gender." *PoLAR: Political and Legal Anthropology Review* 20.2: 115–143.
Convery, Alyson. 2011. "Feminist Theory and Discursive Intersections: Activating the Code of 'Political Correctness.'" PhD diss., University of Newcastle, Australia.
Corrigan, Rose. 2013. *Up Against a Wall: Rape Reform and the Failure of Success*. New York: New York University Press.
Curthoys, Jean. 1997. *Feminist Amnesia: The Wake of Women's Liberation*. New York: Routledge.
Cypher, Louis. 2004. "Bryant Trial: No 'Victim' in the Courtroom." *Major Wager.com*, 1 June. http://www.majorwager.com/forums/mess-hall/9497-bryant-trial-no-victim-courtroom.html.
Danticat, Edwidge. 1994. *Breath, Eyes, Memory*. New York: Vintage Books.
Danto, Bruce. 1981. *Crisis Behind Bars—The Suicidal Inmate: A Book for Police and Correctional Officers*. Warren, MI: Dale Corp.
Davis, Angela Y. 1998. "Masked Racism: Reflections on the Prison Industrial Complex." *Colorlines: News for Action* http://www.colorlines.com/archives/1998/09/masked_racism_reflections_on_the_prison_industrial_complex.html.
Davis-Floyd, Robbie E. 1998. "Ritual in the Hospital: Giving Birth the American Way." *Birth Gazette* 14.4: 12–17.
Deem, Melissa. 1999. "Scandal, Heteronormative Culture, and the Disciplining of Feminism." *Critical Studies in Mass Communication* 16.1: 1–10.
de Jonge, Ank, Birgit van der Goes, Anita C. Ravelli, Marianne P. Amelink-Verburg, Ben Willem Mol, Jan G. Nijhuis, Jack Bennebroek Gravenhorst, and Simone E. Buitendijk. 2009. "Perinatal Mortality and Morbidity in a Nationwide Cohort of 529,688 Low-Risk Planned Home and Hospital Births." *BJOG: An International Journal of Obstetrics & Gynaecology* 116.9: 1177–1184.
De Lauretis, Teresa. 1985. "The Violence of Rhetoric: Considerations on Representation and Gender." *Semiotica* 54.1–2: 11–31.

Didion, Joan. 2005. *The Year of Magical Thinking*. New York: Alfred A. Knopf.

Donnell, Alison. 2005. *Twentieth-Century Caribbean Literature: Critical Moments in Anglophone Literary History*. New York: Routledge.

Donovan, Jenny. 1995. "The Process of Analysis during a Grounded Study of Men during Their Partners' Pregnancies." *Journal of Advanced Nursing* 21.4: 708–715.

Dorr, Lisa Lindquist. 2004. *White Women, Rape, and the Power of Race in Virginia, 1900–1960*. Chapel Hill: University of North Carolina Press.

Doyle, Laura. 2007. *Freedom's Empire: Race and the Rise of the Novel in Atlantic Modernity, 1640–1940*. Durham, NC: Duke University Press.

Doyle, Sady. 2009. "Trading on Our Fear of Rape." *The Guardian*, 1 December. http://www.guardian.co.uk/commentisfree/cifamerica/2009/nov/30/rape-beck-limbaugh-savage.

D'Souza, Dinesh. 1992. *Illiberal Education: The Politics of Race and Sex on Campus*. New York: Vintage Books.

Duden, Barbara. 1993. *Disembodying Women: Perspectives on Pregnancy and the Unborn*. Cambridge, MA: Harvard University Press.

Dumond, Robert W., and Doris A. Dumond. 2002. "The Treatment of Sexual Assault Victims." In *Prison Sex: Practice and Policy*, ed. Christopher Hensley. Boulder, CO: Lynne Rienner Publishers.

Dunn, Jennifer L. 2010. *Judging Victims: Why We Stigmatize Survivors, and How They Reclaim Respect*. Boulder, CO: Lynne Rienner Publishers.

Durand, Mark A. 1992. "The Safety of Home Birth: The Farm Study." *American Journal of Public Health* 82.3: 450–453.

Dyer, Richard. 1986. *Heavenly Bodies: Film Stars and Society*. New York: St. Martin's.

Ebert, Roger. 1996. "Jerry Maguire." Roger Ebert.com. http://www.rogerebert.com/reviews/jerry-maguire-1996.

Ebert, Teresa L. 1996. *Ludic Feminism and After: Postmodernism, Desire, and Labor in Late Capitalism*. Ann Arbor: University of Michigan Press.

Edmondson, Belinda. 1999. *Making Men: Gender, Literary Authority, and Women's Writing in Caribbean Narrative*. Durham, NC: Duke University Press.

Edwards, David. 2013. "CNN Grieves That Guilty Verdict Ruined 'Promising' Lives of Steubenville Rapists." *The Raw Story*, 17 March. http://www.rawstory.com/rs/2013/03/17/cnn-grieves-that-guilty-verdict-ruined-promising-lives-of-steubenville-rapists/.

Elia, Nada. 2000. "'A Man Who Wants to Be a Woman': Queerness as/and Healing Practices in Michelle Cliff's *No Telephone to Heaven*." *Callaloo* 23.1: 352–365.

Faludi, Susan. 2007. *Terror Dream: Fear and Fantasy in Post-9/11 America*. New York: Metropolitan Books.

Faulkner, Jeanne. 2012. "It's Not Birth Rape; It's Birth Trauma." *FitPregnancy*, 17 May. http://www.fitpregnancy.com/labor-delivery/ask-labor-nurse/its-not-birth-rape-its-birth-trauma.

Filipovic, Jill. 2012. "The Real Republican Rape Platform." *The Guardian*, 25 October. http://www.guardian.co.uk/commentisfree/2012/oct/25/real-republican-party-rape-platform.

Flax, Jane. 1990. *Thinking Fragments: Psychoanalysis, Feminism, and Postmodernism in the Contemporary West*. Berkeley: University of California Press.

Fleisher, Mark S., and Jesse L. Krienert. 2006. "The Culture of Prison Sexual Violence." https://www.ncjrs.gov/pdffiles1/nij/grants/216515.pdf.

Foucault, Michel. 1978. *The History of Sexuality: An Introduction*. Vol. 1. New York: Random House.

———. 1986. *The Use of Pleasure*. New York: Vintage.

———. 1988. "Confinement, Psychiatry, Prison." In *Politics, Philosophy, Culture: Selected Interviews and Other Writings, 1977–1984*, ed. Lawrence D. Kritzman, 178–211. New York: Routledge.

Frederick, Brian. 2009. "Conservative Media Frequently Accuse Progressives of 'Raping' Americans." *Media Matters*, November 19. http://mediamatters.org/research/2009/11/19/conservative-media-frequently-accuse-progressiv/157280.

Freeh Sporkin and Sullivan, LLP. 2012. *Report of the Special Investigating Counsel Regarding the Actions of The Pennsylvania State University Related to the Child Sexual Abuse Committed by Gerald A. Sandusky*. http://progress.psu.edu/assets/content/REPORT_FINAL_071212.pdf.

Friedman, Jaclyn. 2013. "Toxic Masculinity." *The American Prospect*, 13 March. http://prospect.org/article/toxic-masculinity.

Gabbidon, Shaun L., and Helen Taylor Greene, eds. 2005. *Race, Crime, and Justice: A Reader*. New York: Routledge.

Gavey, Nicola. 1999. "'I Wasn't Raped, but . . .': Revisiting Definitional Problems in Sexual Victimization." In *New Versions of Victims: Feminists Struggle with the Concept*, ed. Sharon Lamb, 57–82. New York: New York University Press.

———. 2005. *Just Sex? The Cultural Scaffolding of Rape*. New York: Routledge.

George, Rosemary Marangoly. 2007. "(Extra)ordinary Violence: National Literatures, Diasporic Aesthetics, and the Politics of Gender in South Asian Partition Fiction." *Signs: Journal of Women in Culture and Society* 33.1: 135–159.

Glaze, Lauren, and Laura M. Maruschak. 2008. *Parents in Prison and Their Minor Children*. Washington, DC: Bureau of Justice Statistics Special Report.

Gornick, Vivian. 1997. *Approaching Eye Level*. Boston: Beacon.

Graham, Lucy Valerie. 2012. *State of Peril: Race and Rape in South African Literature*. Oxford: Oxford University Press.

Gray, John. 1993. *Men Are from Mars, Women Are from Venus: A Practical Guide for Improving Communication and Getting What You Want in Your Relationships*. New York: HarperCollins.

Grossberg, Lawrence. 1992. *We Gotta Get Out of This Place: Popular Conservatism and Postmodern Culture*. New York: Routledge.

Gunn, Janet Varner. 1998. "Book Review: Maxine Sheets-Johnstone. The Roots of Thinking. Philadelphia: Temple University Press, 1990. And Maxine Sheets-Johnstone. The Roots of Power: Animate Form and Gendered Bodies. Chicago: Open Court, 1994." *Hypatia* 13.3: 177–181.

Gunne, Sorcha, and Zoe Brigley Thompson, eds. 2011. *Feminism, Literature, and Rape Narratives: Violence and Violation*. New York: Routledge.

Haag, Pamela. 1996. "'Putting Your Body on the Line': The Question of Violence, Victims, and the Legacies of Second-Wave Feminism." *differences* 8.2: 23–68.

Haaken, Janice. 1996. "The Recovery of Memory, Fantasy, and Desire: Feminist Approaches to Sexual Abuse and Psychic Trauma." *Signs: Journal of Women in Culture and Society* 21.4: 1069–1095.

———. 1999. "Heretical Texts: The Courage to Heal and the Incest Survivor Movement." In *New Versions of Victims: Feminists Struggle with the Concept*, ed. Sharon Lamb, 13–42. New York: New York University Press.

Haire, Doris. 1999. "Focal Point on Childbirth Education: A History of Childbirth Education." *International Journal of Childbirth Education* 12.4: 26–28.

Halberstam, Judith. 1998. *Female Masculinity*. Durham, NC: Duke University Press.

Hall, Stuart. 1980a. "Cultural Studies: Two Paradigms." *Media, Culture, Society* 2: 57–72.

———. 1980b. "Encoding/Decoding." In *Culture, Media, Language: Working Papers in Cultural Studies, 1972–1979*, ed. Stuart Hall, Dorothy Hobson, Andrew Lowe, and Paul Willis, 128–138. London: Hutchinson.

———. 1992. "Cultural Studies and Its Theoretical Legacies." In *Cultural Studies*, ed. Lawrence Grossberg, Cary Nelson, and Paula Treichler, 277–286. Urbana: University of Illinois Press.

Hamill, Jasper. 2012. "Faith in Our Youth." *The Big Issue*, 2 August. http://www.bigissue.com/features/1260/faith-our-youth.

Hanrahan, Robb. 2012. "Freeh Report Calls Out Failure to Protect Children by Four PSU Leaders." 12 July, http://www.whptv.com/content/Sandusky/story/Freeh-Report-calls-out-failure-to-protect/fPLY_rbOZE29ggMk3qDXnA.cspx.

Harmon, Steven. 2013. "Leader of California Republican Group Steps into Rape Pregnancy Controversy." *Mercury News*, 1 March. http://www.mercurynews.com/california-budget/ci_22701070/california-gop-leader-steps-into-rape-pregnancy-controversy.

Harper, Shaun R., and Frank Harris III, eds. 2010. *College Men and Masculinities: Theory, Research, and Implications for Practice*. San Francisco: Jossey Bass.

Hawkesworth, Mary. 2005. "Theorizing Globalization in a Time of War." *Studies in Political Economy* 75 (Spring): 127–139.

Hayes, Lindsay M. 2010. *National Study of Jail Suicide: 20 Year Later*. Washington, DC: National Institute of Corrections. http://nicic.gov/Library/024308.

Heberle, Renee. 1996. "Deconstructive Strategies and the Movement against Sexual Violence." *Hypatia* 11.4: 63–76.

Heller-Nicholas, Alexandra. 2011. *Rape-Revenge Films: A Critical Study*. Jefferson, NC: McFarland.

Hesford, Wendy. 2001. "Reading 'Rape Stories': Material Rhetoric and the Trauma of Representation." In *Haunting Violations: Feminist Criticism and the Crisis of the 'Real,'* ed. Wendy S. Hesford and Wendy Kozol, 13–47. Urbana: University of Illinois Press.

hooks, bell. 1984. *Feminist Theory: From Margin to Center*. Boston: South End Press.

Horeck, Tanya. 2004. *Public Rape: Representing Violation in Fiction and Film*. New York: Routledge.

Howe, Keith A. 1988. "Home Births in South-West Australia." *Medical Journal of Australia* 149.6: 296–297, 300, 302.

Huffington Post. 2011. "New York City Rapes Increase, Murders Drop in 2011." *The Huffington Post*, 4 April. http://www.huffingtonpost.com/2011/04/04/new-york-city-rapes-incre_n_844363.html.

Hughes, Karen. 2004. *Ten Minutes from Normal*. New York: Penguin Books.

Human Rights Watch Women's Rights Project. 1996. *All Too Familiar: Sexual Abuse of Women in U.S. State Prisons*. New York: Human Rights Watch.

Hunter, Latham. 2003. "The Celluloid Cubicle: Regressive Constructions of Masculinity in 1990s Office Movies." *Journal of American Culture* 26.1: 71–87.

In My Country. 2004. Dir. John Boorman. DVD. Sony Home Pictures Entertainment.

Irving, Toni. 2007. "Borders of the Body: Black Women, Sexual Assault, and Citizenship." *Women's Studies Quarterly* 35.1–2: 67–92.

Jacobs, Janet Liebman. 1990. "Reassessing Mother Blame in Incest." *Signs: Journal of Women in Culture and Society* 15.3: 500–515.

———. 1993. "Victimized Daughters: Sexual Violence and the Empathic Female Self." *Signs: Journal of Women in Culture and Society* 19.1: 126–146.

James, Joy. 1996. *Resisting State Violence: Gender and Class in U.S. Culture*. Minneapolis: University of Minnesota Press.

Jeffords, Susan. 1994. *Hard Bodies: Hollywood Masculinity in the Reagan Era.* New Brunswick, NJ: Rutgers University Press.
Jehl, Douglas. 1999. "Arab Honor's Price: A Woman's Blood." *New York Times,* 20 June, 1.
Jerry Maguire. 1996. Dir. Cameron Crowe. DVD. Sony Pictures Home Entertainment.
Johanson, Richard, Mary Newburn, and Alison Macfarlane. 2002. "Has the Medicalisation of Childbirth Gone Too Far?" *British Medical Journal* 324.7342: 892–897.
John, Marie-Elena. 2006. *Unburnable: A Novel.* New York: Amistad.
———. 2007. Interview with Nealeigh Mitchell. YouTube video, 25 June. http://www.youtube.com/watch?v=ueRwNT6P-zA.
Johnson, Leola A. 1995. "Forum on Feminism and the Media: Afterword." *Signs: Journal of Women in Culture and Society* 20.3: 711–720.
Johnston, Garth. 2011. "NYPD: Crime Down, Rape Up in the First Quarter of 2011." Gothamist Web site, 4 April. http://gothamist.com/2011/04/04/nypd_crime_down_rape_up_in_the_firs.php.
Johnson, Martin P. 2002. "An Exploration of Men's Experience and Role at Childbirth." *Journal of Men's Studies* 10.2: 165–183.
Johnson, Paula C. 2003. *Inner Lives: Voices of African American Women in Prison.* New York: New York University Press.
Jones, Kathleen B. 1997. "The Politics of Responsibility and Perspectives on Violence against Women." In *Feminism and the New Democracy: Re-Sitting the Political,* ed. Jodi Dean, 13–29. London: Sage.
Jungle Fever. 1991. Dir. Spike Lee. DVD. Universal Studios.
Jurney, Florence Ramond. 2006. "The Island and the Creation of (Hi)story in the Writings of Michelle Cliff and Jamaica Kincaid." *Anthurium: A Caribbean Studies Journal* 4.1. http://anthurium.miami.edu/volume_4/issue_1/jurney-theisland.html.
Kaiser, David, and Lovisa Stannow. 2010. "The Rape of American Prisoners." *New York Review of Books,* 57.4: 16–20.
Kapur, Ratna. 2012. "Rape and the Crisis of Indian Masculinity." *The Hindu,* 19 December. http://www.thehindu.com/opinion/op-ed/rape-and-the-crisis-of-indian-masculinity/article4214267.ece.
Karmel, Marjorie. 1959. *Thank You, Dr. Lamaze: A Mother's Experience in Painless Childbirth.* Philadelphia: B. Lippincott Co.
Kennell, John, Marshall Klaus, Susan McGrath, Steven Robertson, and Clark Hinkley. 1991. "Continuous Emotional Support during Labor in a U.S. Hospital: A Randomized Controlled Trial." *JAMA, The Journal of the American Medical Association* 265.17: 2197–2203.
Kimball, Roger. 1990. *Tenured Radicals: How Politics Has Corrupted Our Higher Education.* New York: Harper and Row.
Kincaid, Jamaica. 1996. *The Autobiography of My Mother.* New York: Farrar, Straus and Giroux.
Kitzinger, Sheila. 1995. *Ourselves as Mothers: The Universal Experience of Motherhood.* New York: Addison-Wesley.
Klein, Ellen R. 1998. "Can Feminism Be Rational?" *Journal of Interdisciplinary Studies* 10.1–2: 17–29.
Kramer, Lawrence. 2000. *After the Lovedeath: Sexual Violence and the Making of Culture.* Berkeley: University of California Press.
Krog, Antjie. 1998. *Country of My Skull: Guilt, Sorrow, and the Limits of Forgiveness in the New South Africa.* New York: Broadway Books.
Kruttschnitt, Candace, and Rosemary Gartner. 2003. "Women's Imprisonment." *Crime and Justice* 30.1: 1–81.

Kubitschek, Missy Dehn. 1988. "Subjugated Knowledge: Toward a Feminist Exploration of Rape in Afro-American Fiction." In *Black Feminist Criticism and Critical Theory*, ed. Joe Weixlmann and Houston A. Baker Jr., 43–56. Greenwood, FL: Pankevill Publishing Co.

Kurshan, Nancy. 2006. "Women and Imprisonment in the US: History and Current Reality." *Zine Distro*. http://zinedistro.org/zines/18/women-and-imprisonment-in-the-us/by/nancy-kurshan.

Lakoff, George. 2004. *Don't Think of an Elephant! Know Your Values and Frame the Debate*. White River Junction, VT: Chelsea Green Publishing.

Lamb, Sharon.1996. *The Trouble with Blame: Victims, Perpetrators, and Responsibility*. Cambridge, MA: Harvard University Press.

———. 1999. "Constructing the Victim: Popular Images and Lasting Labels." In *New Versions of Victims: Feminists Struggle with the Concept*, ed. Sharon Lamb, 108–139. New York: New York University Press.

———, ed. 1999. *New Versions of Victims: Feminists Struggle with the Concept*. New York: New York University Press.

Larsson, Stieg. 2008. *The Girl with the Dragon Tattoo*. New York: Random House.

Ledent, Bénédicte. 1997. "Remembering Slavery: History as Roots in the Fiction of Caryl Phillips and Fred D'Aguiar." In *The Contact and the Culmination: Essays in Honour of Hena Maes-Jelinek*, ed. Marc Delrez and Bénédicte Ledent, 271–281. Liège, Belgium: Liège Language and Literature.

Lesage, Julia. 1978. "Disarming Film Rape." *Jump Cut* 19 (December): 14–16.

Lew, Mike. 2004. *Victims No Longer: The Classic Guide for Men Recovering from Sexual Child Abuse*. New York: Harper Perennial.

Lisak, David. 1991. "Sexual Aggression, Masculinity, and Fathers." *Signs: Journal of Women in Culture and Society* 16.2: 238–263.

Loftus, Geoff. 2012. "Show Me the Money." *Forbes*, 16 February. http://www.forbes.com/sites/geoffloftus/2012/02/16/show-me-the-money/.

Lothian, Judith A. 1995. "Home Birth: How Can the Information Be Included in Class?" *Journal of Perinatal Education* 4.1: v–vi.

MacKinnon, Catharine A. 1989. *Toward a Feminist Theory of the State*. Cambridge, MA: Harvard University Press.

McCarthy, Mary. 1967. *Vietnam*. New York: Harcourt, Brace & World.

McClintock, Anne. 1997. "'No Longer in a Future Heaven': Gender, Race, and Nationalism." In *Dangerous Liaisons: Gender, Nation, and Postcolonial Perspectives*, ed. Anne McClintock, Aamir Mufti, and Ella Shohat, 89–113. Minneapolis: University of Minnesota Press.

McCulloch, Jude, and Amanda George. 2009. "Naked Power: Strip Searching in Women's Prisons." In *The Violence of Incarceration*, ed. Phil Scraton and Jude McCulloch, 107–124. New York: Routledge.

McGuire, Danielle. 2010. *At the Dark End of the Street—Black Women, Rape, and Resistance- A New History of the Civil Rights Movement from Rosa Parks to the Rise of Black Power*. New York: Alfred A. Knopf.

McWatt, Mark. 1982. "The Preoccupation with the Past in West Indian Literature." *Caribbean Quarterly* 28.1–2: 12–19.

Mahoney, Martha R. 1994. "Victimization or Oppression? Women's Lives, Violence, and Agency." In *The Public Nature of Private Violence: The Discovery of Domestic Abuse*, ed. Martha Albertson Fineman and Rozanne Mykitiuk, 59–93. New York: Routledge.

Malinen, KellyAnne. 2007. "'The Lesbian Phallus': Deconstruction, Subversion . . . and Rape?" PhD diss., Dalhousie University, Canada.

Marable, Manning, Keesha Middlemass, and Ian Steinberg, eds. 2007. *Racializing Justice, Disenfranchising Lives: The Racism, Criminal Justice, and Law Reader*. New York: Palgrave Macmillan.

Marcus, Sharon. 1992. "Fighting Bodies, Fighting Words: A Theory and Politics of Rape Prevention." In *Feminists Theorize the Political*, ed. Judith Butler and Joan W. Scott, 385–404. New York: Routledge.

Marecek, Jeanne. 1999. "Trauma Talk in Feminist Clinical Practice." In *New Versions of Victims: Feminists Struggle with the Concept*, ed. Sharon Lamb, 158–183. New York: New York University Press. 1999

Mariner, Joanne. 2001. *No Escape: Male Rape in US Prisons*. New York: Human Rights Watch.

Martin, Emily. 1987. *The Woman in the Body: A Cultural Analysis of Reproduction*. Boston: Beacon Press.

Martin, Patricia Yancey. 2005. *Rape Work: Victims, Gender, and Emotions in Organization and Community Context*. New York: Routledge.

May, Vivian. 2004. "Dislocation and Desire in Shani Mootoo's Cereus Blooms at Night." *Studies in the Literary Imagination* 37.2: 97–122.

Mazza, Brittney. 2006. "Women and the Prison Industrial Complex: The Criminalization of Gender, Race, and Class in the 'War on Drugs.'" *Dialogues Journal* 5: 79–90. http://dialogues.rutgers.edu/all-journals/cat_view/12-volume-v.

Meijer, Maaike. 1993. "Countering Sexual Violence: On the Critique of Representation and the Importance of Reading Its Methods." *Women's Studies International Forum* 16.4: 367–379.

Midmer, Deana. 1992. "Does Family-Centered Maternity Care Empower Women? The Development of the Woman-Centered Childbirth Model." *Family Medicine* 24.3: 216–221.

Milman, Louis. 2013. "Steubenville Accuser Told Friend She Couldn't Remember What Happened." *Akron News Now*, 16 March. http://akronnewsnow.com/news/national-news/item/78486-steubenville-rape-accuser-told-friend-she-couldn-t-remember-what-happened.

Millhiser, Ian. 2013. "Fox News Guest Receives Racist Rape and Death Threats after Arguing Guns Aren't the Solution to Rape." *ThinkProgress*, 9 March. http://thinkprogress.org/justice/2013/03/09/1695891/fox-news-guest-receives-racist-rape-and-death-threats-after-arguing-guns-arents-the-solution-to-rape/.

Mills, Jane. 1995. "Screening Rape." *Index on Censorship* 24.6: 38–41.

Minnich, Elizabeth Kamarck. 1998. "Feminist Attacks on Feminisms: Patriarchy's Prodigal Daughters." *Feminist Studies* 24.1: 159–176.

Moi, Toril. 2006. "'I Am Not a Feminist, But . . .' How Feminism Became the F-Word." *PMLA* 121.5: 1735–1742.

Molland, Judy. 2013. "17-Yr-Old Girl Kills Herself after Rape Photo Goes Viral." *Care2 Make a Difference*, 10 April. http://www.care2.com/causes/17-yr-old-girl-kills-self-after-rape-photo-goes-viral-2.html.

Mooney, Carolyn. 1988. "Conservative Scholars Call for a Movement to 'Reclaim' the Academy." *Chronicle of Higher Education* 35.13: A1, A11.

Mootoo, Shani. 1999. *Cereus Blooms at Night*. New York: Harper Perennial.

Muhammed, Khalil Gibran. 2010. *The Condemnation of Blackness: Race, Crime, and the Making of Modern Urban America*. Cambridge, MA: Harvard University Press.

Narayan, Uma. 1997. *Dislocating Cultures: Identities, Traditions, and Third World Feminism*. New York: Routledge.

Naughton, Kerry. 2009. "Prison Rape Elimination Act: Eliminating Sexual Violence in Oregon's Correctional Institutions." *PSJ: Partnership for Safety and Justice*, 16 June.

http://www.safetyandjustice.org/news/prison-rape-elimination-act-eliminating-sexual-violence-oregon%E2%80%99s-correctional-institutions.

Ng, Vivien. 1994. "Sexual Abuse of Daughters-in-Law in Qing China: Cases from the Xing' An Huilan." *Feminist Studies* 20.2: 373–392.

Nicholson, Linda, ed. 1989. *Feminism/Postmodernism*. New York: Routledge.

Nietzsche, Friedrich. 1967. *On the Genealogy of Morals: Ecce Homo*. New York: Random House.

NOW. 2010. "End Shackling Now! A NOW Activist Leader's Guide to Eliminating Shackling of Incarcerated Women Pre, During and Post Labour and Delivery." www.now.org/issues/violence/AntiShacklingKit.pdf.

Nunez, Elizabeth. 2006. *Prospero's Daughter: A Novel*. New York: Ballantine Books.

O'Brien, Mary. 1981. *The Politics of Reproduction*. London: Routledge.

Olsen, Ole. 1997. "Meta-Analysis of the Safety of Home Birth." *Birth* 24.1: 4–13.

Paglia, Camille. 1990. *Sexual Personae: Art and Decadence from Nefertiti to Emily Dickinson*. New Haven: Yale University Press.

Perez, Loida Maritza. 2000. *Geographies of Home*. New York: Viking.

Pew Center on the States. 2008. "One in 100: Behind Bars in America 2008." 28 February. http://www.pewtrusts.org/uploadedFiles/wwwpewtrustsorg/Reports/sentencing_and_corrections/one_in_100.pdf.

Phillips, Celeste R. 1999. "Family Centered Maternity Care: Past, Present, Future." *International Journal of Childbirth Education* 14.4: 6–11.

Pidd, Helen. 2010. "Teenager Jailed for Murder over Facebook Insult." *The Guardian*, 22 June. http://www.guardian.co.uk/uk/2010/jun/22/teenager-jailed-facebook-insult.

Picart, Caroline Joan. 2003. "Rhetorically Reconfiguring Victimhood and Agency: The Violence Women Act's Civil Rights Clause." *Rhetoric and Public Affairs* 6.1: 97–125.

Pinard, Michael. 2010. "Collateral Consequences of Criminal Convictions: Confronting Issues of Race and Dignity." *New York University Law Review* 85 (May): 457–534.

Pinkerton, Steven D., Carol L. Galletly and David W. Seal. 2007. "Model-Based Estimates of HIV Acquisition Due to Prison Rape." *Prison Journal* 87.3: 295–310.

Plaza, Monique. 1980. "Our Costs and Their Benefits." *m/f* 4: 28–39.

President's Task Force on Victims of Crime. 1982. *Final Report of the President's Task Force on Victims of Crime*. http://www.ojp.usdoj.gov/ovc/publications/presdntstskforcrprt/front.pdf.

Projansky, Sarah. 2001. *Watching Rape: Film and Television in Postfeminist Culture*. New York: New York University Press.

Pullum, Geoffrey. 2012. "Shock: Writer Avoids Mentioning Passive." *Lingua Franca* 27 January. http://chronicle.com/blogs/linguafranca/2012/01/27/shock-writer-avoids-mentioning-passive/.

Quaker United Nations Office. 2005. "Violence against Women and Girls in Prison." 6 October. http://www.quno.org/humanrights/women-in-prison/womenPrisonLinks.htm.

Rape, Abuse & Incest National Network. N.d. "Why Will Only 3 Out of Every 100 Rapists Serve Time?" RAINN Web site, http://www.rainn.org/get-information/statistics/reporting-rates.

Rapping, Elayne. 2003. *Law and Justice as Seen on TV*. New York: New York University Press.

Razack, Sherene. 1994. "What Is Gained by Looking White People in the Eye? Culture, Race, and Gender in Cases of Sexual Violence." *Signs: Journal of Women in Culture and Society* 19.4: 894–924.

Reddy, Chandan. 2011. *Freedom with Violence: Race, Sexuality, and the US State*. Durham, NC: Duke University Press.

Reeser, Todd. 2010. *Masculinities in Theory: An Introduction*. Chichester, West Sussex: John Wiley & Sons.

Reid, Maire. 1997. "The Disappearance of Birth: Language versus Reality in Modern Childbirth." *Birth Gazette* 13.1: 15–21.
Rentschler, Carrie. 2011. *Second Wounds: Victims' Rights and the Media in the U.S.* Durham, NC: Duke University Press.
Rich, Adrienne. 1976. *Of Woman Born: Motherhood as Experience and Institution.* New York: Bantam Books.
Richie, Beth. 1996. *Compelled to Crime: The Gender Entrapment of Black Women.* New York: Routledge.
Riley, Jason. 2012a. "Contempt Charges Withdrawn for Assault Victim Savannah Dietrich." *Courier-Journal* (Louisville, Ky.), 23 July.
———. 2012b. "Contempt Motion Withdrawn for Assault Victim Savannah Dietrich." *Courier-journal.com* 23 July 2012, http://www.courier-journal.com/apps/pbcs.dll/article?AID=2012101070002.
———. 2012c. "Sexual Assault Victim's Tweets about Attackers Prompt Contempt Charges against Louisville's Savannah Dietrich." *Courier-Journal* (Louisville, Ky.), 28 August 2012.
Roiphe, Katie. 1993. *The Morning After: Sex, Fear, and Feminism on Campus.* Boston: Little, Brown.
Russell, Dominique. 2010. *Rape in Art Cinema.* New York: Continuum International Publishing Group.
Samuel, Shirley. 2004. *Facing America: Iconography and the Civil War.* Oxford: Oxford University Press.
Sapphire. 1997. *Push: A Novel.* New York: Vintage.
Satran, Joe. 2012. "'You Had Me at Hello' Study Reveals Secrets of Memorable Movie Lines." *The Huffington Post*, 20 April. http://www.huffingtonpost.com/2012/04/20/you-had-me-at-hello-study_n_1441247.html.
Scarce, Michael. 2001. *Male on Male Rape: The Hidden Toll of Stigma and Shame.* New York: Basic Books.
Scott, Joan. 1992. "Experience." In *Feminists Theorize the Political*, ed. Judith Butler and Joan Scott, 22–41. New York: Routledge.
Scraton, Phil, and Jude McCulloch, eds. 2009. *The Violence of Incarceration.* New York: Routledge.
Sears, William, and Martha Sears. 1993. *The Baby Book: Everything You Need to Know About Your Baby—From Birth to Age Two.* New York: Little, Brown and Company.
Sedgwick, Eve Kosofsky. 1992. *Between Men: English Literature and Male Homosocial Desire.* New York: Columbia University Press.
———. 1993. *Tendencies.* Durham, NC: Duke University Press.
Selverston, Aaron. 2012. "Eshoo Slams Effort to Weaken Violence Against Women Act." *CampbellPatch*, May 21. http://campbell.patch.com/groups/politics-and-elections/p/eshoo-slams-effort-to-weaken-violence-against-women-adac4cf5370.
Shapiro, Bruce. 1997. "Victims and Vengeance: Why the Victim's Rights Amendment Is a Bad Idea." *The Nation*, 10 February: 11–20.
Shropshire, Kenneth. 1996. *In Black and White: Race and Sports in America.* New York: New York University Press.
Sielke, Sabine. 2002. *Reading Rape: The Rhetoric of Sexual Violence in American Literature and Culture, 1790–1990.* Princeton, NJ: Princeton University Press.
Simkin, Penny. 1999. "Labor Support: Where Has It Been and Where Is It Going?" *International Journal of Childbirth Education* 12.4: 22–23.
Skomba, Anne, and Annie Chen. 2001. "FBI: Violent Crimes Down, Forcible Rape Up." *The Hoya*, 22 September. http://www.thehoya.com/fbi-violent-crimes-down-forcible-rape-up-in-dc-1.2608038#.UBiPkXCmCX8.

Sleepers. 1996. Dir. Barry Levinson. DVD. Warner Home Video.
Smith, Brenda. 1998. *An End to Silence: Women Prisoners' Handbook on Identifying and Addressing Sexual Misconduct*. Washington, DC: National Women's Law Center.
Smith, S. E. 2013. "Audrie Pott, Only 15 Years Old, Killed Herself After Being Raped." *Care2 Make a Difference*, 14 April. http://www.care2.com/causes/audrie-pott-only-15-years-old-killed-herself-after-being-raped.html.
Solnit, Rebecca. 2013. "A Rape a Minute, a Thousand Corpses a Year." *Aljazeera*, 13 February. http://m.aljazeera.com/story/201327114230765738.
Sommers, Christina Hoff. 1994. *Who Stole Feminism? How Women Have Betrayed Women*. New York: Simon and Schuster.
Southern Poverty Law Center. 2010. "SPLC Files Federal Lawsuit Targeting State-Funded Juvenile Facility in Florida." 8 October. http://www.splcenter.org/get-informed/news/southern-poverty-law-center-files-federal-lawsuit-targeting-state-funded-juvenile-. Accessed 12 January 2013.
Stand and Deliver. 2009. "Dutch Home Birth Study." Stand and Deliver Web site. 16 April. http://rixarixa.blogspot.com/2009/04/dutch-home-birth-study.html.
Stanworth, Michelle. 1997. "Reproductive Technologies: Tampering with Nature?" In *Feminisms*, ed. Sandra Kemp and Judith Squires. Oxford: Oxford University Press.
Stealing Sinatra. 2003. Dir. Ron Underwood. DVD. Showtime Entertainment.
Steinberg, Suzanne, Laurence Kruckman, and Stephanie Steinberg. 2000. "Reinventing Fatherhood in Japan and Canada." *Social Science and Medicine* 50.9: 1257–1272.
Stewart, Mary White, Shirley A. Dobbin, and Sophia I. Gatowski. 1996. "'Real Rapes' and 'Real Victims': The Shared Reliance on Common Cultural Definitions of Rape." *Feminist Legal Studies* 4: 159–177.
Stockton, Sharon. 2006. *The Economics of Fantasy: Rape in Twentieth-Century Literature*. Athens: Ohio State University Press.
Struckman-Johnson, Cindy, and David Struckman-Johnson. 2006. "A Comparison of Sexual Coercion Experiences Reported by Men and Women in Prison." *Journal of Interpersonal Violence* 21.12: 1591–1615.
Sudbury, Julia, ed. 2005. *Global Lockdown: Race, Gender, and the Prison Industrial Context*. New York and London: Routledge.
Suleri, Sara. 1993. *The Rhetoric of English India*. Chicago: University of Chicago Press.
Summer, Nicole. 2008. "Powerless in Prison: Sexual Abuse against Incarcerated Women." *AlterNet*, 15 January. www.alternet.org/reproductivejustice/73784/page3.
Sweeney, Megan. 2004. "Prison Narratives, Narrative Prisons: Incarcerated Women Reading Gayl Jones's 'Eva's Man.'" *Feminist Studies* 30.2: 456–482.
Tew, Marjorie. 1986. "Do Obstetric Intranatal Interventions Make Birth Safer?" *British Journal of Obstetrics and Gynaecology* 93.7: 659–674.
———. 1990. *Safer Childbirth? A Critical History of Maternity Care*. London: Chapman and Hall.
———, and Sonja Damstra-Wijmenga. 1991. "Safest Birth Attendants: Recent Dutch Evidence." *Midwifery* 7.2: 55–63.
Tjaden, Patricia, and Nancy Theonnes. 1998. *The Prevalence, Incidence, and Consequence of Violence against Women: Findings from the National Violence against Women Survey*. Washington, DC: National Institute of Justice and Center for Disease Control and Prevention. https://www.ncjrs.gov/pdffiles/172837.pdf.
Underwood, Thomas L., and Christine Edmunds, eds. 2002. *Victim Assistance: Exploring Individual Practice, Organizational Policy, and Societal Responses*. New York: Springer Publishing Company.

United Nations. 1999. "Integration of the Human Rights and Women and the Gender Perspective: Violence against Women: Report of the Special Rapporteur on Violence against Women, Its Causes and Consequences." Economic and Social Council document E/CN.4/1999/68/Add.2, 4 January, http://www.unhchr.ch/Huridocda/Huridoca.nsf/0/7560a6237c67bb118025674c004406e9#IVF.

United Nations Commission on Human Rights. 1955. "Standard Minimum Rules for the Treatment of Prisoners." 30 August. http://www.unodc.org/pdf/criminal_justice/UN_Standard_Minimum_Rules_for_the_Treatment_of_Prisoners.pdf.

Valente, Joseph. 2011. *The Myth of Manliness in Irish National Culture, 1880–1922*. Urbana: University of Illinois Press.

Vehvilainen-Julkunen, Katri, and Anja Liukkonen. 1998. "Fathers' Experiences of Childbirth." *Midwifery* 14.1: 10–17.

Vernon, David, ed. 2001. *Men at Birth: Stories of Men's Experiences of the Birth of Their Children*. Sydney, Australia: Finch Publishing.

Vigarello, George. 2001. *A History of Rape: Sexual Violence in France from the 16th to the 20th Century*. Malden, MA: Blackwell Publishers.

Wallace, Karen. 2000. "Focal Point on Childbirth Education: The Bradley Method." *International Journal of Childbirth Education* 11.1: 9–10.

Walters, Suzanna Danuta. 1995. "Introduction." In *Material Girls: Making Sense of Feminist Cultural Theory*. Berkeley: University of California Press.

Warshaw, Robin. 1988/1994. *I Never Called It Rape: The Ms. Report on Recognizing, Fighting, and Surviving Date and Acquaintance Rape*. New York: Harper Perennial.

Washington Post. 2001. "Cruel and Usual." *Washington Post*, 23 April, A14.

Weedon, Chris. 1999. *Feminism, Theory, and the Politics of Difference*. Oxford: Blackwell Publishers.

Wertz, Richard W., and Dorothy C. Wertz. 1989. *Lying In: A History of Childbirth in America*. New Haven, CT: Yale University Press.

White, Phillip, and Genny White. 2009. *Men at Birth: Guide to a Successful Childbirth Experience*. Orange, CA: Navigate Press.

Whitehead, Stephen, ed. 2006. *Men and Masculinities*. New York: Routledge.

Wickham, Sara. 1999. "Homebirth: What Are the Issues?" *Midwifery Today* 50 (Summer): 16–18.

Wiegman, Robyn. 1995. *American Anatomies: Theorizing Race and Gender*. Durham, NC: Duke University Press.

Wolf, Naomi. 1993. *Fire with Fire: The New Female Power and How to Use It*. New York: Random House.

———. 2001. *(Mis)conceptions: Truth, Lies, and the Unexpected on the Journey to Motherhood*. New York: Doubleday.

Yablonsky, Lewis. 1998. *Gangsters: 50 Years of Madness, Drugs, and Death on the Streets of America*. New York: New York University Press.

———. 2008. *Gangs in Court*. New York: Lawyers & Judges Publishing Co.

Young, Charlotte. 2011. "Number of Young African American Women in Prison Rises." *Atlanta Post*, 16 March. http://atlantapost.com/2011/03/16/numbers-of-young-african-american-women-in-prison-rise/.

Young, Iris Marion. 1990. *On Female Body Experience: "Throwing Like a Girl" and Other Essays*. Oxford: Oxford University Press.

Žižek, Slavoj. 1994. *The Metastases of Enjoyment*. New York: Verso.

———. 2008. *Violence*. New York: Picador.

INDEX

Abdullah-Khan, Noreen, 137n11
Abele, Elizabeth, 142n8
Abrams, Kathryn, 92
Abu Ghraib, 8
agency, 13–15, 18–23, 26, 28, 31–37, 39, 41–46, 49, 51–54, 57, 59, 64, 66, 69–70, 88, 89, 92, 94, 97, 113, 116, 123, 124, 125, 126, 128, 130, 131, 133, 137n2, 138n3
Akin, Todd, 28, 138n4
Alcoff, Linda, 138n6, 139n3, 140n16, 145n2
Arms, Suzanne, 79, 80
Armstrong, Nancy, 57

Badinter, Elizabeth, 31
Bahar, Saba, 138n6
Barak, G., 142n3
Barclay, Lesley, 141n7
Bart, Pauline, 139n8
Bartky, Sandra, 1
Bassett, Laura, 28
Baumgardner, Jennifer, 145n4
Beck, Allen J., 90, 95
Beck, Glenn, 16
Becker, Dana, 32, 138n8
Becker, Maki, 35
Beebe, Michael, 35
Beech, Beverley Lawrence, 87
Benhabib, Seyla, 36
Bennett, William, 32
Berlant, Lauren G., 39, 42, 138n2
Bernstein, Richard, 30
Bevacqua, Maria, 37, 52, 94, 115, 138n1
Bike Path Rapist, 35
Bloom, Mia, 113
Bongie, Chris, 144n6
Bordo, Susan, 56, 71, 140n13
Bourke, Joanna, 137n1, 140n10
Bradley, Robert A., 72
Bradley method, 69, 70, 72, 73, 82, 83, 86, 141n4
Braidotti, Rosi, 52
Brand, Dionne, 144n9
Brontë, Emily, *Wuthering Heights*, 120

Brown, Wendy, 20, 44, 57, 59–66, 108, 144n1
Brownmiller, Susan, 8, 51
Bruce, Elizabeth, 80
Bryant, Kobe, 24, 26, 30, 33, 34
Bush, George W., 25, 29, 142n7
Butler, Judith, 15, 36, 48, 52, 75, 102, 123, 140n13

Cagle, Daryl, 34
Cahill, Ann, 1, 8, 20, 44, 51–54, 62
Calling the Ghosts: A Story About Rape, War, and Women (documentary film), 143n4
Carle, Susan, 36
Christiansë, Yvette, 113, 124, 125; *Unconfessed*, 113, 124, 125–126
Clark, Vévé, 128
Clarke, Austin, 115, 116, 124; *The Polished Hoe*, 116, 124
Cliff, Michelle, 114, 122, 144n5; *No Telephone to Heaven*, 122
Cobham, Rhonda, 124, 125
Coetzee, J. M., 22, 128
Cohen, Theodore F., 127n7
Cole, Alyson M., 25, 29, 31, 32, 33
Condé, Maryse, 115; *I, Tituba, Black Witch of Salem*, 115
Connell, Patricia, 92
Convery, Alyson, 30, 31, 35, 92, 138n6
Corrigan, Rose, 12
Courier, Michael, 2
Curthoys, Jean, 61, 66
Cypher, Louis, 27

Danticat, Edwidge, 112, 116, 117, 120–121, 125, 144n6, 144n8; *Breath, Eyes, Memory*, 112, 116, 117–118, 120–121, 144n6
Danto, Bruce, 141n1
Davis, Angela Y., 142n3
Davis-Floyd, Robbie E., 80
De Beauvoir, Simone, 23
Deem, Melissa, 139n5
de Jonge, Ank, 87
De Lauretis, Teresa, 4, 27

Didion, Joan, 27; *The Year of Magical Thinking*, 27, 137n1
Dietrich, Savannah, 53, 134
Dobbin, Shirley A., 95
Donnell, Alison, 143n3
Donovan, Jenny, 141n7
Dorr, Lisa Lindquist, 144n7
doubling, 22, 125–128, 131
Doyle, Laura, 17
Doyle, Sady, 137n10
D'Souza, Dinesh, 18, 30
Duden, Barbara, 140n1
Dumond, Robert W. and Doris A., 141n1
Dunn, Jennifer L., 138n6
Dworkin, Andrea, 51
Dyer, Richard, 109

Ebert, Roger, 107
Ebert, Teresa L., 134
Edmondson, Belinda, 143n3
Edmunds, Christine, 25

Faludi, Susan, 142n4
Faulkner, Jeanne, 69
FBI, 1, 3, 4, 46, 47
Filipovic, Jill, 28, 138n3
Flavin, J., 142n3
Flax, Jane, 36
Fleisher, Mark S., 97, 98
Foucault, Michel, 6–8, 20, 22, 42, 57, 58, 59, 62, 64, 75, 140nn14,15, 144n1
Freeh Sporkin and Sullivan, LLP, 3
Friedman, Jaclyn, 10–11, 137n6

Gabbidon, Shaun L., 142n3
Gartner, Rosemary, 93
Gatens, Moira, 52
Gatowski, Sophia I., 95
Gavey, Nicola, 17, 140n13, 145n3
Genovese, Ann, 141n7
George, Amanda, 95, 142n2
George, Rosemary Marangoly, 123
Glaze, Lauren, 96
Goodson, Lorna, 144n9
Gornick, Vivian, 114
Graham, Lucy Valerie, 17
Gravelle, Peter, 50
Gray, John, 141n12
Greene, Helen Taylor, 142n3
Grossberg, Lawrence, 119

Grosz, Elizabeth, 52
Gunn, Janet Varner, 138n6
Gunne, Sorcha, 17

Haag, Pamela, 139n3
Haaken, Janice, 65, 139n3
Haire, Doris, 141n4
Halberstam, Judith, 137n8
Hall, Stuart, 38, 44, 92
Hamill, Jasper, 5
Harmon, Steven, 28, 138n4
Harrison, Paige M., 90, 95
Hawkesworth, Mary, 25
Hayes, Lindsay M., 142n1
Heberle, Renee, 20, 44, 61, 62, 139n8
Heller-Nicholas, Alexandra, 16
Hesford, Wendy, 112
Hollywood, 19, 21, 39, 40, 90, 91, 100, 101, 108, 142n7, 143n10
hooks, bell, 137n5
Horeck, Tanya, 17
Hughes, Karen, 25, 26, 27, 30, 33
Hunter, Latham, 101

In My Country (film), 32
Irigaray, Luce, 52
Irving, Toni, 94, 96, 142n4

Jacobs, Janet Liebman, 139n1
James, Joy, 96, 114
Jeffords, Susan, 101, 142n7
Jehl, Douglas, 63
Jerry Maguire (film), 101, 102, 105–111, 143n9
John, Marie-Elena, 112, 116, 118–119, 144n6, 144n8; *Unburnable: A Novel*, 112, 116, 118–120, 144n6
Johnson, Leola A., 139n4
Johnson, Martin P., 141n7
Johnson, Paula C., 93
Jones, Kathleen B., 64, 139n7
Jungle Fever (film), 143n10
Jurney, Florence Ramond, 144n5

Kaiser, David, 98
Kapur, Ratna, 10, 11
Karmel, Marjorie, 72
Kennell, John, 83
Kimball, Roger, 30
Kincaid, Jamaica, 113, 115, 124–125, 126,

127, 144n5, 144n9; *The Autobiography of My Mother*, 113, 124–125, 126
Kitzinger, Sheila, 78, 80
Klein, Ellen R., 30
Koss, Mary, 46
Kramer, Lawrence, 6, 8, 119, 120, 122, 123, 137n4
Krienert, Jesse L., 97, 98
Krog, Antjie, 32, 138n7
Kruttschnitt, Candace, 93
Kubitschek, Missy Dehn, 112, 143n1
Kurshan, Nancy, 93

Lakoff, George, 22, 24, 26
Lamb, Sharon, 55, 138n5, 139n9, 140n12, 140n18
Larsson, Stieg, 33
Ledent, Bénédicte, 112, 143n2
Lee, Spike, 143n10
Leighton, P., 142n3
Lesage, Julia, 139n4
Lew, Mike, 137n11
Limbaugh, Rush, 16
Lisak, David, 139n3

MacKinnon, Catherine A., 51, 59, 61, 66
McCarthy, Mary, 68, 89
McClintock, Anne, 13
McCulloch, Jude, 95, 142n2
McGuire, Danielle, 115
McWatt, Mark, 144n5
Mahoney, Martha R., 92
Malinen, KellyAnne, 137n3
Marable, Manning, 142n3
Marcus, Sharon, 13, 20, 44, 48, 49, 51–53, 56, 62, 132, 139n8
Marecek, Jeanne, 145n3
Mariner, Joanne, 90
Martin, Emily, 140n1
Martin, Patricia Yancey, 17
Maruschak, Laura M., 96
masculinity, 3, 5, 6, 9–17, 19, 21, 22, 39, 51, 69, 70–79, 83, 85–87, 90, 91, 95, 99, 100–111, 119, 120, 122, 123, 130, 133, 134, 137nn6–9, 137n11, 139n3, 141n2 (ch. 3), 141n1 (ch. 4), 142nn7,8
Maxwell, Zerlina, 51
May, Vivian, 127
Mazza, Brittney, 93, 94
Meijer, Maaike, 139n4

Middlemass, Keesha, 142n3
Midmer, Deana, 141n8
Millhiser, Ian, 51
Mills, Jane, 139n4
Minnich, Elizabeth Kamarck, 47, 138n5
Moi, Toril, 23
Molland, Judy, 53
Mooney, Carolyn, 30
Mootoo, Shani, 127, 144nn8,9; *Cereus Blooms at Night*, 127, 144n8
Mourdock, Robert, 28
Muhammed, Khalil Gibran, 96, 142n3

Narayan, Uma, 63
Naughton, Kerry, 90
Ng, Vivien, 138n3
Nicholson, Linda, 138n10
Nietzsche, Friedrich, 60, 61, 108
Nunez, Elizabeth, 115; *Prospero's Daughter*, 115

O'Brien, Mary, 140n1
O'Brien, Patricia, 139n8
Olsen, Ole, 87

Paglia, Camille, 18, 46, 77, 91
Pandey, Jyoti Singh, 10
Parsons, Rehtaeh, 53
Paterno, Joe, 3
Perez, Loida Maritza, 112, 116–117, 118, 120–122; *Geographies of Home*, 112, 116–117, 120–122
Phillips, Celeste R., 8, 141n4
Picart, Caroline Joan, 92
Pidd, Helen, 5
Pinard, Michael, 100
Plaza, Monique, 8, 140n15
Pott, Audrie, 53
Projansky, Sarah, 17, 115
Pullum, Geoffrey, 15

rape: birth rape, 17, 20, 68–90; child sexual assault, 3, 4; decriminalization of, 6, 7; gang rape, 9–11, 51; and heteronormativity, 4, 21, 51, 91, 95, 105; and the law, 4, 7, 10, 11–12, 18, 59, 92, 99–100, 138n11, 140n17, 144n4; and nationalism, the nation, 5, 13, 14, 16, 17, 18, 21, 22, 25–26, 28, 33, 34, 37, 40, 90–91, 93, 94, 96, 101, 105, 113–115, 123, 129, 138n9, 142n4, 142n7;

rape (continued): and passivity, 2, 8, 13–15, 18, 22, 31–34, 39, 41, 50, 52–55, 66, 94, 109, 113, 123, 124, 128, 130, 131, 133; and politics, 14, 24, 28, 37, 60, 116; prison rape, 21, 90–101, 102; and race, 4–5, 27, 29, 32, 37, 38, 40, 92–96, 100–102, 105–111, 112–128, 134, 138n2 (ch. 1), 138n1 (ch. 2), 142n3, 143nn10,11, 143n1, 144n7; script, 13, 14, 39, 42, 49–51, 55, 65; vs. sexualized violence, 4–10, 14, 15, 17, 18, 24; statistics, 1, 7–8, 46–47, 90, 93; in Steubenville, 11, 53, 140n11; and subjectivity, 6, 10, 12, 15, 22, 33, 34, 39, 41, 45, 51, 52, 54, 57, 58, 104, 111, 119, 120, 124, 127, 128, 131, 135; and vulnerability, 9, 10, 11, 15, 18, 22, 62, 110, 120, 131; as weapon of war, 16, 113

Rape, Abuse, and Incest National Network, 7–8

rape culture, 8, 16, 17, 134, 137n5

Rapping, Elayne, 37

Razack, Sherene, 139n3

Reagan, Ronald, 28, 37, 101, 142n7

Reddy, Chandan, 94

Reeser, Todd, 9, 12

Reid, Maire, 80

Rhys, Jean, 144n9

Rich, Adrienne, 79, 80

Richie, Beth, 93

Riley, Jason, 53, 134

Roiphe, Katie, 1, 18, 46, 48, 91

Russell, Dominique, 17

Samuel, Shirley, 138n9

Sandusky, Jerry, 3, 4

Sapphire, 115

Savage, Michael, 16

Scarce, Michael, 137n11

Scott, Joan, 43, 48, 63, 144n1

Scraton, Phil, 95, 142n2

Sean Hannity Show (radio program), 51

Sears, William and Martha, 73, 80, 82, 83–86, 141n13

Sedgwick, Eve Kosofsky, 102, 111

Selverston, Aaron, 18

Senior, Olive, 144n9

Shakespeare, William, *The Tempest*, 115

Shapiro, Bruce, 37

Sielke, Sabine, 17, 114, 115, 116

Simkin, Penny, 83, 141n7

Sleepers (film), 101–105, 107, 108, 110, 111

SlutWalk, 2, 50

Smith, Brenda, 99

Smith, S. E., 53

Solnit, Rebecca, 11

Sommers, Christina Hoff, 1, 18, 46, 48, 91

Southern Poverty Law Center, 99–100

Stannow, Lovisa, 98

Stanworth, Michelle, 141n1

Stealing Sinatra (film), 129–130

Steinberg, Ian, 142n3

Stewart, Jon, 34

Stewart, Mary White, 95

Stockton, Sharon, 17

Stone, Cynthia, 27

Struckman-Johnson, Cindy and David, 90, 94

Sudbury, Julia, 93

Suleri, Sara, 137n10

Summer, Nicole, 90

Sweeney, Megan, 92

Tew, Marjorie, 87

Theonnes, Nancy, 47

Thompson, Zoe Brigley, 17

Tjaden, Patricia, 47

Underwood, Thomas L., 25

U.S. military, 8, 51, 142n2

Valente, Joseph, 12, 137n9

Vernon, David, 141n6

Vigarello, George, 140n17

Wallace, Karen, 141n3

War on Terror, 29

Warshaw, Robin, 88

Weedon, Chris, 86, 141n9

Wertz, Richard W. and Dorothy C., 140n4

White, Phillip and Genny, 141n6

Whitehead, Stephen, 137n7

Wickham, Sara, 141n5

Wiegman, Robyn, 102, 109, 143n11

Wolf, Naomi, 42, 70, 74, 78, 80, 81, 87, 141n7, 141n10

Yablonsky, Lewis, 5, 9

Young, Charlotte, 96

Young, Iris Marion, 1

Žižek, Slavoj, 6, 9, 45, 65, 137n2, 137n4

ABOUT THE AUTHOR

CARINE M. MARDOROSSIAN teaches feminist and postcolonial studies at the University at Buffalo, New York. Her first book, *Reclaiming Difference: Caribbean Women Rewrite Postcolonialism*, was published by the University of Virginia Press in 2005. Her articles have appeared in *Callaloo, Signs, Hypatia, College Literature,* the *Journal of Caribbean Literatures, Small Axe,* and various anthologies. She is completing a book manuscript on ecocriticism and Caribbean literature entitled "Creolized Ecologies."

www.ingramcontent.com/pod-product-compliance
Ingram Content Group UK Ltd.
Pitfield, Milton Keynes, MK11 3LW, UK
UKHW041428180426
11947UKWH00007B/350